CAMBRIDGE LIBRARY COLLECTION

Books of enduring scholarly value

Music

The systematic academic study of music gave rise to works of description, analysis and criticism, by composers and performers, philosophers and anthropologists, historians and teachers, and by a new kind of scholar - the musicologist. This series makes available a range of significant works encompassing all aspects of the developing discipline.

Alfred Day's Treatise on Harmony

Alfred Day (1810–49) first published this controversial work in 1845 to substantial negative criticism. He was encouraged in his enterprise by the composer George Alexander Macfarren (1813–87) who remained a staunch supporter of Day's theories. The work begins with an introduction to Day's new approach to the figured bass and then moves on to set out his concept of diatonic (or strict) harmony and chromatic (or free) harmony. Each is discussed in depth, with sections devoted to common chords and their inversions, discords, pedals and modulation together with a large number of musical examples. This second edition of 1885 by Macfarren includes an additional preface discussing the genesis of the work and supporting its basic premise, together with an extensive appendix presenting his additions and differences of view, developed during the intervening period. Despite its complexity, Day's thinking had considerable influence on later writers on harmony.

Cambridge University Press has long been a pioneer in the reissuing of out-of-print titles from its own backlist, producing digital reprints of books that are still sought after by scholars and students but could not be reprinted economically using traditional technology. The Cambridge Library Collection extends this activity to a wider range of books which are still of importance to researchers and professionals, either for the source material they contain, or as landmarks in the history of their academic discipline.

Drawing from the world-renowned collections in the Cambridge University Library, and guided by the advice of experts in each subject area, Cambridge University Press is using state-of-the-art scanning machines in its own Printing House to capture the content of each book selected for inclusion. The files are processed to give a consistently clear, crisp image, and the books finished to the high quality standard for which the Press is recognised around the world. The latest print-on-demand technology ensures that the books will remain available indefinitely, and that orders for single or multiple copies can quickly be supplied.

The Cambridge Library Collection will bring back to life books of enduring scholarly value (including out-of-copyright works originally issued by other publishers) across a wide range of disciplines in the humanities and social sciences and in science and technology.

Alfred Day's
Treatise on Harmony

EDITED, WITH AN APPENDIX,
BY G.A. MACFARREN

 CAMBRIDGE
UNIVERSITY PRESS

CAMBRIDGE UNIVERSITY PRESS

Cambridge, New York, Melbourne, Madrid, Cape Town,
Singapore, São Paolo, Delhi, Tokyo, Mexico City

Published in the United States of America by Cambridge University Press, New York

www.cambridge.org
Information on this title: www.cambridge.org/9781108038607

© in this compilation Cambridge University Press 2011

This edition first published 1885
This digitally printed version 2011

ISBN 978-1-108-03860-7 Paperback

ALFRED DAY'S

TREATISE ON HARMONY.

ALFRED DAY'S

TREATISE ON HARMONY.

Edited, with an Appendix,

BY

G. A. MACFARREN,

(Mus. D., M.A. Cantab., et Mus. D. Oxon.)

PROFESSOR OF MUSIC IN THE UNIVERSITY OF CAMBRIDGE AND
PRINCIPAL OF THE ROYAL ACADEMY OF MUSIC.

LONDON:
HARRISON & SONS, 59, PALL MALL.

1885.

HARRISON AND SONS,
PRINTERS IN ORDINARY TO HER MAJESTY,
ST. MARTIN'S LANE.

CONTENTS.

PART I.

DIATONIC HARMONY, OR HARMONY IN THE STRICT STYLE.

PART II.

CHROMATIC HARMONY, OR HARMONY IN THE FREE STYLE.

PREFACE.

As the Introductions to the Chapters in the following work contain such matter as is usually comprised in a preface, but placed immediately before that part of the subject to which it refers, the preface itself will naturally be short. There are, however, a few points to which it is necessary to call the reader's attention.

It is exceedingly probable that the notation used in the following work will—by players on stringed instruments—be said to be incorrect, because, when playing according to it they play out of tune. This I have myself experienced; still the fault is not in the notation, but in the false position in which the fingers are placed for the chromatic notes on those instruments. This I shall now prove.

Supposing on the violin, a performer, playing in the key of C, take on the E string the following notes—G, A♭, A♮, he would play them thus: G, second finger;* A♭, third finger, nearly close to the second finger; A♮, third finger in its proper place (at a distance from the nut equal to a quarter of the distance from the nut to the bridge): this (if the basses were C, C, F) would be out of tune, the A♭ being too flat. In the ordinary method of noting the same passage, G, G♯, A, the G♯ would be played with the second finger nearly close to the third, and therefore nearer to the bridge than the A♭: this (with the same bass) would be in tune.

The relative pitch of different notes is in proportion to the number of vibrations made by each in a given time, the lower the note the smaller the number of vibrations. The number or ratio of vibrations is in inverse proportion to the length of string.

It is proved in a note to Chap. XXI., sect. 16, of this book, that the diatonic semitone above any note is larger or sharper than the chromatic: that is, that E♭ is sharper than D♯, and the same with the other chromatic and diatonic semitones.

If on any stringed instrument (say the violin), two notes, the above-mentioned A♭ and G♯, be played, the A♭ being proved to be sharper than G♯—the sharper note making more vibrations in a given time than the flatter —the length of any string being smaller in proportion as the vibrations are more rapid—and the portion of any string the vibration of which forms the

---

* The English method of numbering the fingers is here used, the thumb not being counted.

note, being that lying between the two points stopping the vibration (which in this case are the bridge and the finger), it follows that the finger should be placed higher up the string or nearer to the bridge for the A♭ than for the G♯, and the same with all other notes relatively situated, the position of the fingers being now exactly the reverse of what it should be when playing such notes; but even this would not be practically of much importance were the notes always written alike, but from want of any decided system of notation, not only do different composers note the same passages differently, but even the same composer notes them sometimes one way and sometimes another, especially when occurring in different keys, being as often wrong as right, and *vice versá*, so that the performer can never be certain of perfect intonation, and very frequently the reproach of playing out of tune rests with him when in justice it should be on the shoulders of the composer.

As it is proved above that the position of the fingers on stringed instruments when playing chromatic notes is wrong,—why should error be perpetuated?—why should not the composer be taught what is the proper note to write, and the player the exact spot on which the finger should be placed?

Although it is several times observed in the book itself, yet, as I think it cannot be too much impressed on the student, I shall here mention that the chromatic common chords, and *all the fundamental discords*, more especially those forms of them in which two notes occur, which, counting from the root, form with each other the interval of the ninth, *should be used very sparingly*, and most especially when such ninth is minor.

The Examples are by no means to be looked on as specimens of either composition or melody, but merely of the progression of the chords treated of to their allowable places; had any examples of such progression, sufficiently lengthy to be intelligible and agreeable, been extracted from the great writers, the expense of the book would have been multiplied at least by four, which certainly would not have been desirable.

Although the following work is the result of immense labour during the leisure time of many years, yet, considering how much in it is new in theory, however old in practice, it is hardly to be expected that it shall be without errors; that not anything essential shall have been overlooked. For such errors and omissions, when occurring, the reader's indulgence is requested; should the book reach a second edition, it will then probably be as free from faults as it will ever be in the power of its Author to make it.

The subjoined Letter from Mr. G. A. Macfarren (a Professor of Harmony in the Royal Academy of Music of London), whose opinion, from the extent of his teaching, must necessarily be of some value, will show that *the following Treatise is not a mere Theory, visionary, useless, and incapable of being reduced to practice, but that it has really been found, by him, of considerable practical utility.*

With these few remarks I submit the following System to the musical profession and the public, satisfied that, if true, as I believe it to be, it will at some time make its way.

ALFRED DAY.

15, *Margaret Street, Cavendish Square,*
AUGUST 4, 1845.

73, Berners Street, July 12, 1845.

MY DEAR FRIEND,

In giving an opinion of your Theory of Harmony, there are two lights in which I may speak of it; as regards my own comprehension of it—and as regards my explanation of it to others. In the first place, I am happy to own that in becoming acquainted with your principles, I found my ideas of the resources of Harmony greatly to expand; and my facility and confidence in the practical application of them is now much greater than I believe it could possibly be, had I not the advantage of the peculiar view of the subject which is opened by your new System;—above all, I am gratified by it, insomuch as I find in it an explanation of and a rule for many of the greatest beauties of the best Masters, which formerly appeared to violate all the rules of music, and which were sanctioned as the unaccountable aberrations of genius, but which could only be imitated to be plagiarised. In the second place, since I have become familiar with your System, feeling as I have done that it was true, and that as Truth is single, so none but yours could be true, I have taught upon it, and have found it most easily comprehended by pupils who had no foreknowledge of the subject; and by those who have come to me with a small acquaintance with other works, it has been admitted to explain many points of Harmony, which had been to them before quite unintelligible. It is a Theory, in my opinion, of peculiar advantage to the student, as comprising the laws of counterpoint with all those of the chromatic or free style; and, for the first time to my knowledge, distinguishing between these very dissimilar schools of harmony. I firmly believe that should your Theory be generally read, it would greatly improve and facilitate the study of Harmony.

I am, my dear Friend,

Very sincerely yours,

G. A. MACFARREN.

To Alfred Day, Esq., M.D.

PREFACE TO THE SECOND EDITION.

BY THE EDITOR.

WHAT is stated in this Preface is, for convenience of diction, said in the first person. Elsewhere throughout the book, save only in the letter appended to the author's Preface, the word "I" signifies the writer of the original work.

In the autumn of 1838 my previous acquaintance with Alfred Day sprang into closest intimacy. He then propounded to me his theory of harmony, which I combated point by point, as each point differed from views I had hitherto learned, and every opposing argument successively fell under the convincing weight of his novel principles. I was engaged in teaching, and I could but communicate, so far as I was able, to those who trusted me for instruction, the convictions I received. As yet the theory was wholly unwritten, and, in the belief that its promulgation would throw invaluable light on the study of harmony, I persuaded my reluctant friend to commit it to paper. Conceiving a hypothesis is a different mental process from that of formulating the same, and though the idea was distinct in the mind of the author, or let me say the discoverer, of this system, the methodical arrangement of it was a task of great difficulty and proportionate time. Constantly, throughout the constructing of the book, Day read to me his growing work, and more than once he recast the plan of the whole and began the writing anew from the beginning. The Treatise was at length published in the autumn of 1845. It was received worse than coldly by the heads of the musical profession, and the probably injudicious arrangement with the original publishers impeded, still more than the opposing of musicians, the circulation of the book and the propagation of its principles. The author died after long illness, at the age of 39, in the February of 1849, supposing his theory to have been still-born. It fell not, however, wholly upon barren soil, and some few, who had profited by its lessons, requested me, in order to make these more generally accessible than they had been to set them forth afresh in a book of less extent and smaller price than DAY'S TREATISE, wherein rules should be stated but no arguments given for, their support, wherein the points of least frequent application should be omitted, and wherein a series of illustrative exercises should be included for practical service to the student. Accordingly, in 1860, THE RUDIMENTS OF HARMONY was issued; at first with the provision (on the publishers' part) that Alfred Day should not be named in the course of the book, and that

I might only declare myself not to be the originator of the theory it enunciates; in after editions, however, and always by word of mouth, the best possible amends have been made for this injustice. Perhaps a worthier tribute to the memory of my friend than the declaration of his name has been the promulgation of his principles; and this, I flatter myself, the little book in question has to some extent effected. SIX LECTURES ON HARMONY, delivered in 1866 at the Royal Institution, were framed with the avowed design of expounding Day's theory, and they perhaps have tended to further the object in view, especially by their containing extracts from standard compositions that exemplify all the points of the novel chromatic system. During recent years a demand has arisen for the original work, the long-shelved copies have been all dispersed, and the production of the present edition is thus rendered desirable.

The speciality of the Treatise is twofold: Firstly, the standard laws of the ancient, strict, diatonic, artificial, or contrapuntal style are collected and systematically codified with such clearness and consistency as I have not found in earlier works, and they are distinguished entirely from those of the modern, free, chromatic, natural, or harmonic style; Secondly, though the natural chord of the dominant seventh had been more or less freely used for two, or, as lately proved, three and a half centuries prior to the appearance of this book, and though general views had grown into acceptance as to its constitution and treatment, no systematic principles of fundamental harmony had ever been deduced from the phenomena that bring that remarkable chord within the resources of the musician. Every guideless application of them was tentative in those composers who had the genius to conceive and the boldness to practise it; and those of less power copied their examples or framed empirical rules for the peculiar treatment of every special instance. Day perceived that the acoustical laws of harmonic evolution were the genesis of all music; that the natural chords springing from the dominant were imitable by the appropriation of the chromatic element upon other notes in the key; and that these chromatic imitations of the dominant harmonies were identified with the key by their resolution upon, or progression into, other chords common to the same tonality. Mainly, he thus distinguishes the ancient and modern styles: in the former, discords differ in the quality of their intervals according to the degree of the scale from which each is reckoned, but are all governed by one series of rules for their preparation and resolution; in the latter, the fundamental discords consist of the same intervals by whichever of the notes in a key they are generated, but each differs from the others by radical progressions and by resolutions of its discordant notes peculiar to itself in its key relationship. Lastly, whereas the term diatonic defines notes according to the key signature,[*] the term

---

[*] The occasional inflection of the sixth and seventh degrees of the minor scale, and the more rare alteration of the third, are apparent but not genuine exceptions from this statement.

chromatic signifies notes that can only be expressed by accidentals but induce no change of key, and the two styles of music admit respectively the use of the one or the other genus of notes.

Objection has been made to Day's statement that the fundamental discords are "prepared by nature"—objection that the word "prepared" means a note sounded in one part previously to the sounding of a note in another part against which the first is to form a discord, whereas the notes of the harmonic column are not sounded previously to, but coincidently with, if not subsequently to, their generator. Obviously this refers to a term and not to a principle; let the word "prepared" be exchanged for "generated" and the sense is indisputable. No musical sound is onefold, but as every ray of light includes all gradations of colour, so every musical sound includes the boundless harmonic prism. This truth was not perceived in early ages; and, when perceived, it was regarded for its bearing on physics and not on music, and it was not applied to art. Without this guide to musical organisation, arbitrary rules were framed for combining notes in concords and discords, and for treating them in respect to what preceded and followed each. It must be supposed that intuition, rather than science, first prompted an artist to employ chords of natural evolution. In so doing particular notes in each key are selected as the available fundamental notes or generators of the chords in question, and further selection is made of some or other particular notes derived from each generator as being pertinent to the expression of the prevailing idea; such selection and sub-selection are analogous to the painter's process, who, in like manner, selects one of the seven primitive colours or any of the graduated tints between them as appropriate to the object he aims to represent. Day gives technical reasons for the selection of certain fundamental roots and the disregard of others. His reasons for the employment in composition of more or less complete chords derived from these roots, according to the circumstances of each instance, are self-obvious. So far as I can perceive, this view of the subject places harmony on a scientific basis, distinct from the accidental or capricious footing it would have were its assignment to psychological causes to be accepted, assuming that such or such things are written because the composer likes them better than other things, without rule for justification of his preference, or guidance from courses that would be offensive to the general ear.

A seemingly valid objection to the "fundamental" theory is that it involves several variations of pitch for every degree but one of the chromatic scale. Practically, while keyed instruments are tuned by equal temperament, according to which no interval but the octave is true, this objection is a fancy and not a fact. Theoretically, the statement deserves and shall have consideration. The tables given in the Appendix* to the present edition not

---

* Appendix A and V.

only acknowledge but define the alleged variations. I affirm that the employment of the minutely modified notes therein described, enhances the beauty
of the chords to which they belong, and greatly enhances the beauty of the
progression from these chords to those others which naturally succeed to
them. Surely, then, the objection in question is an argument in favour of the
theory it pretends to denounce, and it points to an excellence that might
be, and not to an existing defect. I, for one, am thankful to equal temperament for the music it renders practicable upon keyed instruments; but,
though I bow to the necessity of limiting the sounds within an octave to 12,
I insist that this expedient conventionality affects not the laws of nature upon
which alone sound theory can be based, and that the student ought to know
what *should* be, though forced to practice what *must* be.

The author's entirely original method of figuring the bass to denote the
chords that accompany it claims a different consideration. It is adopted
incompletely in the so-called Tonic Sol-fa Notation, but this may have been
without knowledge of its being set forth in the present book, and, if so, its
having been twice independently invented must be a testimony to its merit.
Let me explain the term Thorough (through) Bass in English, General Bass
in German, Basso Continuo in Italian, or Art d'Accompagnement in French.
When the practice was for an organist or clavecinist to accompany a vocal
or instrumental performance from the score, he read only the bass part and
played harmony according to figures which corresponded with the intervals
above the bass that were to be played. If the part for the bass voices or
the bass orchestral instruments had rests, the part for the tenors or whatever
voices or instruments then stood lowest in the score was transcribed on the
staff whence the organist read, such part being then practically the bass of
the music. Thus, however low or high the notes, the real bass throughout
the composition was always presented on this one staff, which was hence
thorough, or general, or continuous, and reading from it was the art of
accompaniment. Many books in present use in cathedrals are printed in
this species of shorthand, and it is employed also for the organ part in
compositions of past times and of our own. To understand the single or
grouped figures at a glance is therefore indispensable for an organist in
choral performances; many such persons protest against the difficulty of
learning two methods of figuring, and, taking these musicians at their word,
one supposes the implied difficulty may exist though wondering at the fact.
For the sake of avoiding a possible, if only imaginary, obstacle to the
acceptance of DAY'S HARMONY, his method of figuring was not employed in
the book of RUDIMENTS. That it was not, must not be interpreted as an
admission of its impracticability, but as a concession to established habit if
not to prejudice. I am none the less certain that the method in question is,
for the purpose of study, not only superior to the old method, but as perfect
in itself as is anything but the science of numbers. In justice to the author,

then, and also in justice to those who study his theory, his method of figured bass is retained in the present edition : but as the method of figuring is altogether independent of the chords denoted, and does not therefore affect the theory of harmony, I by no means urge the acceptance of Day's method of figuring as necessary to the understanding of his work.

When the book was first published, Day gave me an interleaved copy and requested me to insert on the blank pages any suggestions for modifying the printed matter that might arise from daily observation of the working of the system. This accordingly I did, sometimes by amplifying, sometimes by changing the words of the original explanations, and very often by extending the musical examples. From time to time I submitted my suggestions to him, we discussed them largely, and he adopted them fully. Reference to him was stopped by his death ; but not so my opportunities of observation. It may be that constant practice and constant exposition of his principles have given me a broader and deeper insight into them than I gained during my years of intercourse with the author, and the experience of the subsequent thirty-six years is embodied in the present issue.

Let me now speak of this Second Edition. I have just avowed its somewhat alteration from the original book and stated my licence for such alteration. Let me also state one omission for which I solely am responsible, that, namely, of the intermediate chapter between the First and Second Parts, describing what the author called " Diatonic Free Music." The twilight between the prevalence of the ancient and modern styles in music has so many examples of each, the strict and the free so continually overlap each other in the music produced throughout what may be assumed as the transition period, that to date the dawning of the one or the setting of the other is impossible. When once the concordance of the note at a fourth above the bass as the inversion of the fifth was admitted, in distinction from the discordance of the fourth as the substitute for the third of a chord, and when once, almost co-incidently, the use of the fundamental discords derived from the dominant in any key was practised, the floodgates of free thought were opened, and while always quoting the still standard rules of past times composers overstepped these with broader or narrower latitude, and nothing can be distinctly stated as marking a style which prevailed between that of the past and that of the present. Much music was written and much is now produced that comprises the elements above-named, but is not essentially chromatic in comprising notes foreign to the diatonic scale ; whatever rules are special to the free style apply as fully to this class of music as to that which comprises chromatic chords—the class largely presented in works of two centuries ago, if less frequently than in productions of our own time. As all the matter of the omitted chapter is included in the Second Part of the book, its prior statement was redundant if not confusing. A few points that are integral to the theory had not risen to the surface while my friend lived, but have since become manifest; from some of his views—these by far the least important—I have learned to dissent. My own additions and my own differences of opinion are given in a copious Appendix.

It may be deemed that I, who from time to time offer musical compositions for censure, am presumptuous in enunciating laws for the direction of composers. This might be just, were the laws of my own devising; but, as I have adopted, not invented them, I trust I am exempt from any charge of egotistic dictation, and, as I have profited most largely in my own practice from my comprehension of Day's theory, I feel it to be my duty to musicians who accept me in their number, to set this theory before them in as clear a light as experience enables me to do.

Here, then, is the Second Edition which was hypothetically prognosticated in the author's Preface. If it be not, to cite his words, " as free from faults as it " would have been " in the power of the author to make it," it as nearly represents his views as up to the present I am able to display them. I dedicate it to the use of those musicians of the rising generation who have founded their art practice on the principles it inculcates, and I submit it to the consideration of those elder practitioners, who have most liberally cast aside prejudices which at first were barriers to their perception, and give now their support to the theory. Emphatically I disclaim any merit of authorship, but I trust that I am doing the best I may to disseminate a system which, if true, as I believe it to be, must in course of time supersede all other theories of harmony.

G. A. MACFARREN.

7, HAMILTON TERRACE, N.W.,
July, 1885.

GENERAL INTRODUCTION.

OF THOROUGH BASS.

SECTION 1. Thorough Bass (as it is called) being only a musical short hand, it may be thought of no consequence what the arbitrary signs representing the notes may be, so that those signs are understood; but as the figuring used in thorough bass is taken as the index of all chords written above any given bass in exercises, it is absolutely necessary that the figuring should indicate the real nature and derivation of those chords. The received system of thorough bass has been found utterly insufficient for this purpose because chords entirely different in their nature are figured the same; as for example (Ex. 1), in the following all the chords on the seven notes of the scale of C minor are composed of different intervals, or have different

Ex. 1.

resolutions, and are therefore essentially different chords; yet all these chords are, under the old method figured alike with a 7: this must have a tendency to mislead the student as to the real root and nature of the several chords.

2. To prevent the confusion which this old system induces, a new code of thorough bass is offered in this work, of which the following are the principles:—

3. Any chord will have one figuring in all its inversions unless a discord be in the bass.

4. It will be expressed by letters, as A, B, C, &c., what interval from the root of the chord is in the bass; the following is a table of the letters which are used as arbitrary characters for that purpose:

A	always indicates that the root of a chord is in the bass.					
B	,,	,,	,,	3rd	,,	,,
C	,,	,,	,,	5th	,,	,,
D	,,	,,	,,	7th	,,	,,
E	....	....	....	....	9th (essential)	,,
F	....	....	....	....	11th	,,	,,
G	....	....	....	....	13th	,,	,,
M	indicates the suspended		4th		,,	
N	,,	the suspended	9th		,,	,,

When the bass has a letter expressing a discord, the figure representing that interval of course will not appear.

5. In the second part of this book two chords are described having both primary and secondary roots, and primary and secondary harmonics, or notes generated by each root respectively: the manner of indicating those secondary roots and harmonics will be explained in the chapter treating of the chords to which they belong.

6. The intervals indicated by the figures must be taken according to the signature of the piece of music, if not otherwise expressed.

7. If any interval is to be varied from the pitch which according to the signature it would have, a ♯, ♭, or ♮, is placed before the figure naming or describing that interval.

8. The third may be represented by the ♯, ♭, or ♮, intended to affect it, without any figure whatever: thus when a ♯, ♭, or ♮, is placed over a bass note, it means that a third to that note is to be taken, which third is to be either a ♯, ♭, or ♮ note, according to the accidental marked.

9. If a common chord be intended, the letter A will be placed to the bass without any figure; if the first inversion, the letter B; if the second, the letter C; unless either the third or fifth differs from the signature, in

which case, whichever interval be affected, it will be expressed in the manner above described (Ex. 2).

Ex. 2.

Ex. 3.

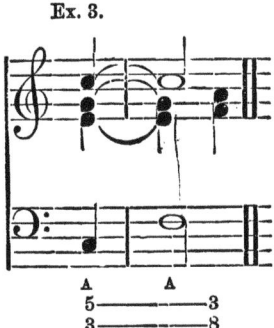

10. A horizontal line drawn from a figure, signifies that the note indicated by that figure is to continue so long as that line lasts, and the figure following such line signifies the note to which such continued note is to proceed (Ex. 3).

11. None of the concords are to be figured unless they be suspended over the resolution, or unless they differ from the signature of the piece of music, excepting in some particular fundamental chords, which will be noticed in the introductions to the chapters containing those chords.

PART I.

DIATONIC HARMONY, OR HARMONY IN THE STRICT STYLE.

CHAPTER I.

OF INTERVALS.

INTRODUCTION.

THIS first chapter, only treating of intervals, contains only one thing new, that is, making the inversion of an octave an octave, instead of an unison, as is usually done; the reason of which is this, to invert does not necessarily mean to move one part an octave up, or the other an octave down, because in that manner of proceeding a ninth could not be inverted, as whichever part were moved it would be a second; but to invert the position of the notes with regard to one another, placing that above which was below, and *vice versâ*. This condition is not fulfilled in making the octave an unison, but is perfectly fulfilled in inverting the octave as an octave, as is done in the following chapter.

SECTION 1. An interval is the distance, or space, between any two notes.

2. Intervals are named seconds, thirds, fourths, fifths, sixths, sevenths, eighths, and ninths, according to the distance of the notes composing those intervals on the staff. The note from which an interval is counted is the first, and hence arise the numbers of all the intervals. Two parts in harmony often proceed to the same note or first, which throughout this book is called the unison.

Ex. 1.

3. Intervals are reckoned from the lower note to the upper, both inclusive. The interval C E is always to be considered a third, although the pitch is varied by the ♯, ♭, or ♮ placed before the notes (Ex. 1), because an interval is numbered according to the relative situation on the staff of the notes composing that interval, without any reference to their positive sound.

4. It may be as well here to observe that from C to E is considered a third, whether the notes be placed at the distance of a third simply, or of one octave and a third, two octaves and a third, or any greater distance; and the same with all other intervals, with the exception of the second, which differs from a ninth (or octave and second), as will be explained hereafter.

5. Either the second or ninth may be taken at (or at a greater distance than) the octave and second, but the uninverted interval of the ninth should never be taken nearer than the octave and second, though this has been done by some writers. The figuring to be used in such a case will be stated when speaking of the first species of discords.

6. A semitone is the distance between any one sound and the nearest sound on an ordinary pianoforte; it follows, therefore, that from C to C♯, D to E♭, or C to B, is one semitone (Ex. 2), and not two, as has been some-times stated.

Ex. 2.

7. A tone is two semitones.

Ex. 3.

8. Intervals are divided into perfect and imperfect.

9. The perfect intervals are the fourth, fifth, and eighth.

10. The imperfect intervals are the second, third, sixth, seventh, and ninth.

11. The imperfect intervals may be either major or minor.

12. The second, fourth, and fifth may be augmented.

13. The fourth, fifth, and seventh may be diminished.

14. No other interval than those named above can occur in diatonic harmony.

15. The intervals in the following table are all in the key of C major or minor.

TABLE OF INTERVALS.*

Ex. 4.

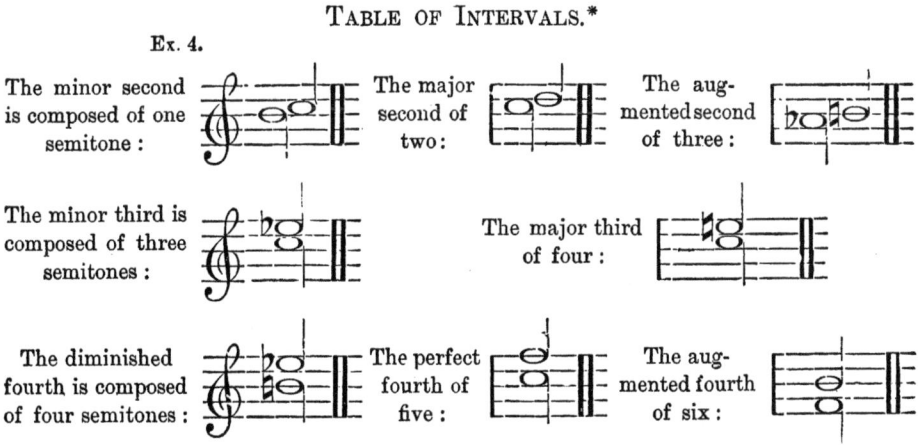

The minor second is composed of one semitone :

The major second of two:

The aug-mented second of three:

The minor third is composed of three semitones :

The major third of four :

The diminished fourth is composed of four semitones :

The perfect fourth of five :

The aug-mented fourth of six :

---

* Appendix A.

TABLE OF INTERVALS—*continued.*

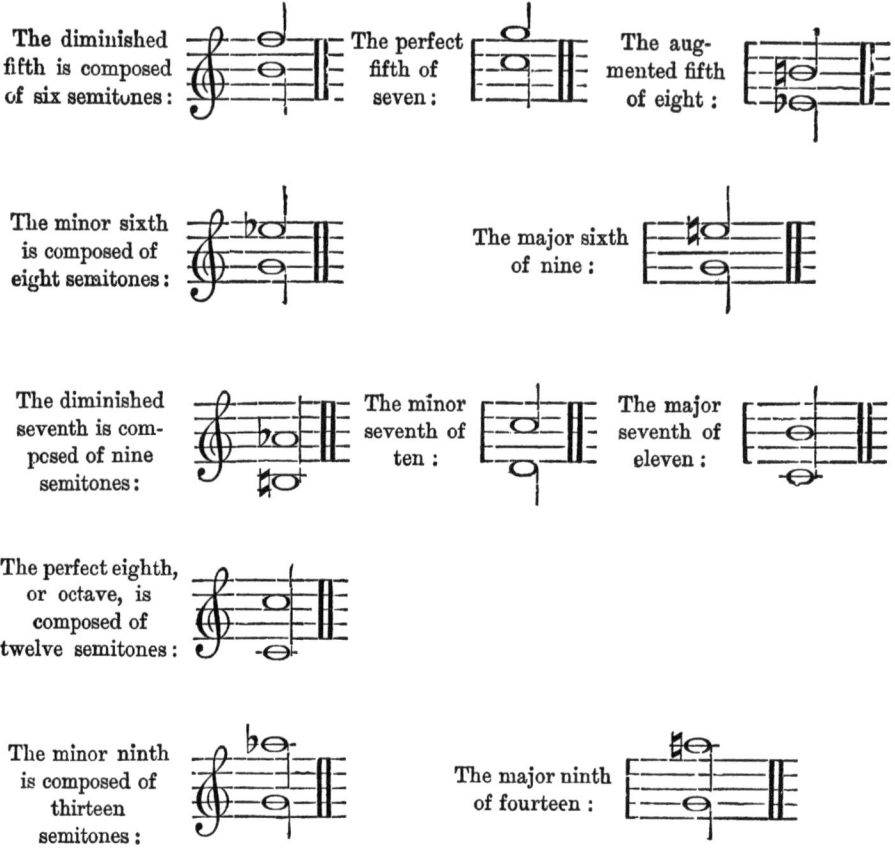

The diminished fifth is composed of six semitones:

The perfect fifth of seven:

The augmented fifth of eight:

The minor sixth is composed of eight semitones:

The major sixth of nine:

The diminished seventh is composed of nine semitones:

The minor seventh of ten:

The major seventh of eleven:

The perfect eighth, or octave, is composed of twelve semitones:

The minor ninth is composed of thirteen semitones:

The major ninth of fourteen:

INVERSION OF INTERVALS.

16. The inversion of an interval is the changing the relative position of the notes composing that interval, either by placing the upper note beneath the lower, or the lower above the upper (Ex. 5).

Ex. 5.   Ex. 6.

17. Perfect intervals, when inverted, remain perfect, the octave an octave, the fifth a fourth, the fourth a fifth (Ex. 6).

18. Major intervals by inversion become minor, and minor intervals major. In the example, the major second C D becomes, by inversion, a

minor seventh D C; the major third C E, a minor sixth E C; the minor second E F, a major seventh F E; the minor third D F, a major sixth F D; the major ninth C D, a minor seventh D C.

Ex. 7.

19. Augmented intervals, by inversion, become diminished, and diminished intervals augmented; the augmented second A♭ B♮, becomes a diminished seventh B♮ and A♭; the diminished fifth B F, an augmented fourth F B; and the augmented fifth E♭ B, the diminished fourth B E♭.

Ex. 8.

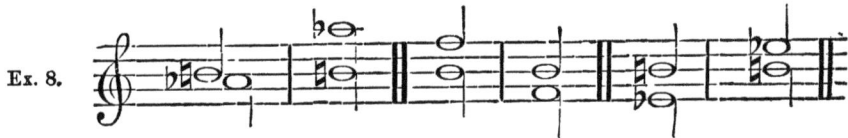

Chapter II.

SCALES AND KEYS.

Introduction.

In this chapter the scales, major and minor, are written: the minor in a manner which is becoming both practically and theoretically more common than it was some few years back; I mean writing it with a minor sixth and major seventh both ascending and descending. The reason of doing so is this: the foundation of the major scale is the common chord of the tonic, which supplies the first, third, and fifth of the key; of the dominant, which supplies the seventh and second; and of the subdominant, which supplies the fourth and sixth. The minor scale is formed in a similar manner: from the minor common chord of the tonic which gives the minor third and fifth; the major common chord of the dominant which gives the major seventh and second of the scale (the third of the dominant being always major); and the minor common chord of the subdominant which gives the fourth and minor sixth of the scale. Here no major sixth or minor seventh is to be found; and, strictly speaking, no major sixth nor minor seventh should be used, though custom has somewhat sanctioned their use, and the particular instances in which they may be used are noticed in future chapters. The reason which is given against writing the minor scale as it is written in this chapter, viz., that the step from the minor sixth to the major seventh is too great, is no reason at all; if all the other steps of the ladder or scale were at equal distances, there might be some show of sense, but in the mixture of whole tones and semitones, I can see no reason why an augmented second should not be introduced. This scale may not be so easy to some instruments and to voices as the old minor scale; therefore, let all those who like it, practise that form of passage, but let them not call it the minor scale. Even as a point of practice I deny the old minor scale to be the better, as practice is for the purpose of overcoming difficulties, and not of evading them.*

SECTION 1. A diatonic scale is a succession of notes following in regular order; by regular order is meant that no line or space be skipped: if either a line or space be skipped, the succession of notes ceases to be a scale.

---

* Appendix B.

2. Scales are the same both ascending and descending.

3. A key has seven notes.

4. The first is called the key note or *tonic*.

5. The second is called the *supertonic*.

6. The third is called the *mediant*.

7. The fourth is called the *subdominant*.

8. The fifth is called the *dominant*.

9. The sixth is called the *submediant*.

10. The seventh is called the *leading* or sensitive note; it cannot ever be doubled excepting in one of the transpositions of a passage in sequence, or as a passing note, or else in an arpeggio against a sustained chord.

11. Scales are of two kinds, major and minor, which are distinguished by the third and sixth.

12. In the major scale, every interval is either major or perfect, when reckoned *upward* from the key note.

Ex. 1.

13. In the minor scale, the third and sixth are minor; the other notes as in the major, counting upwards from the key note.

Ex. 2.

14. As a scale may be commenced on any note, modified in any way by sharps or flats, and as the notes composing the diatonic scales *must* follow in the order above named, therefore it is necessary to introduce sharps in some keys, and flats in others: hence the difference in the signatures of keys.

15. There being more notes in common between the above two keys of C major and A minor, than between C major and any other minor key, or A minor and any other major key, those two keys are therefore called relative major and minor; this is a mere matter of words, and of no practical utility.

Chapter III.

OF THE PROGRESSION OF PARTS IN THE DIATONIC OR STRICT STYLE.

Introduction.

This chapter, as the first, contains little that is new; and, for the most part, the reason for such novelty is given at the time. With regard to the doctrine of false relation, which has been usually treated of under two laws, it is here divided into three; one as affecting the false relations between two parts in the same chord, another between two consecutive chords, and the other between two chords with one intervening: that it is not done so without reason, I think will be evident.

SECTION 1. A chord is two or more notes sounded together.

2. Each note is a separate part; and as the number of notes sounded simultaneously, so is the number of parts.

3. Chords consist of concords and discords.

4. The concords are the unison, major and minor thirds, perfect fifth, major and minor sixths, and perfect eighth between any parts; also the perfect and augmented fourths, and the diminished fifth between any two upper parts: of these the unison, fifth, and eighth are called perfect concords, the third and sixth imperfect.

5. The discords are the second, seventh, ninth, augmented fifth, and diminished fourth between any parts; also the fourth, all augmented and diminished intervals, and the fifth of the mediant, between any upper part and the bass.

6. In passing from chord to chord, the different parts are susceptible of three motions with relation to each other, the similar, contrary, and oblique.

7. Similar motion is two parts moving the same way, that is, both ascending or both descending (Ex. 1).

8. Contrary motion is the parts moving contrary ways, that is, one ascending and the other descending (Ex. 2).

9. Oblique motion is one part remaining and the other moving.

Ex. 3.

Ex. 4.

10. No two parts are allowed to move in perfect fifths; the reason of this is, that two perfect fifths following, in most cases, give the idea of two different keys.*

11. No two parts are allowed to move in octaves on account of the thinness thereby produced, the parts lying between the octaves being scarcely heard; in the example (5), the forbidden octaves are between the first and fourth parts of the third and fourth chords.

Ex. 5.   Ex. 6.

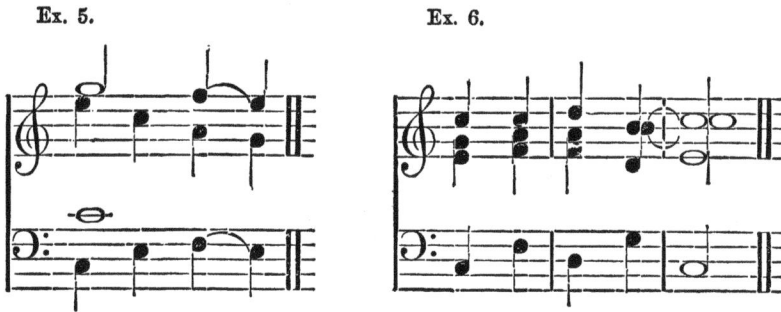

12. No two parts are allowed to move in unison, the clearness of the part writing being thereby destroyed; the first and second parts in the example (6), move in unisons at the fourth and fifth chords.

13. Fifths by contrary motion should not be used (although by most writers allowed), as the reason given why fifths by similar motion should not be used (sect. 10) is equally applicable to fifths by contrary motion (Ex. 7).

Ex. 7.   Ex. 8.

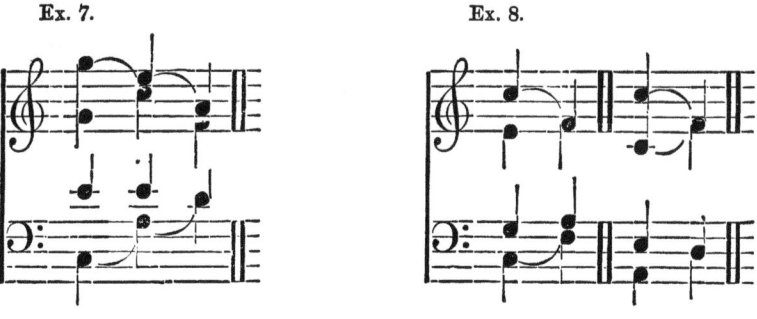

---

* Appendix C.

14. Octaves by contrary motion, or what is equivalent thereto, the progression from an octave to an unison or from an unison to an octave (though allowed by most writers), should not be used, as the richness of the harmony would be thereby destroyed (Ex. 8).

Ex. 9.

15. It is not allowable to come on a perfect concord by similar motion, in two-part writing (Ex. 9).

16. It is not allowable to come on a perfect concord by similar motion, between the extreme parts, whatever be the number of parts (Ex. 10).

Ex. 10.

17. It is not allowable, between any of the parts, to come on an unison by similar motion, whatever be the number of parts (Ex. 11).

Ex. 11.

Ex. 12.

18. It is not allowable, even by contrary motion, and whatever be the number of parts, to skip to the octave or unison of the bass, in the top part, when the bass moves (Ex. 12).*

---

* Appendix D.

19. No two notes next each other in alphabetical order can ever be allowed to go to the unison or octave by similar motion* (Ex. 13).

Ex. 13.   Ex. 14.

20. It is not allowable between any parts to go by similar motion to the unison or octave of any note which resolves a discord (Ex. 14).

21. It is not allowable to move an augmented interval unless it occur in a sequence (Ex. 15). It is not allowable to move a diminished interval except in sequence, unless the melody of the part return to some note within such interval (Ex. 16).

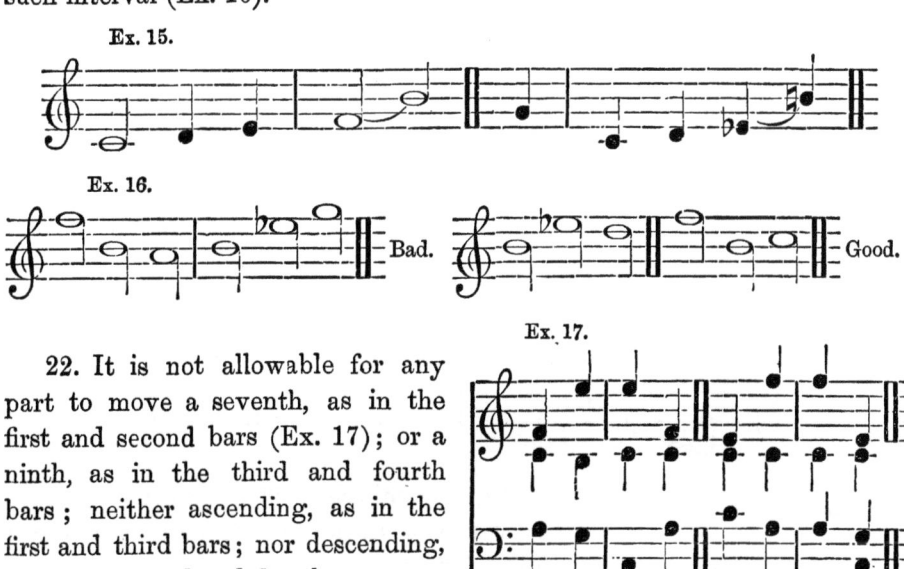

Ex. 15.

Ex. 16.   Bad.   Good.

22. It is not allowable for any part to move a seventh, as in the first and second bars (Ex. 17); or a ninth, as in the third and fourth bars; neither ascending, as in the first and third bars; nor descending, as in the second and fourth.

Ex. 17.

Ex. 18.

23. Two major thirds by similar motion, in two-part writing, are not allowed to follow at the step of a major second (Ex. 18).

24. No upper part should move to a note below the note which an under part has just quitted, nor should a lower part proceed to a note above the note which an upper part has just quitted† (Ex. 19).

---

* Appendix E.   † Appendix F.

Ex. 19.

Ex. 20.

25. In two-part writing, the third on the dominant, in either major or minor key, cannot be followed by the fifth on the subdominant; nor can the third on the sixth of the minor scale be followed by the fifth on the dominant; nor is it desirable in two-part writing, in any case, to move from the third to the fifth by step of a second, in both parts (Ex. 20).*

26. A lower part may not cross a higher, and a higher part may not cross a lower (Ex. 21). The upper notes are heard as one melody, and the under notes are heard as another melody,

Ex. 21.

whoever may sing them; and, besides the confusion thus induced in the part writing, such faulty progression as that in the third bar of the example has the same bad effect as if the two parts preserved their natural position. The sole exception from this rule is when shorter notes in one part cross longer notes in another (Ex. 22).

Ex. 22.

Ex. 23.

27. A diminished fifth may not proceed by step of a second in both parts to a perfect fifth. An exception is that the fifth of the leading note may be followed by the fifth of the tonic in upper parts when the bass is the supertonic followed by the mediant (Ex. 23).

28. False relation between any two parts is not allowable.

29. Notes are falsely related when two notes of the same name, but of a different quality, are either sounded together, or in such succession on the ear, as to confuse, either the progression of the parts, or the key in which such progression may be.

---

* Appendix G.

30. No two notes of the same name, but of a different quality, can occur simultaneously, as in the example (24) where the B♭ and the B♮ are sounded together.

Ex. 24.

Ex. 25.

31. When in two consecutive chords, two notes of the same name occur, but with an alteration by the addition or subtraction of a ♯, ♭, or ♮, such two notes must be in the same part, as in the first bar, and not the original note in one part, and the alteration in another, as in the second (Ex. 25).

32. Where the note which has to be varied is doubled, one only of those notes moves to the altered note, as in the first bar (Ex. 26); when the converse of this progression is taken, as in the second bar (that is, where the note when altered is doubled), not only is the original note allowed to move to the altered note, but also any other note, which does not, by so doing, make false progression.

Ex. 26.

33. False relation also exists between two notes varied in quality, if one note intervene (as in the first bar) (Ex. 27), excepting in two instances. One of these occurs in the minor key, in passing from the first inversion on the minor seventh of the scale to the major common chord of the dominant, whose third is the major seventh of the scale (as in the second and third bars). The other instance occurs in passing from common chords of the first

Ex. 27.

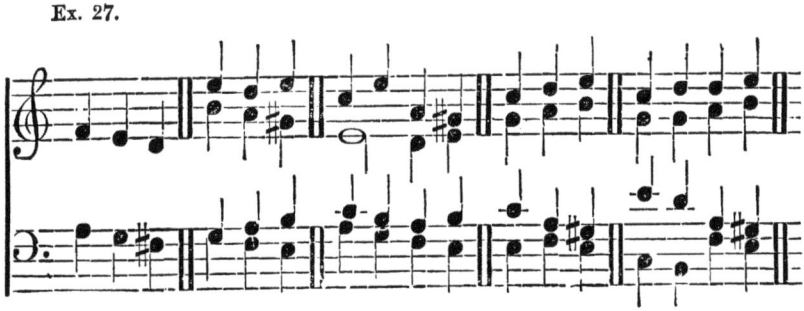

and fifth of the major scale, or their first inversions, to the common chord
of the fifth of the relative minor (as in the fourth and fifth bars), or any of
their inversions.   The false relations in the second and third bars occur from
the defective manner of writing the minor scale as it is frequently written,
with the seventh minor when it falls, major only when it rises; this, though
somewhat sanctioned by long use, is by no means recommended.   Why
those in the fourth and fifth bars are allowable, will be explained in the
Second Part of this book; suffice it here to say that they are so.

Ex. 28.

34. No part may approach the eighth of a
note by similar motion, which note is approached
in another part by descent of a chromatic semitone (Ex. 28).

CHAPTER IV.

OF COMMON CHORDS AND THEIR INVERSIONS.

INTRODUCTION.

THE only thing in which this chapter departs from the orthodox doctrine, is in forbidding the use of the common chord on the third of the major scale in its original position; but be it understood, that although positively forbidden in the text, the student is only *recommended not to use it.*   There are numerous instances in which the best writers (Handel especially) use it; but I always think with bad effect, the chord having nothing whatever to do with the key.   It would not be in place here, nor would it be understood, were the reasons for its prohibition given; but in the Second Part of this book, in the introduction to the chapter treating of the chromatic scale, those reasons will be found.

SECTION 1. A triad consists of any bass note and its third and fifth.   This bass note is called the root of the chord; it is lettered A.

2. A common chord is a triad with a perfect fifth.

3. The third may be either major or minor; and as the third, so is the chord called, that is, either major or minor.

4. The third of the chord should not be omitted as in the first bar, because it leaves an uncertainty whether the chord be major as in the second bar, or minor as in the third (Ex. 1).   The fifth or even the root of a chord may be omitted.

Ex. 1.

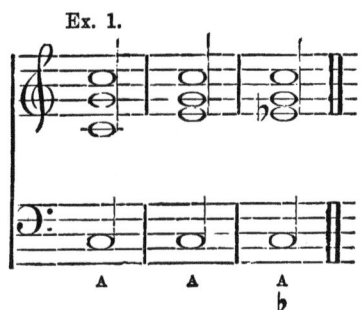

Ex. 2.

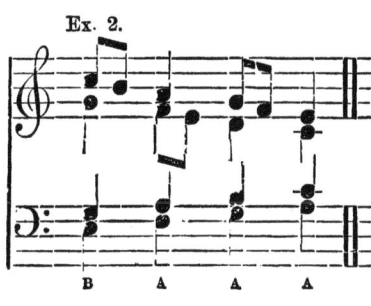

5. It is desirable not to double the *major* third of the chord, because the harmonic fifth of that third (the vibration of which may be distinctly heard), destroys the distinctness of the chord.*

6. It is not objectionable to double the major third of the chord, if the third be both approached and quitted by contrary motion, and by a step of one degree of the scale in both parts (Ex. 2).

* Appendix H.

C

7. The common chord on the mediant or third of the major scale, is not allowable, excepting in the repetitions of a sequence, and therefore the fifth on the third of the scale can never be taken as a concord. No unprepared augmented or diminished interval can be taken, unless in sequence, excepting the augmented fourth, or its inversion the diminished fifth, formed by the third and sixth of the subdominant in the minor key, or of the supertonic in either minor or major.

8. Ancient rule required, and modern practice admits, that a passage in a minor key close with a major chord, the third in which chord is called the *Tierce de Picardie* (Ex. 3).

Ex. 3.

9. The inversion of a chord is the placing any other of its notes than the root in the bass.

10. The first inversion is when the third is in the bass, when the root becomes a sixth to that bass, and the fifth a third; this is usually called the chord of the sixth.

11. When this chord occurs B is placed to the bass, which shows that the bass is the third from the root (Ex. 4).

Ex. 4.   Ex. 5.

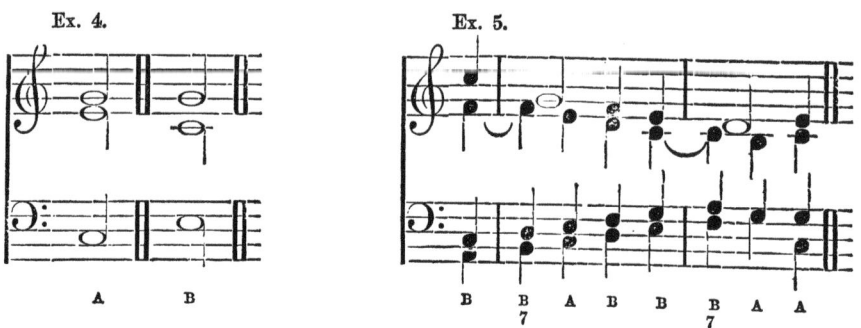

12. In this chord, as in the common chord, the root or fifth of the chord may be doubled.

13. When this chord is an inversion of a major common chord, the bass, the major third from the root, should not be doubled, unless it be both approached and quitted by contrary motion, as in **Ex. 5**, and by step of only one degree of the scale in both parts.

14. The reason for not doubling the bass of this chord is the same as that given for not doubling the major third of the common chord, and in this case the reason is even stronger, as the harmonics of a bass note come out much more strongly than those of any other part. The reason why the passage in Ex. 5 is correct is that the doubled third (from the contrary motion of the parts) sounds more like part of a passage belonging to the fourth species of discords (Chap. X.) than an actual major third of a common chord. The doubling of the bass when it is a minor third in a common chord is less objectionable; and the doubling of the bass when it is the third of a diminished triad is quite unobjectionable.

15. No form of the common chord of the second of the scale can be followed by any form of the common chord on the tonic, unless both be in their first inversion, as in Ex. 6.

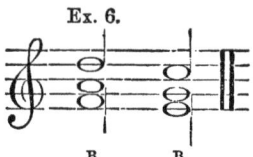

Ex. 6.

16. Though the triads on the third and seventh of the major scale, and on the second and seventh of the minor scale, are not allowed as concords in pure diatonic harmony, yet the first inversion of these chords is allowed; but in that which forms the sixth on the supertonic in major or minor, the sixth, *being the leading note*, cannot be doubled, and in that which forms the sixth on the dominant in major, the third, being the leading note, cannot be doubled.

17. The chords of the sixth, on the second of either major or minor key, and on the fourth of the minor (which form the link between the diatonic and chromatic schools), are the only cases where an augmented or diminished interval can be taken without preparation. The reason will be given in the Second Part of this book, when the chords from which they are derived are treated of.*

18. The first inversion of the incomplete triad of the mediant in the minor key, omitting the augmented fifth of the root, may be taken on the

Ex. 7.

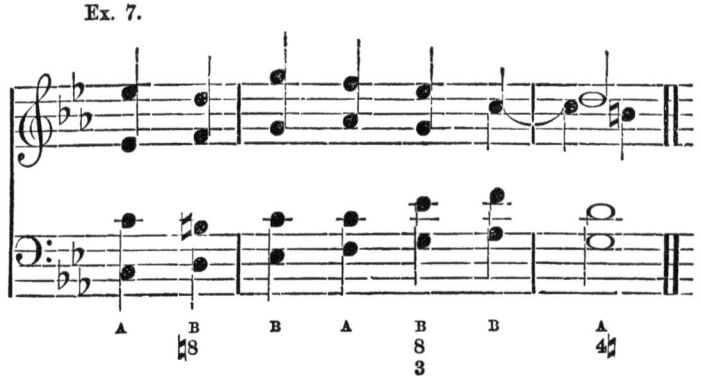

* Appendix I.

dominant, in which chord either or both of the notes may be doubled. The bass is lettered B, with the figures $\frac{6}{3}$, implying the absence of the fifth, which would be discordant against the inverted root (Ex. 7).

19. If the chord of the sixth on the third of the scale either major or minor (being the first inversion of the common chord of the tonic), be followed by that of the sixth on the leading note (the first inversion of the common chord of the dominant), as in the first bar of Ex. 8, the bass should fall, or if the order be reversed should rise, as in the second bar. If the sixth on the

Ex. 8.

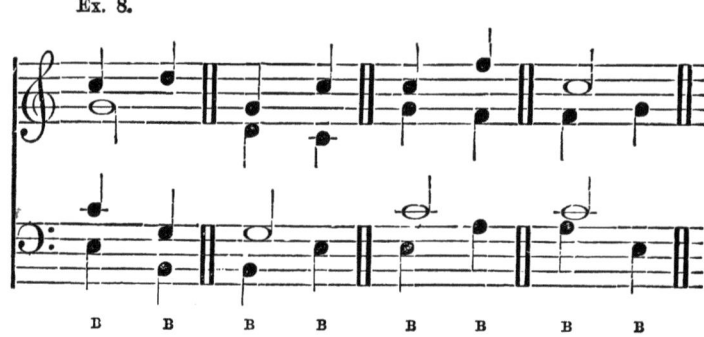

third of either major or minor key (the first inversion of the tonic major or minor common chord) be followed by the sixth on the sixth of the scale (the first inversion of the subdominant major or minor common chord), the bass should rise as in the third bar, or if the order be reversed should fall, as in the fourth bar.

20. The second inversion of a common chord is when the fifth is in the bass, when the root becomes a fourth, and the third a sixth.

21. This chord can never occur in *strict* diatonic music; it will, therefore, not be treated of here.*

---

* Appendix J.

CHAPTER V.

OF SEQUENCE.

INTRODUCTION.

THIS chapter, which treats of sequence, will, I think, be enough to decide the writing of the minor scale. In the diatonic school, at the repetitions in a sequence, all idea of the quality of the intervals, that is, whether they be perfect, major, minor, augmented, or diminished, is lost, and all intervals are treated the same; on which principle the sequence in C minor in the following chapter is written; supposing which sequence altered to suit the more common minor scale, as the sixth and seventh of the scale both ascend, they must be major, and the following sequence would be formed, the objections

Ex. 1.

to which are so numerous and palpable, that I think one glance will be sufficient to determine the fate of the old minor scale. How the keys are confused in the above example I shall now proceed to show. The first three chords taken in succession could only belong to Bb major; the third and fourth chords to C major; the fourth and fifth chords to C minor; the fifth and sixth chords it is utterly impossible to connect in any key, the fifth chord belonging only to C minor, as a diatonic chord, and the sixth chord belonging only to Bb; the sixth and seventh chords taken together could only belong to Bb; the seventh and eighth to C major; the eighth and ninth to C major or minor; and the last two chords only to C minor. It will be seen by this how the old minor scale confuses the key, and in itself entirely refutes all arguments used in its favour. It has been said that any minor scale, say C minor, is only a portion of its relative (as it is called) major (Eb), the minor beginning on the sixth of the major scale; but as the fourth and fifth of such major, when occurring as parts of the ascending minor scale, are uniformly augmented in the old

method of writing the minor scale, therefore it cannot belong to that major
(E♭); it appears to be nearer to B♭ than to any other key, but as the B,
whenever it occurs, is ♮, it cannot belong to B♭.   The descending scale
might be a portion of E♭ were it never harmonized, but unfortunately the
B♮ is made use of occasionally, even by the greatest advocates for the old
form of minor scale.   It follows, therefore, that such descending scale of C
minor bears a great resemblance to E♭, so much so as to render it particularly
easy to confuse the two keys in such a manner as to make it doubtful in
which key any progression may be, and that the old ascending minor scale
cannot by any possibility belong, nor does it bear any great resemblance, to
any key at all.   The real fact is, that any minor key is an arbitrary, not a
natural, change of the major third and sixth of the scale into the minor by
means of the tonic and subdominant minor common chords, the dominant
harmony remaining major, natural, and unchanged; otherwise the key would
be undetermined.

SECTION 1. A sequence is the repetition of any progression of harmony on
different notes of the scale, the bass rising or falling in equal gradation in
each repetition *

2. The progression may consist of two chords, as in Ex. 2 ; of three
chords, as in Ex. 3, or of even more chords.

Ex. 2.   Ex. 3.

3. The chords composing a sequence may be either concords or discords,
or a mixture of both.   Sequences of common chords alone will be noticed
here.

4. In sequence a *diatonic* third and fifth to any note of the diatonic scale,
major or minor, may be taken, and the chord so formed may be treated as
though it were a common chord; by this means are obtained the triad with
a diminished fifth on the leading note, and the discordant triad on the
mediant of the major key, as in the example in the major; also the triads with
a diminished fifth on the leading note and second, and the triad with an
augmented fifth on the third, of the minor key, as in the example in the
minor (Ex. 4) ; the * in the example marks the diminished fifth, and the † the
discordant fifth of the mediant.

---

* Appendix K.

Ex. 4.

5. The progression of each part must be in sequence, as well as the bass, that is, in whatever part any interval from the bass be found in the original progression, in the same part must the same interval be found in the repetition thereof.

6. In Ex. 4, in the first chord the third of the chord is in the first part, the octave to the bass in the second part, and the fifth in the third part. In the second chord, which completes the original progression, the octave to the bass is in the first part, the fifth in the second part, and the third in the third part. In the third and fourth chords, which form the repetition of the progression, the notes stand precisely in the same position in regard to the bass as in the original progression.

7. Although the diminished and augmented fifths are allowed as concords in sequence, yet they must not appear in the original progression, but in some one of the repetitions thereof.

8. The same law affects all sequences, that is, that when any chord is allowable only in sequence, it must appear in one of the repetitions, and not in the original progression, therefore the triads on the seventh and third of the major scale, and on the seventh, third, and second of the minor scale, are not allowed (as concords) in the original progression of any sequence.

CHAPTER VI.

ON DISCORDS.

SECTION 1. Discords differ from concords insomuch as that they cannot be taken indiscriminately, but must be taken either by preparation or transition, and must be resolved.

2. Preparation consists in sounding the note forming the discord previously in the same part.

3. A discord may be prepared by sounding the dissonant note previously as a concord with the part with which it afterwards forms the discord (Ex. 1).

Ex. 1.   Ex. 2.

4. A discord may also be prepared by sounding the dissonant note alone, and bringing in the other part afterwards (Ex. 2).

5. Transition is passing from a concord to a discord (by degrees only), which discord must pass on by degrees to the next concord in the same direction, which concord may either belong to the same chord or to any other, or return to the concord whence it came, provided no false progression be made. These discords are not taken notice of in the figuring.

Ex. 3.

6. Resolution is the discordant note passing to the consonant note, to which by the laws of the different discords it is compelled to move (Ex. 4).

Ex. 4.

Ex. 5.

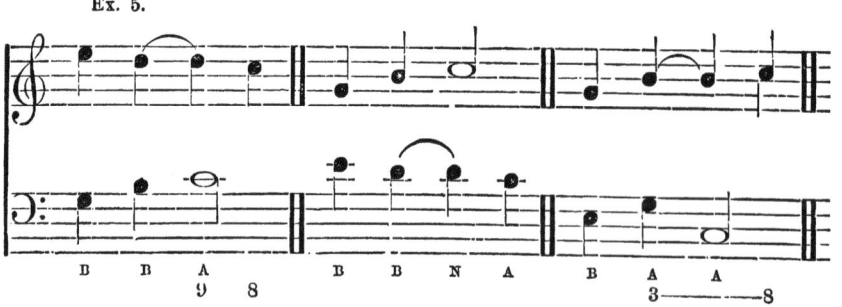

7. No discord can be sounded at the same time as the note on which it resolves, excepting at the distance of a ninth, the discord being in the upper part as in the first bar, or at the distance of a seventh, such seventh being an inversion of a ninth, the discord being in the lower part as in the second bar; or at the distance of a seventh, the discord being in the upper part and rising to the octave as in the third bar (Ex. 5), when in the first species of discords the third of one chord is suspended as the seventh of the next; this will be explained in treating of the first species of discords, with which it forms the dissonance (Chap. VII., sects. 6, 10, 11, 15, 26).*

8. No discord is allowed to be doubled, disallowed octaves being produced by the resolution, as will be seen hereafter.

9. There are four species of diatonic discords.

---

* Appendix L.

Chapter VII.

FIRST SPECIES OF DIATONIC DISCORDS.

INTRODUCTION.

WHATSOEVER in this chapter, regarding the inversions of single or double discords, is heterodox in words and theory, as a matter of notes and practice is perfectly orthodox. The law respecting prepared discords, as deduced from the best writings, appears to be very simple; a discord may be taken in any part, whether top, inner, or bottom, provided that, according to the laws for the progression of parts and preparation of discords, it can be properly prepared in that part, and does not resolve on to another discord. The rules for the resolution of discordant fifths, and those for the suspension of complete chords, are also only novelties in words and theory.*

SECTION 1. That which is here classed as the first species consists of suspended discords. They require to be prepared, and the resolution takes place while the chord against which the discordant note forms the discord remains.†

2. A discord of this species must be taken on a stronger accent than its resolution, as on the first or third division of time having four divisions in the bar, or on the first or second of time having three.

3. The discords which may be taken in this way, are the fourth and ninth, the augmented fifth, the diminished fifth on the leading note, and the fifth on the mediant of the major key.

4. The fourth resolves on the third of the same chord (Ex. 1).

5. The fourth, it will be seen, is a mere retardation of the third of the chord, the bass being the root.

Ex. 1.   Ex. 2.

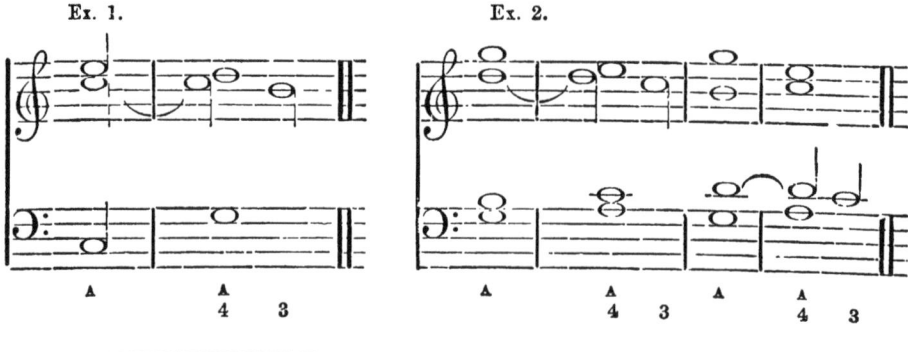

* Appendix M.   † Appendix N.

6. The third and fourth (as in Ex. 2) may be taken together, if the third be approached from the note next below it, and be at the distance of an octave from the resolution of the fourth (Chap. VI., sect. 7), and the same in all the inversions. But it must be observed that this can only be the case where the third may be doubled, never as the third of the dominant, unless in one of the repetitions of a sequence, and it is always more agreeable if the third be minor (Ex. 2).

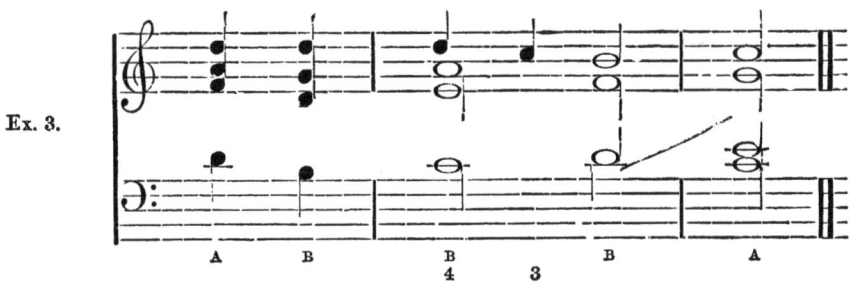

Ex. 3.

7. The first inversion of the chord of the suspended fourth, is when the third is in the bass, when the note which was a fourth becomes a ninth. The bass of this inversion is lettered B, with the figures 4,3; the fourth resolves on the third, the other notes remaining (Ex. 3). This inversion may only be used under the conditions which justify the doubling of the bass of a chord in the first inversion (Chap. IV., sects. 13, 14).

8. The second inversion is with the fifth in the bass; this is never used in strict writing, as the inverted root, being a fourth to the bass, is a dissonance.

9. The third inversion has the fourth in the bass. The bass is lettered M, and, being the suspended fourth, falls one degree to a note lettered B. If the third is to be in the chord, this is denoted by a figure 3 (Ex. 4).

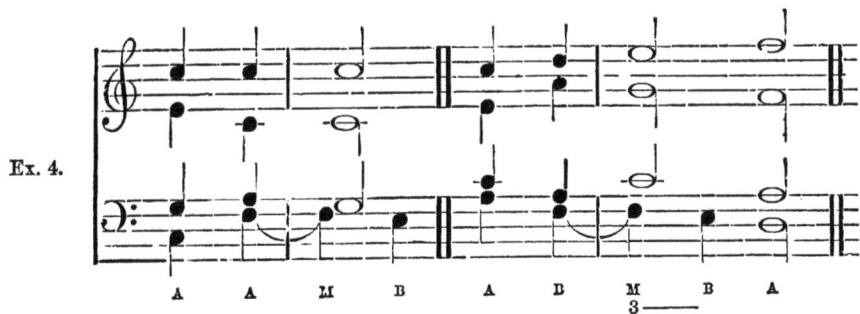

Ex. 4.

10. The suspended ninth cannot be prepared by the eighth; the ninth always resolves on the eighth (Ex. 5).

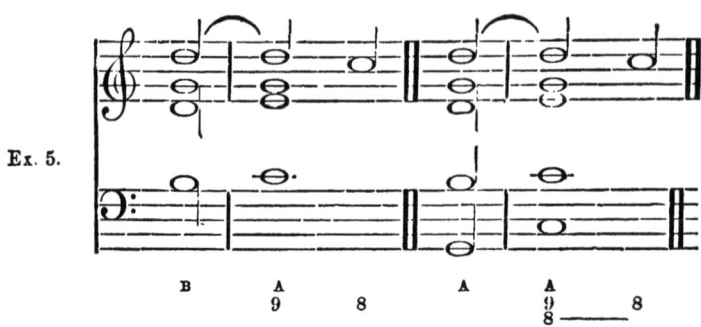

Ex. 5.

11. The first inversion of the chord of the suspended ninth is with the third in the bass. The bass is lettered B, with the figures 9, 8 (Ex. 6), or if the root be in the chord, which it can only be if approached from the note next below it, $\frac{9}{8}$—8 (Chap. VI., sect. 7).

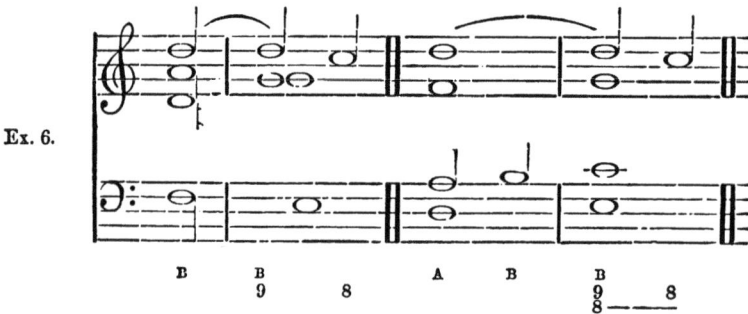

Ex. 6.

12. The second inversion cannot be used, as the suspended ninth in falling to the eighth (its resolution) would form a fourth with the bass, which is no resolution.

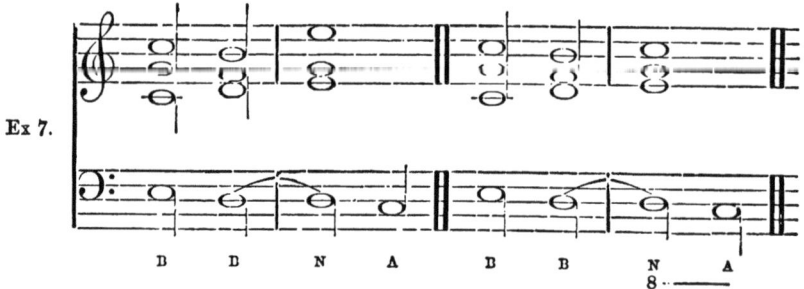

Ex 7.

13. The third inversion has the ninth in the bass. It has the letter N, and being the ninth falls one degree to a note lettered A; if the root is to be in the chord this is denoted by a figure 8 (Ex. 7).

14. A suspended discord prevents not the ill effects of two fifths or two eighths from its notes of preparation and resolution in another part, except only if that other part rise from the note which would become a fifth or an eighth when the suspension resolves. The first two bars in Ex. 8 are bad,

as the fifth would be were there no suspension; the next two bars are good, because A, being a concord with C, is free to go to any other concord while the C continues.

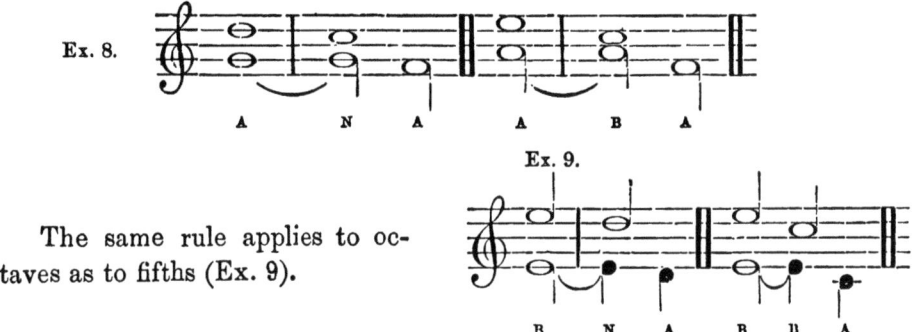

Ex. 8.

The same rule applies to octaves as to fifths (Ex. 9).

Ex. 9.

If the fifth of the chord rise to the root when the ninth is resolved, the effect of consecutive fifths is evaded, as it is if the fifth either rise or fall to the third (Ex. 10).

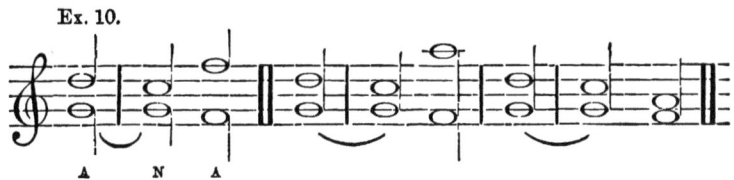

Ex. 10.

15. These two suspended discords may be taken together, and if they can be approached by single step and in contrary motion, &c. (Chap. VI., sect. 7), the eighth and third, or either of them, may exist simultaneously with the fourth and ninth; the fourth resolves on the third, and the ninth on the eighth (Ex. 11).

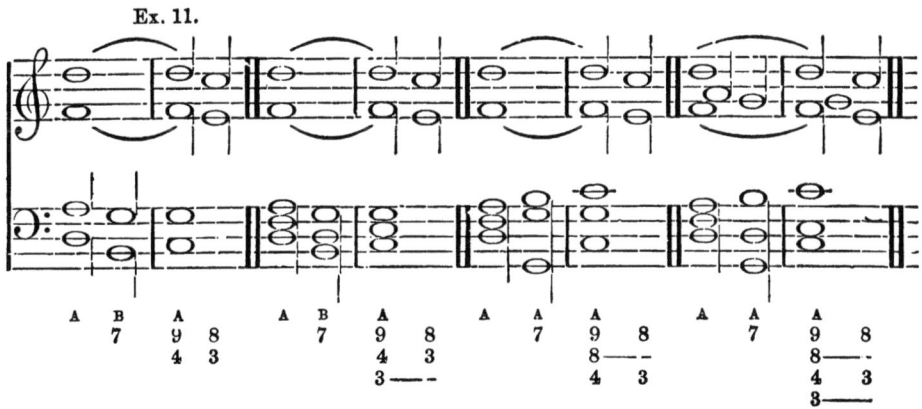

Ex. 11.

16. The first inversion of this double suspended discord has the third in the bass, which is lettered B, with the figures $\frac{9}{\substack{8\\4}}$; the fourth resolves on the third, and the ninth on the eighth (Ex. 12).

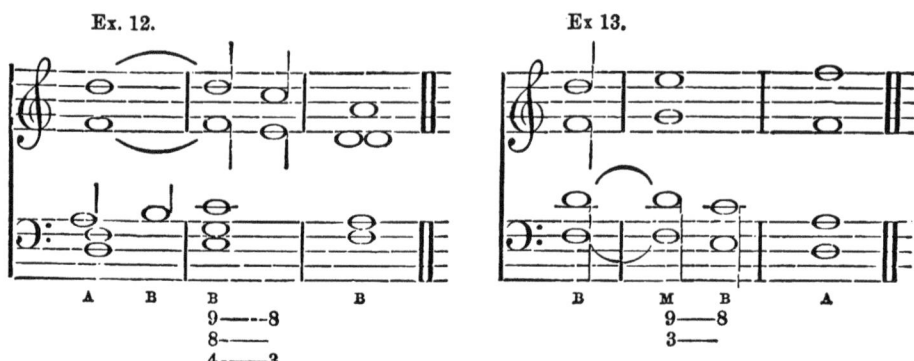

Ex. 12.   Ex 13.

17. The second inversion cannot be used.   (Chap. VII., sects. 8 and 12).

18. The third inversion has the fourth in the bass; it is lettered M, with the figures $\frac{9}{3}$—8; the bass, the original fourth, falls a degree, as does the ninth (Ex. 13).

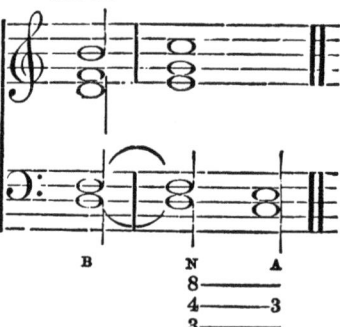

Ex. 14.

19. The fourth inversion has the ninth in the bass, with the letter N, and the figures $\frac{8}{4}{3}$, the bass and fourth both fall one degree (Ex. 14).

20. It will be seen that, in all these inversions, the discordant notes progress exactly in the same way, and to the same places, as in the original position, each inversion of the discord passing to some inversion of that concord on which the discord originally resolved.

21. Those triads which, being discordant in their direct form, cease to be discordant when in their first inversion, may bear the suspension of the fourth, or the ninth, or both, that will be resolved on such first inversions (Ex. 15).

Ex. 15.

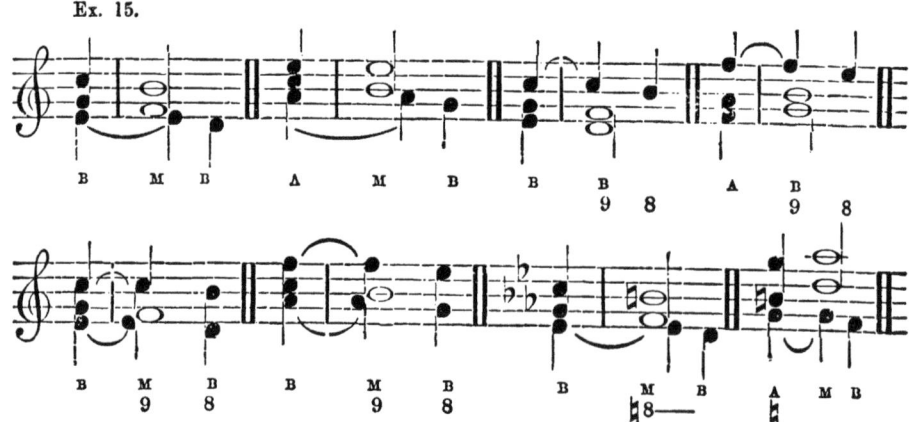

Ex. 15—continued.

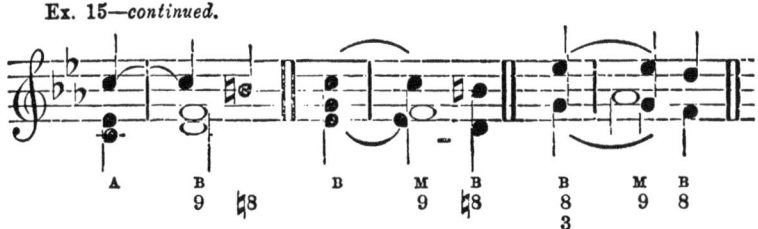

22. The diminished fifth can be taken on the leading note of either major or minor key; its resolution is on the sixth. As the sixth is the real root, the diminished fifth is a note suspended from the previous chord. The bass will be lettered B, with the figures 7—8, indicating the suspended note, which rises to the root of the chord; the seventh, however (which stands as the fifth to the bass) must not be sounded together with the root. It may be accompanied by the inverted ninth and figured accordingly.

Ex. 16.

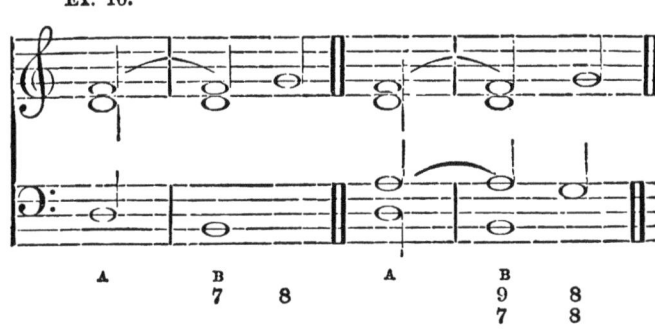

23. The augmented fifth can only be taken on the mediant of the minor scale. It can be accompanied by the third, also by the seventh (which is an

Ex. 17.

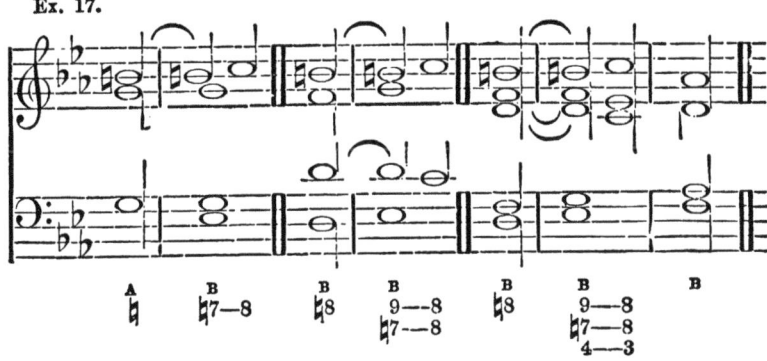

inverted ninth), and by the ninth (which is an inverted fourth), or any combination or variety of them (Ex. 17).

24. The fifth on the third of the major scale, though perfect, is also available as a suspended discord, with the same combination and resolution as the augmented fifth in the minor key. With the change of signature from minor to major, Ex. 17 applies as well to this suspension as to the other.

Ex. 18.

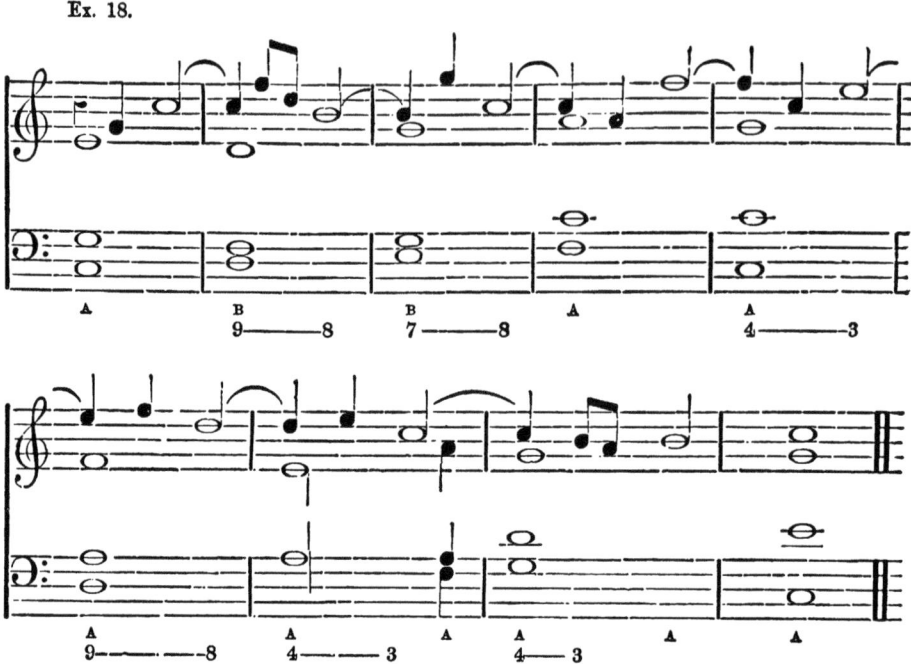

25. A discord of this species may skip to any concord, either above or below it, provided it return to the note which should form its resolution before the rest of the chord be changed (Ex. 18).

26. Any complete chord may be suspended over the root or third of another when the root of the latter is the fourth above the root of the former. The discordant notes may then either rise or fall a second, and the concordant fifth in the latter chord is free. The bass of the chord of preparation has the figures denoting the intervals that are to be suspended; the bass of the suspension has the letter A or B, showing it to be the root or third of the chord of resolution, and it has lines from the figures indicating those intervals in the preceding chord which are suspended to the figures indicating the intervals of the new chord on which they resolve (Ex. 19).

Ex. 19.

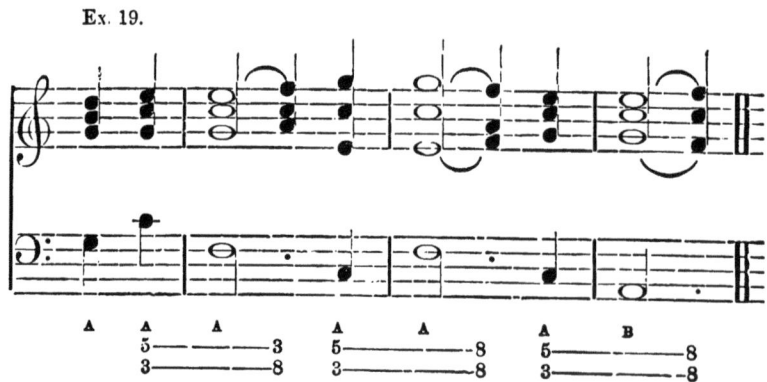

CHAPTER VIII.

THE SECOND SPECIES OF DISCORDS.

INTRODUCTION.

THE novelties in this chapter are: I, When a bass with the intervals $\frac{7}{3}$ is resolved on a chord whose root is a second above the bass of the discord, the said discord is shown to be the first inversion of a chord of the ninth, thus fulfilling the invariable diatonic rule that when a discord is resolved on a chord with another root, the root of the resolution must be a fourth above the root of the discord; and II, the fifth of the mediant is shown to be a discord needing the same radical progression to its resolution.

SECTION 1. Those discords which are here classed as the second species, are those which are prepared, and which are resolved on the following chord.

2. The discords which may be taken in this species are the seventh and ninth, and their inversions; the perfect fifth on the third of the major scale; and the diminished fifth on the second, and the augmented fifth on the third, of the minor scale.

3. Neither seventh nor ninth can be taken on the fourth or seventh of either major or minor key, nor can the seventh be taken on the key note of the minor, nor the ninth on the sixth of the minor.*

4. The seventh and ninth however on these notes, may be taken in the repetitions of a sequence.

5. The seventh may be accompanied by the third, fifth, and eighth, or any variety of them.

6. This chord is resolved on a chord, the root of which is the fourth above or fifth below the root of such seventh (Ex. 1). The seventh must

Ex. 1.

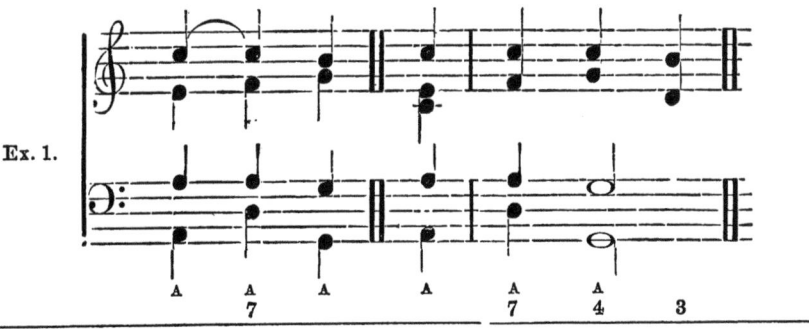

| A | A | A | A | A | A | |
| 7 | | | | 7 | 4 | 3 |

* Appendix O.

fall to the third of the next chord, or be suspended as a fourth. The other intervals are limited in their progression only by the rules for the progression of parts.

7. The third of this chord may prepare a seventh, and a fifth a ninth (Ex. 2).

Ex. 2.

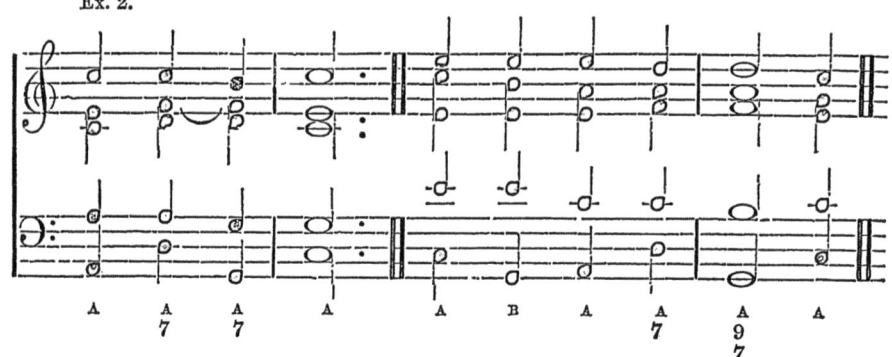

Ex. 3.

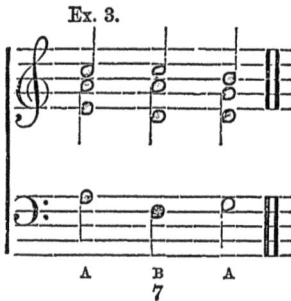

8. The first inversion of this chord has the third in the bass. It is lettered B, with the figure 7; the sixth from the bass is the root, and the fifth is the inversion of the seventh. The resolution of this inversion, is on a chord having the note next above the bass for its root (Ex. 3).

9. The second and third inversions cannot be used, as they each contain two discords, both of which cannot be prepared.*

10. The ninth may be accompanied by the third, fifth, and seventh, or any combination of them; but the root can only be sounded in the bass, and not in any of the upper parts. It will be seen that this chord is, when accompanied by the seventh, merely a ninth added to the chord of the seventh; the chord of the ninth is resolved on a chord the root of which is

Ex. 4.

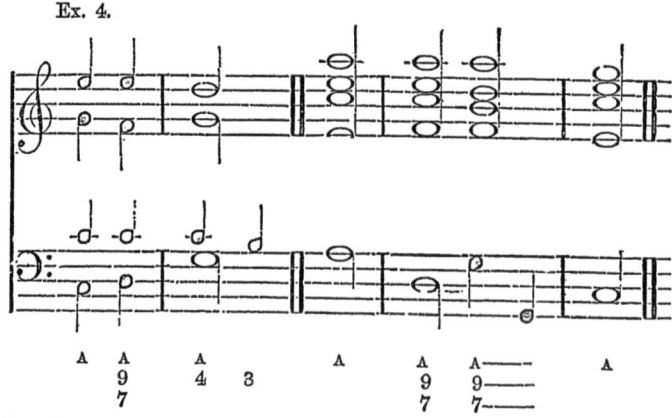

---

* Appendix O.

the fourth above; the ninth is resolved on the fifth of the new root; the rest of the intervals are treated as in the chord of the seventh.

11. The first inversion of this chord, in which the root must be omitted, has the same intervals as a chord of the seventh. The resolution is on the chord of the second above the bass note, and not, as in the original chord of the seventh, on the chord of the fourth above. This chord is marked B $\frac{9}{7}$ (Ex. 5). Every chord of the seventh may be a first inversion of a chord of the ninth, and every first inversion of a chord of the ninth may be a chord of the seventh; for instance, the C, lettered A B, has C for its root, because it is the resolution of the chord of the seventh of G, and has A for its root because it is resolved on the chord of D, and the C lettered B A has A for its root because it is the resolution of the dissonant triad of E, and has C for its root because it is resolved upon the chord of F (Ex. 6). The seventh from the root in this inversion, as it is

Ex. 5.

Ex. 6.

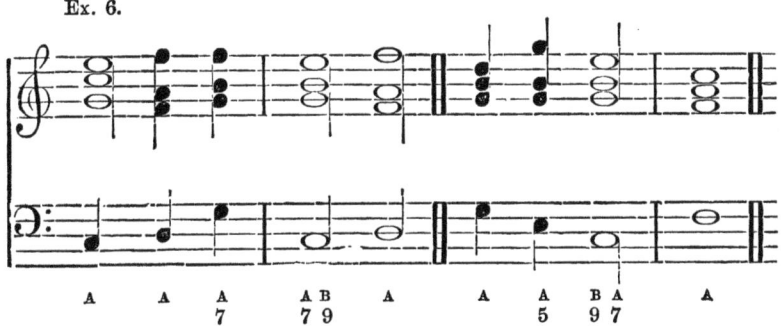

consonant with each note that is sounded, requires not preparation nor resolution, excepting in the first inversion of the $\frac{9}{7}$ of the dominant, in which the seventh forms a diminished fifth with the third, when it requires to be prepared and resolved accordingly (Ex. 7), and excepting also in the first

Ex. 7.

(The Unprepared.)   (The Prepared.)

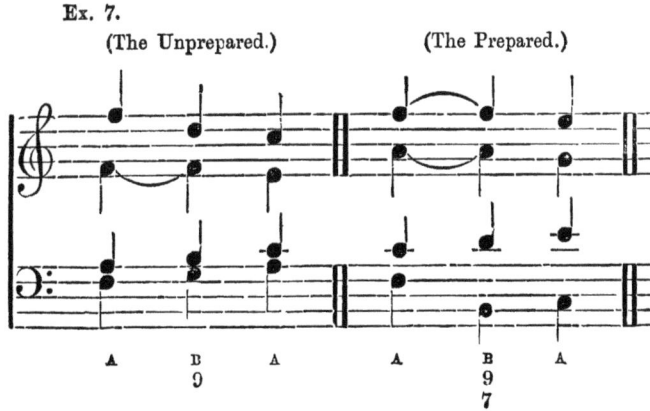

inversion of the ⁹₇ of the tonic in a major key, when the original seventh stands as the dissonant fifth of the mediant (Ex. 8). (Sects. 17 to 19.)

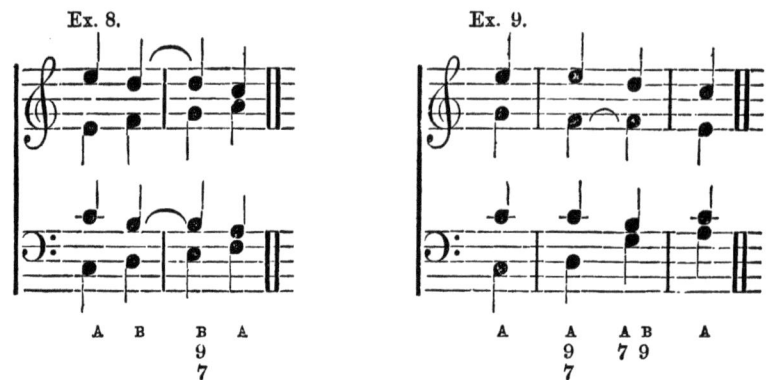

12. When this first inversion of the chord is taken on the dominant, the resolution is known as the interrupted cadence (Ex. 9).

13. The second (and *only other* inversion which can be used in strict music) has the fifth in the bass, marked C ⁹₇. This differs from the first inversion of a seventh, insomuch as its resolution is to a chord whose root is a note below the bass of the inversion, and not a note above, as in the case of the first inversion of a seventh, and any seventh or inversion of a seventh may be treated as a ninth or inversion thereof (Ex. 10).*

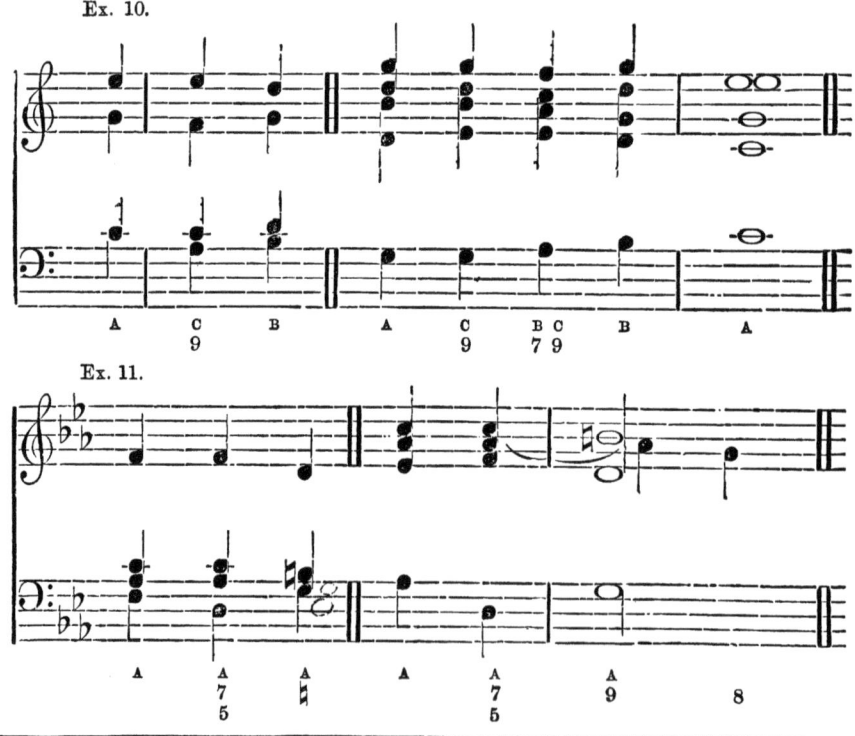

---

* Appendix P.

14. The diminished fifth from the root can only (excepting in sequence) be taken on the second of the minor scale.

15. It must be accompanied by the seventh, which may have either the third or eighth, or both, with it. This chord resolves on a chord the root of which is a fourth above or fifth below: the diminished fifth falls to the new root, or suspends a ninth (Ex. 11).

16. The diminished fifth with seventh may also be accompanied by the ninth. In the inversion of this chord the root is omitted, and the fifth and seventh from the root cease to be discordant, and hence need not preparation (Ex. 12).

Ex. 12.

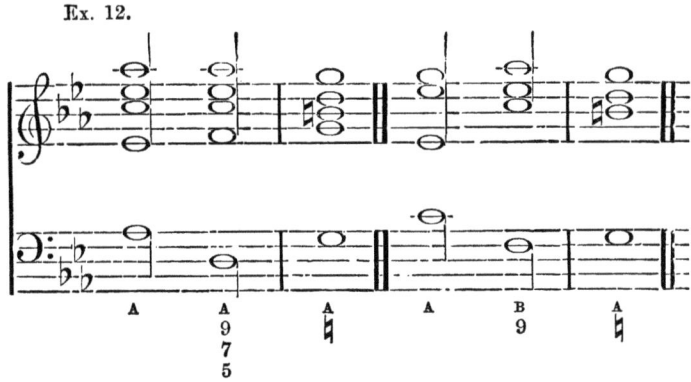

17. The augmented fifth can only be taken on the mediant of the minor key.

18. It may be accompanied by the third, prepared seventh, and ninth, or any combination or variety of them. This chord resolves on a chord the root

Ex. 13.

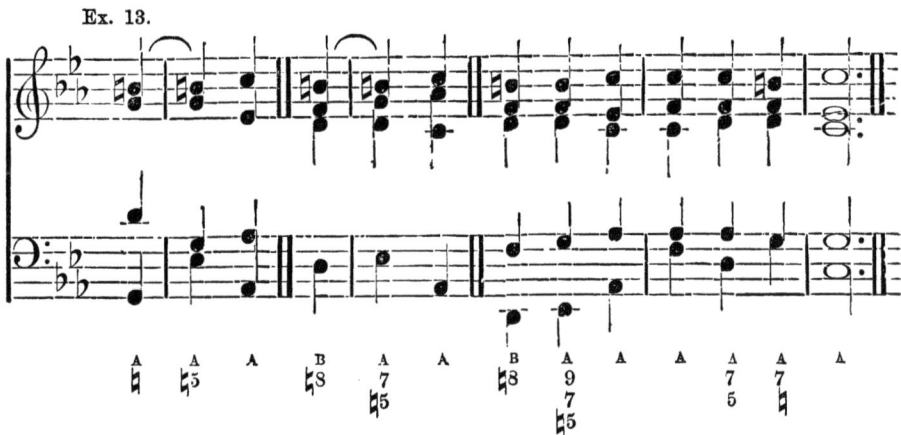

of which is a fourth above or fifth below; the augmented fifth rises to the third of the new root; the other intervals progress as in the chords of the seventh and ninth (Ex. 13).

19. The only inversion of this chord (with its several accompaniments) which can be used, is that which has the third in the bass (Ex. 14).*

Ex. 14.

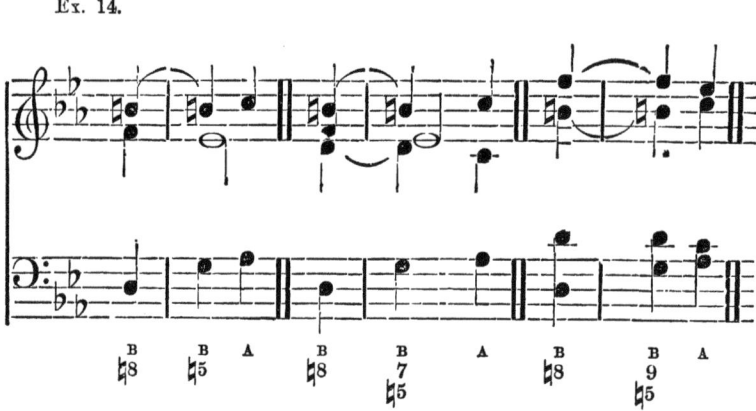

The fifth on the mediant of the major key is in every respect treated as the augmented fifth on the mediant of the minor key, with the exception that the first inversion is not a discord.

20. The dissonant notes of this species may resolve, and the consonant notes prepare other discords of this species (Ex. 15).

Ex. 15.

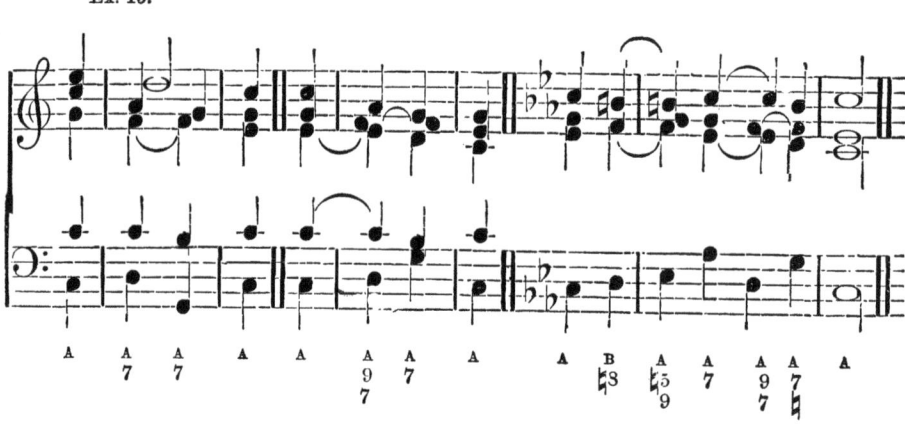

21. As in the first species of discords, any discord of this species may proceed to either of the consonant intervals of the same chord, provided it return to the note which should form its resolution, which in this species of discords will not belong to the same chord, but to another (Chap. VII., sect. 25).

---

* Appendix Q.

Ex. 16.

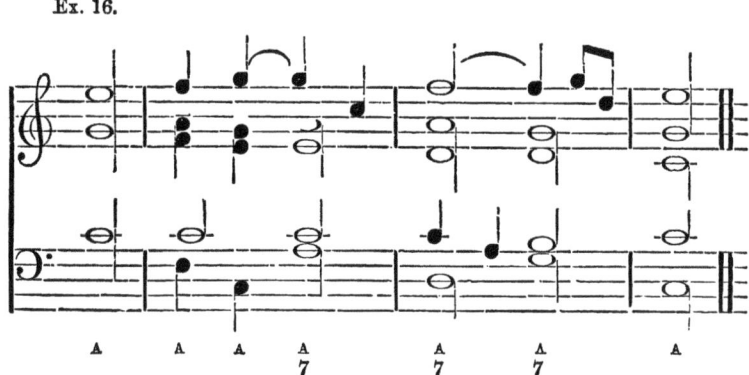

22. Discords both of the first and second species may be used simultaneously; thus an essential seventh, or ninth, or both, may be taken at the same time as a suspended fourth, and an essential seventh may be taken with a suspended ninth, or fourth, or both. Likewise the essential fifth, with seventh, of the supertonic in the minor key may be taken with the suspended ninth, or fourth, or both.

Ex. 17.

23. Any chord of this species, either entire or in part, may be suspended over the root of the chord which follows it, by the same process
as the suspension of complete concords (Chap. VII., sect. 26) (Ex. 18). All
these suspensions, as in the case of discords of the first species, must be on
a stronger accent than their resolution. The new root or third has the letter
indicating that interval, and lines are drawn from the figures indicating those
intervals in the preceding chord which are suspended, to the figures indicating
the intervals of the new chord on which they resolve (Ex. 18).

Ex. 18.

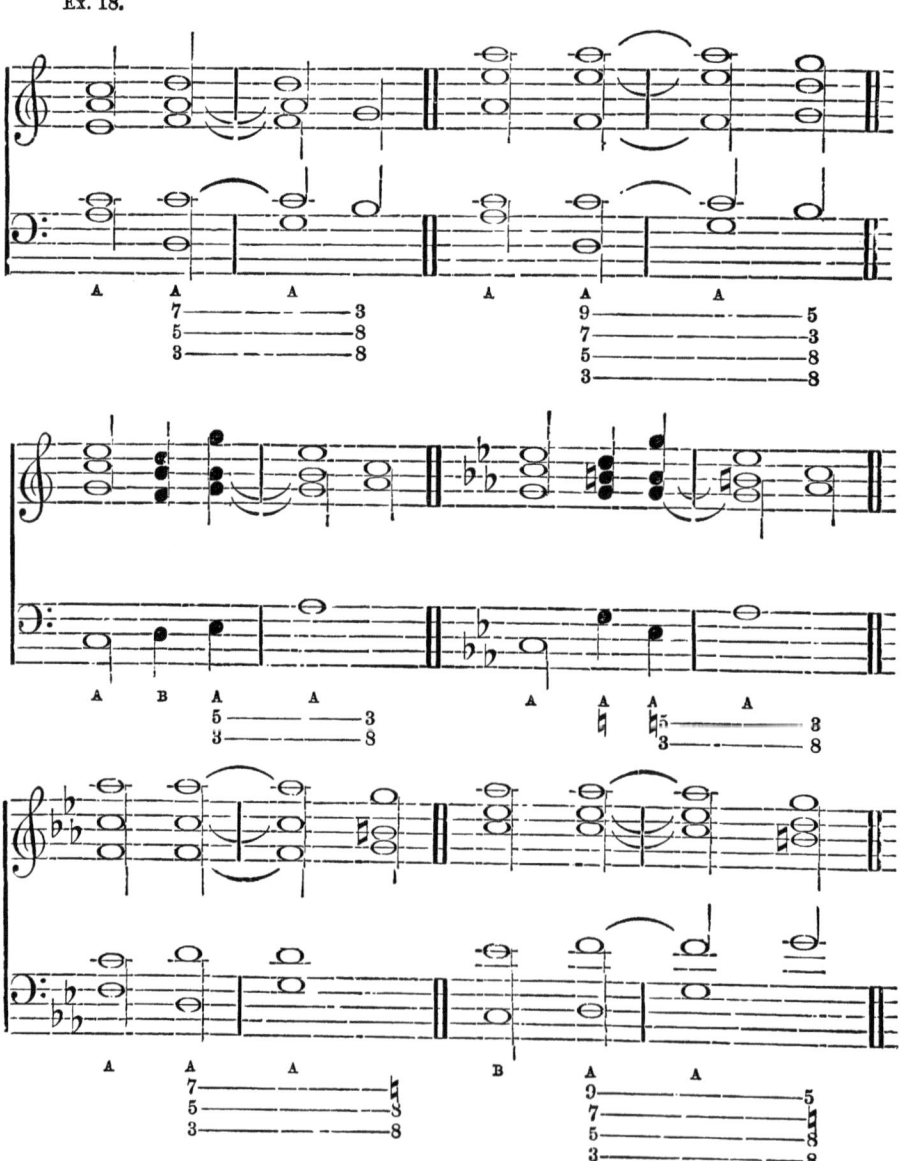

CHAPTER IX.

THE THIRD SPECIES OF DISCORDS.

INTRODUCTION.

IN this chapter are contained the laws affecting transient discords, the passing notes of the diatonic style. Passing notes are not indicated in the figuring, so their employment in exercises is left to the ingenuity of the student. When they occur in the bass, a line is drawn from the essential note whence they proceed, and continued under so many notes, whether one or more, as are foreign to the harmony, the harmony proper to the first note having to be prolonged to the extent of such line. Here also is shown the use of the variable minor scale for notes inessential to the harmony, and rules are enunciated for its treatment.

SECTION 1. The discords, which are here classed as the third species, are discords of transition, where one or more parts remain while the other part or parts move from concord to concord through the intervening discords.

2. Passing notes must be approached and quitted by the interval of a second, upward or downward.

3. A passing note may proceed to a note of the chord against which it is taken (Ex. 1), or to a note of another chord (Ex. 2), or to another passing note (Ex. 3).

Ex. 1.

Ex. 2.

Ex. 3.

4. If one discord follow another, the melody must proceed in the same direction, ascending or descending, until it reach a concord (Ex. 4).

Ex. 4.

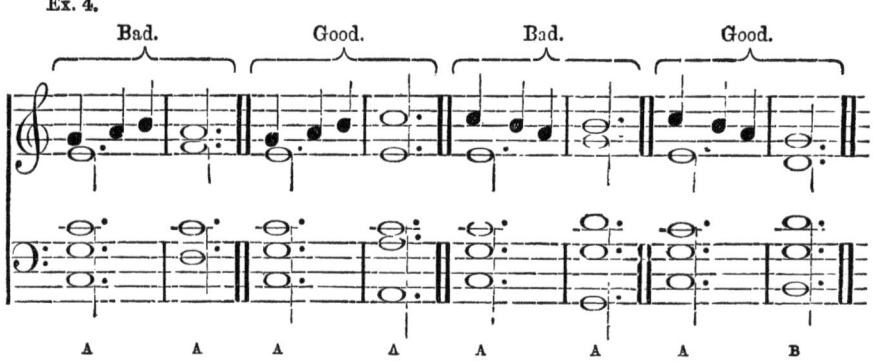

5. The discords of this species must occur on less accented parts of the bar than the harmony note whence they proceed (Ex. 5), unless such

Ex. 5.

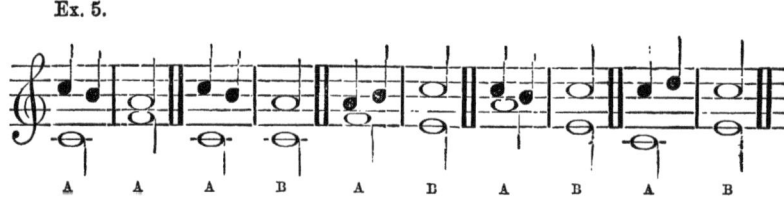

harmony note occur after one or more notes during the continuance of the same chord (Ex. 6); but if there be more than one discord, the first discord of the series must be on the weaker parts.

Ex. 6.

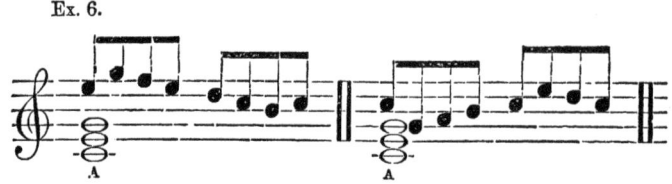

6. Having progressed from concord to discord, it is allowable to move by skip (of a third only) from discord to discord, the chord remaining provided

the second discord move to the concord lying between the two, which concord may belong to the same chord (Ex. 7), or to another chord (Ex. 8).

Ex. 7.

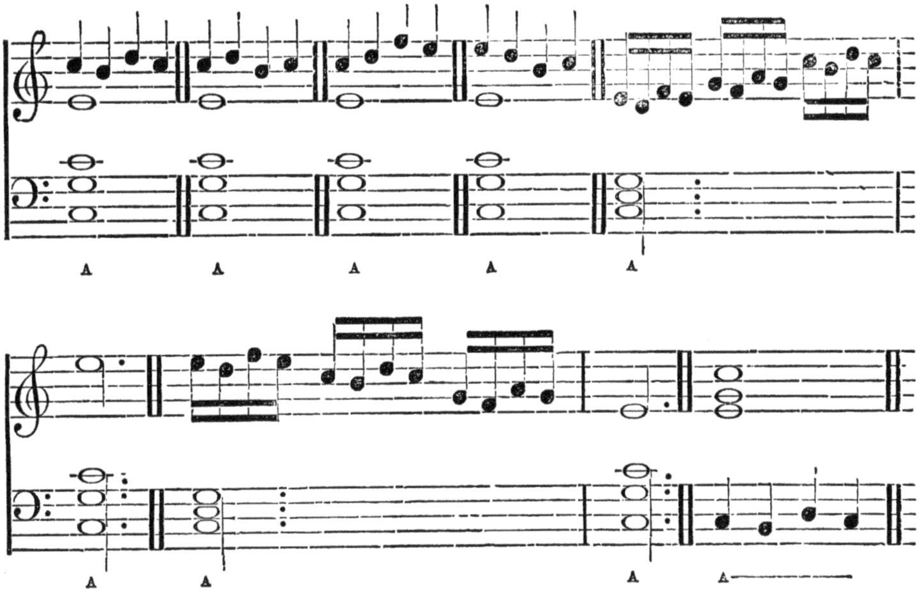

Ex. 8.

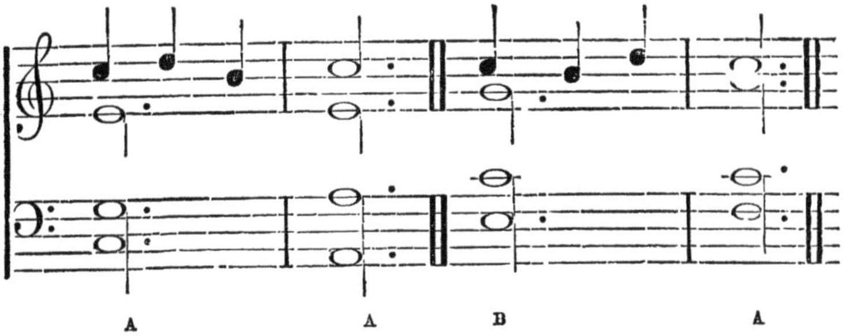

Ex. 9.

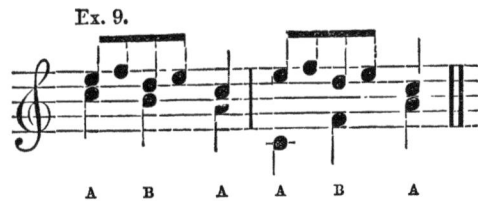

7. It is allowable to skip a third from a discord to a concord, provided that the ascent be to the discord, and the descent to the concord (Ex. 9).

8. Two, or three, or more passing notes may be taken together, provided that however dissonant against the prevailing harmony, the passing notes be all consonant with each other (Ex. 10).

Ex. 10.

9. Any part may step or skip to a concord while another part has a passing note if the notes that are struck together be consonant with each other (Ex. 11).

Ex. 11.

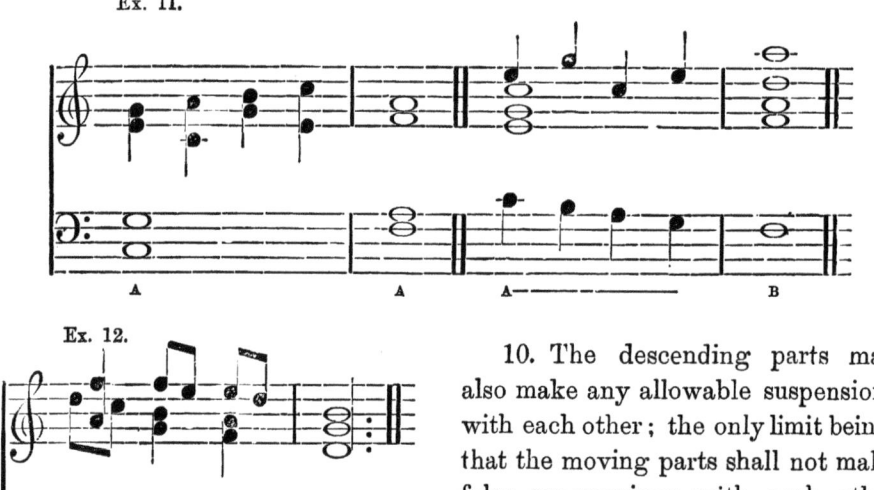

Ex. 12.

10. The descending parts may also make any allowable suspensions with each other; the only limit being, that the moving parts shall not make false progressions with each other (Ex. 12).

11. In a minor key, if the seventh of a scale be taken as a passing note between the sixth and eighth of the scale, or between the sixth of the scale and its repetition, such seventh must be minor (Ex. 13).

Ex. 13.

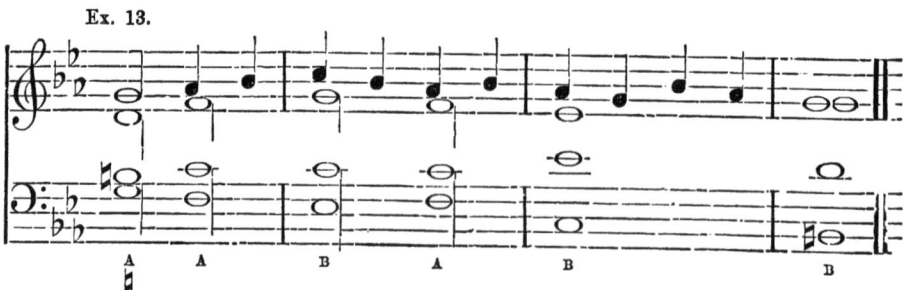

12. In a minor key, if the sixth of the scale be taken as a passing note between the fifth and the seventh, or between the seventh and its repetition, such sixth must be major (Ex. 14).

Ex. 14.

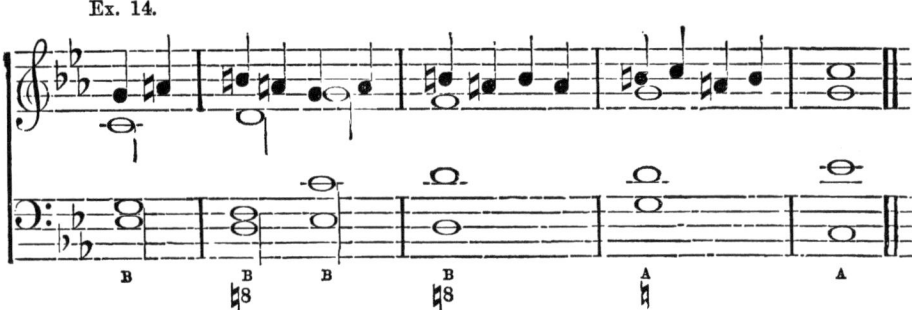

13. In a minor key, if a passage ascend from the fifth to the eighth of the scale, while neither the sixth nor the seventh is in the chord, these two, as passing notes, must be major (Ex. 15).

Ex. 15.

14. In a minor key, if a passage descend from the eighth to the fifth of the scale, while neither the seventh nor the sixth is in the chord, these two as passing notes must be minor (Ex. 16).

Ex. 16.

15. It has been mentioned, when treating of the first and second species of discords, that a discord of either of those species may leap to either of the consonant intervals of the same chord, provided it return to the proper resolution of such discord (Chap. VII., sect. 25, and Chap. VIII., sect. 21). Any passing notes may be taken between such consonant interval and the note which

resolves the discord, either when such discord belongs to the first species (Ex. 17), that is, when it resolves on the same chord, or when it belongs to

Ex. 17.

the second species (Ex. 18), that is, when it resolves on the next chord.

Ex. 18.

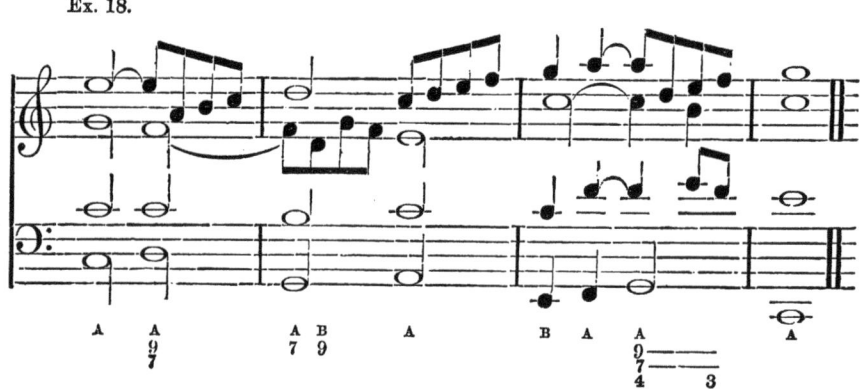

CHAPTER X.

THE FOURTH SPECIES OF DISCORDS.

INTRODUCTION.

THE method of figuring or lettering basses for exercises in the fourth species of discords will be similar to that used for the third species.

SECTION 1. The discords which are here classed as the fourth species are where two or more parts pass by contrary motion and by degrees, from concord to concord, or from a prepared discord to a concord, through all the intervening discords.

2. The discords of this species do not require preparation.

3. They may occur either on the stronger or weaker parts of the bar.

4. The parts must proceed by contrary motion from the discord, and by either contrary or oblique motion to it.

5. A discord of this species may follow any concord (Ex. 1).

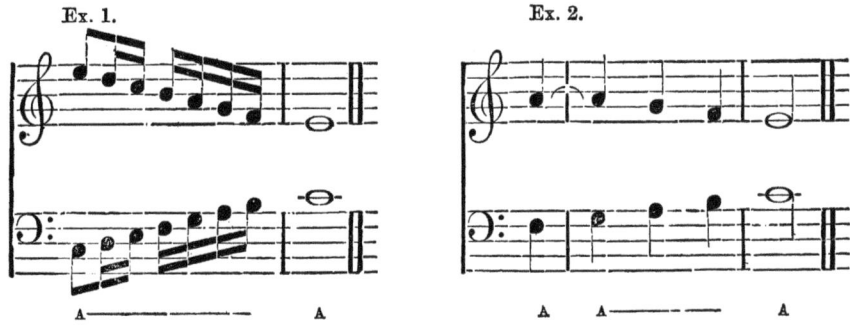

6. It may also follow any prepared discord (Ex. 2).

7. Discords of this species may be used either in two parts, as in Ex. 2, or in more than two parts.

8. When obtained, these discords may either proceed by contrary motion until they reach a concord, as in Ex. 3, or they may be treated as belonging either to the first species of discords, in which case the discord must be on a stronger accent than its resolution (Ex. 4);

Ex. 4.

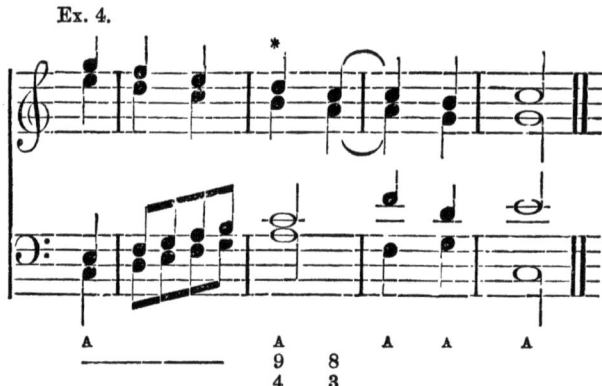

9. Or as belonging to the second species, in which case the resolution may be on either a weaker or stronger accent than the discord (Ex. 5);

Ex. 5.

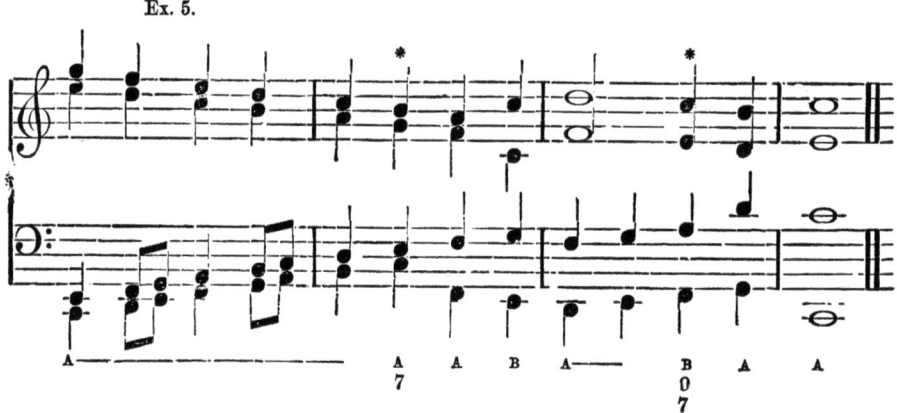

10. Or they may be treated as belonging to the third species of discords, where the discord passes on to the concord, while the note with which it formed the discord remains.

Ex. 6.

11. Any one of the parts in chords containing discords of this species may (descending) be suspended over the note to which it should move (Ex. 7).

Ex. 7.

12. There is one great peculiarity in this species of discords, which is that provided the notes reach their proper place at last, the different parts may be either hurried, or protracted at pleasure; thus we will suppose the progression intended to be from the common chord of F to the common chord of G, in four parts in contrary motion, two above descending, and two below ascending. It is allowable, as in the three following examples, to protract or hurry the movement of any of the parts. The higher and lower parts may be inverted (Ex. 8).

Ex. 8.

E

13. All the parts moving in the same direction must move according to the previously mentioned rules for progression of parts, and the laws affecting the other species of discords; therefore, although in the descending parts any suspensions whatever may be made, they cannot in the ascending parts, as such suspensions would require resolution downwards, whereby the motion of the part would be broken.

14. In this species of discords, the discords are supposed in all cases to be in the descending parts, whether those parts be above the ascending, as

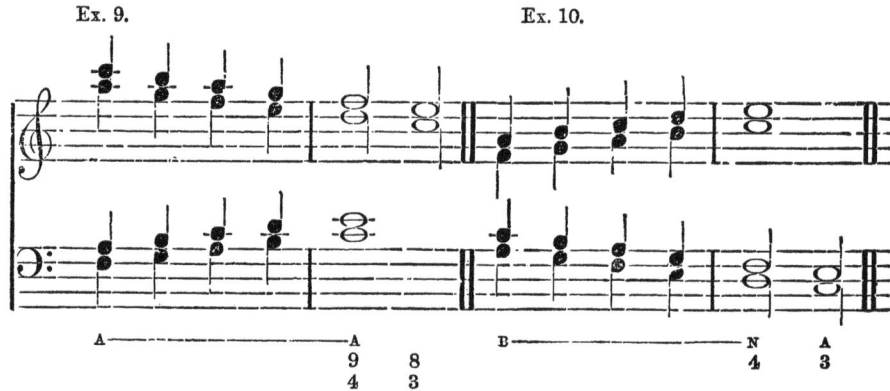

in Ex. 9, or beneath them, as in Ex. 10, the progression in the latter example being an inversion of that in the former, therefore

15. When (both parts moving) a discord is produced, it is not allowable to bring up the ascending part or parts to the concord, and then to treat it as any other concord (Ex. 11);

16. But the ascending parts being raised to concords with the descending, the descending parts must fall to the next concord with the ascending (Ex. 12);

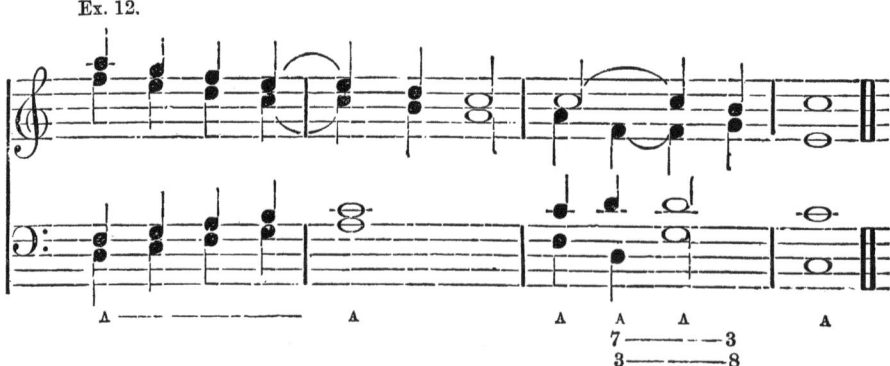

Ex. 13.

17. Or both parts must proceed by contrary motion to a
concord (Ex. 13); or to a discord, when, as has been before
mentioned, such discord may be
treated as belonging to any of
the four species;

18. Or the ascending part or parts may return to the discord, when the
motion of the parts will be reversed, the ascending parts becoming the
descending, and the descending the ascending, because those which were

Ex. 14.

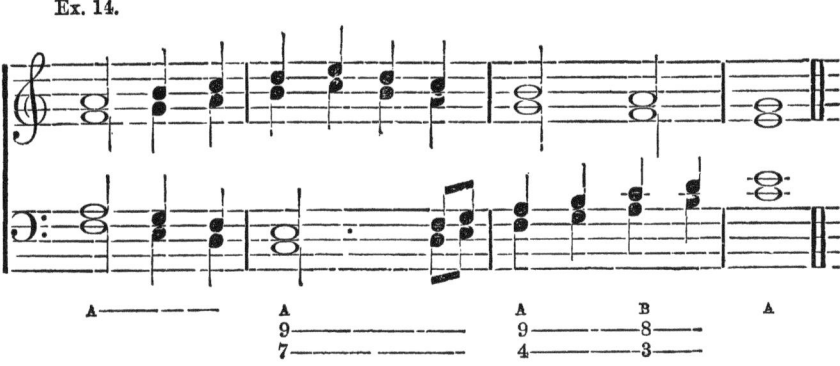

the descending can no longer descend, on account of the false progressions
which would be produced between them and those parts which, by returning
to the discord, had reversed their motion (Ex. 14).

19. Any variety of the third species of discords may be introduced into
this species, that is, while some part or parts remain, others move from
concord to discord, &c.; thus the following and any similar progressions may
be used (Ex. 15).

Ex. 15.

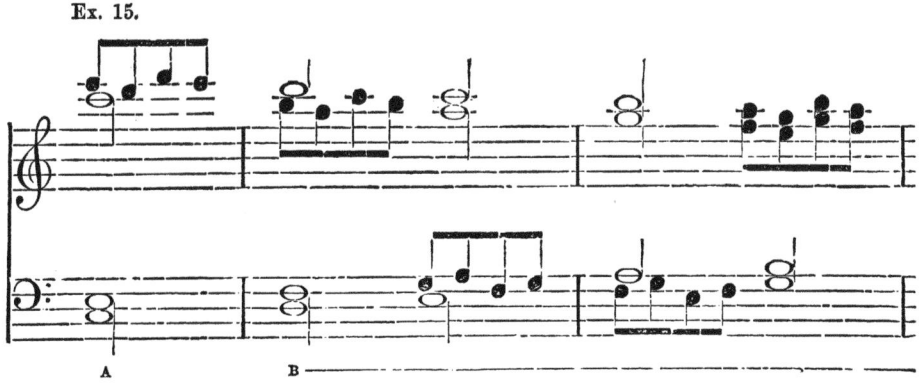

Ex. 15—*continued.*

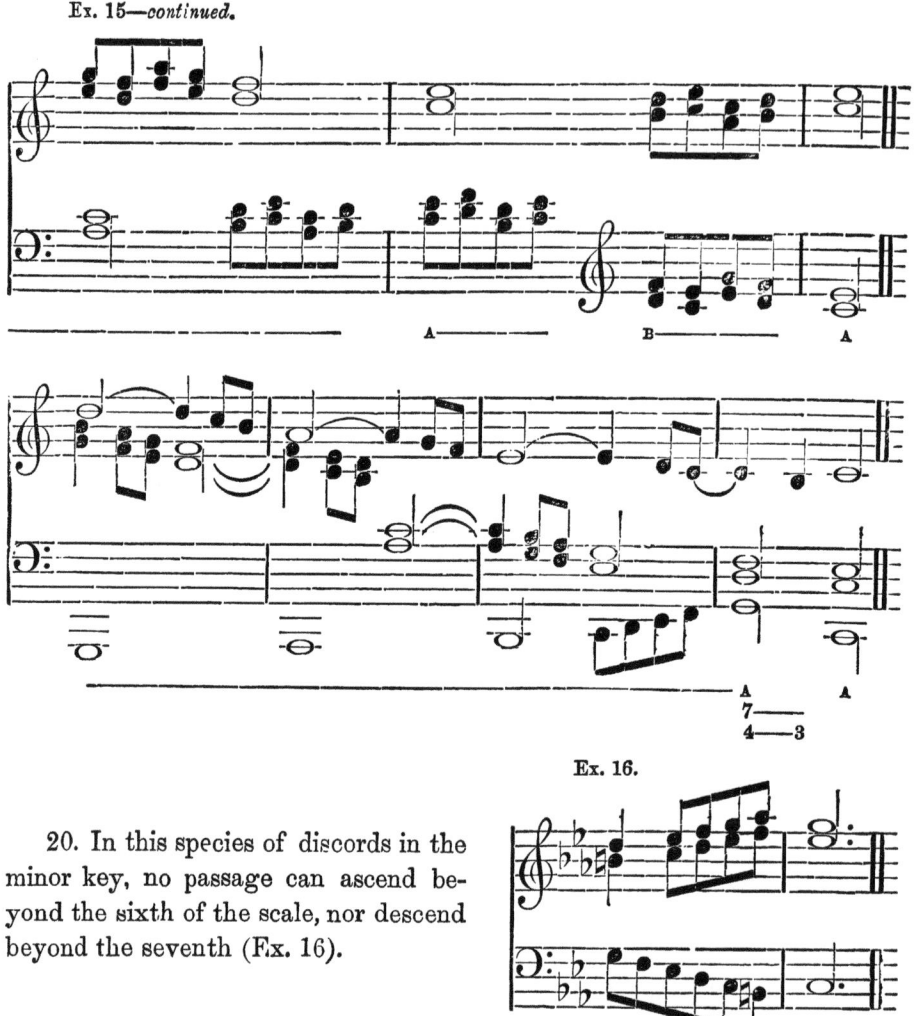

Ex. 16.

20. In this species of discords in the minor key, no passage can ascend beyond the sixth of the scale, nor descend beyond the seventh (Ex. 16).

21. Occasionally the same form of minor scale has been used in this species of discords, as has been mentioned in the third species (Chap. IX., sects. 11—14); but this is not admissible, as false relations of the most disagreeable description are made between the major and minor sixth and seventh of the ascending and descending scales.

CHAPTER XI.

OF PEDALS IN THE STRICT OR DIATONIC STYLE.

INTRODUCTION.

THE general principle that all the notes of the key are subject to uniform laws for their treatment has exception in reference to pedals. The availability as pedals of only two notes in any key is a rule of the ancient style as much as of the modern, and its application to the diatonic style is here explained.

SECTION 1. A pedal is one note continued through several harmonies, such pedal not necessarily being an essential portion of the harmony (Ex. 1).

2. The pedal note can only occur as the bass. It is not lettered or figured.

3. Great care must be taken to distinguish between these "pedal points," as they are called, and the notes held through transient discords of the third species. The key note and fifth can alone be used as pedals (Ex. 1), but

Ex. 1.

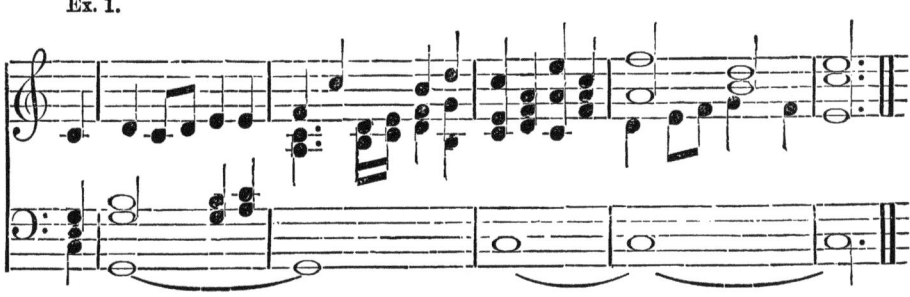

any note, or any chord, may be held through a series of passing notes (Ex. 2).

Ex. 2.

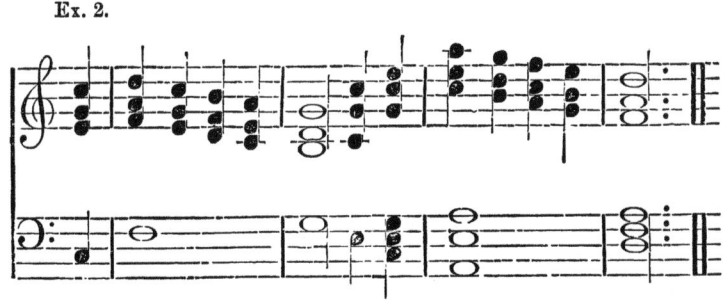

4. Any concords, and any of the four species of discords, in fine, **any** harmonies being strictly in the key, may be taken on a pedal (Ex. 3). In

Ex. 3.

Ex. 3 the first bar contains discords of the first species, the second bar of the second species, the third bar of the third species, and the fourth bar of the fourth species; either the upper or under bass part may be taken as the pedal.

5. A pedal may commence on any con-cord (Ex. 4), or on any prepared discord (Ex. 5).

6. A pedal may be quitted at any con-cord (Exs. 1—5), or on any discord of which the pedal note is essential to the harmony, provided the before-mentioned laws for the resolution of discords be observed (Ex. 6).

Ex. 4.

Ex. 5.

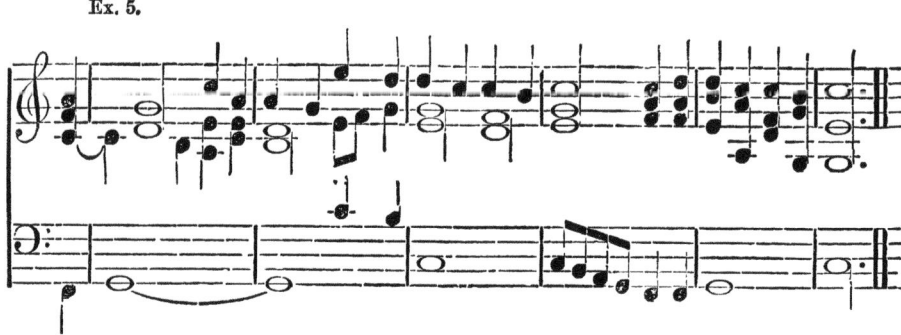

7. The part next above the pedal must practically be the bass to the whole harmony, except where the pedal note is essential to the chord, hence the fourth chord in Ex. 7 is not in the second inversion.

8. The arbitrary minor scale as used in the third species of discords may also be used in the same species on a pedal.

Ex. 6.

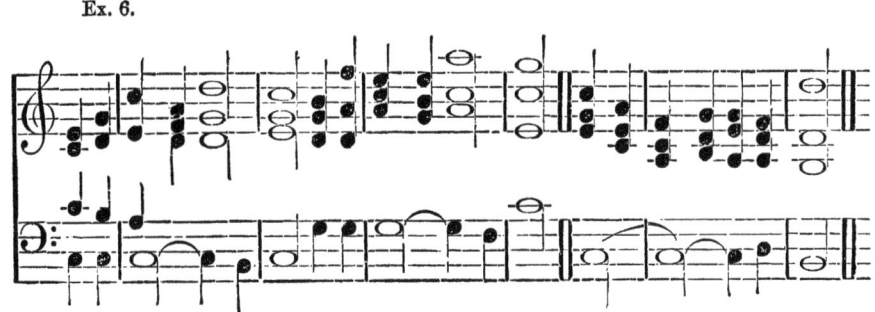

Ex. 7.

CHAPTER XII.

OF MODULATION IN THE STRICT OR DIATONIC STYLE.

INTRODUCTION.

MODULATION is the passing from one key to another, and then the notes inflected by accidentals belong to the diatonic scale of the key newly entered. Confusion occurs in the music of many composers through the want of distinction between the major key and the minor key with the same signature (the so-called relative major and minor), against which the student is most urgently warned. The rules in this chapter may be regarded as recommendatory rather than positive, since, though they all direct to good effect, the practice of even great masters shows that they have not always been punctually observed.

SECTION 1. In the strict style, modulation can be effected by taking any concords sufficient to determine a key as at *, which concord may be delayed by a discord of the first species, as at **, but that chord which determines the new key (that is, which has the first note foreign to the previous key) should have its root in the bass. The † marks the undesirable chords (Ex. 1).

Ex. 1.

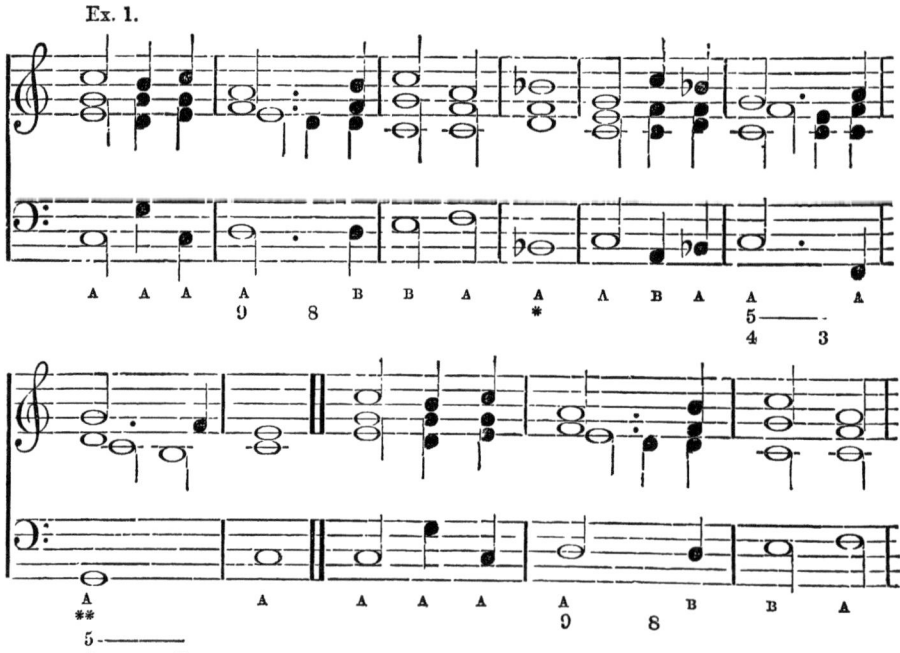

Ex. 1.—*continued.*

2. The first inversion of the diminished triad of the leading note of the new key may be employed to effect modulation, and this is the one exception from the rule against changing the key by an inverted chord (Chap. IV., sect. 16) (Ex. 2).

Ex. 2.

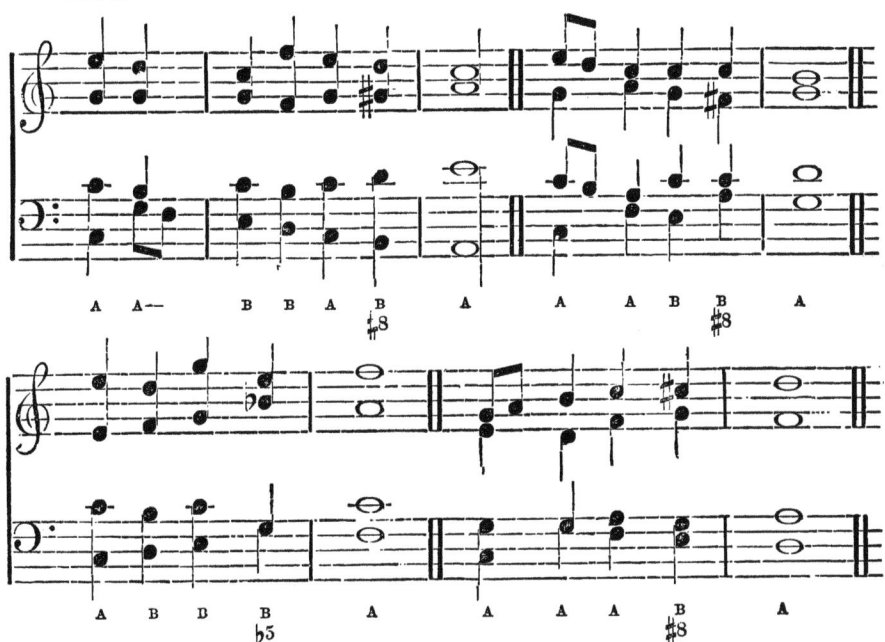

3. The key may be determined by any discord of the second species, and such discord should have the root in the bass (Chap. VIII., sect. 11) (Ex. 3).

Ex. 3.

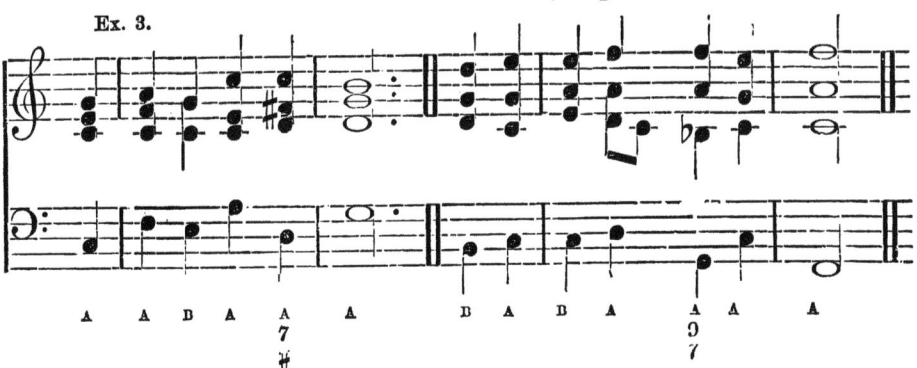

Ex. 3—*continued.*

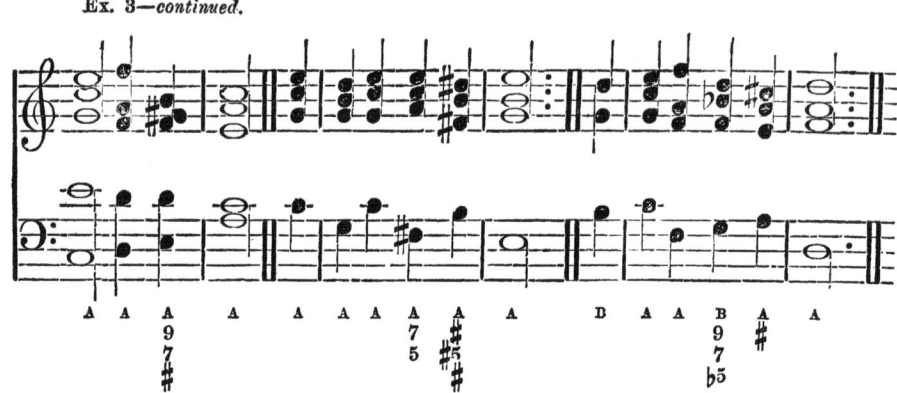

4. In modulating from any key to the dominant of such key, it is not allowable to take the common chord on the sixth of such new key (the disallowed chord of the mediant of the previous key), until a chord including the leading note of the new key has been taken. The * marks the disallowed chord (Ex. 4).

Ex. 4.

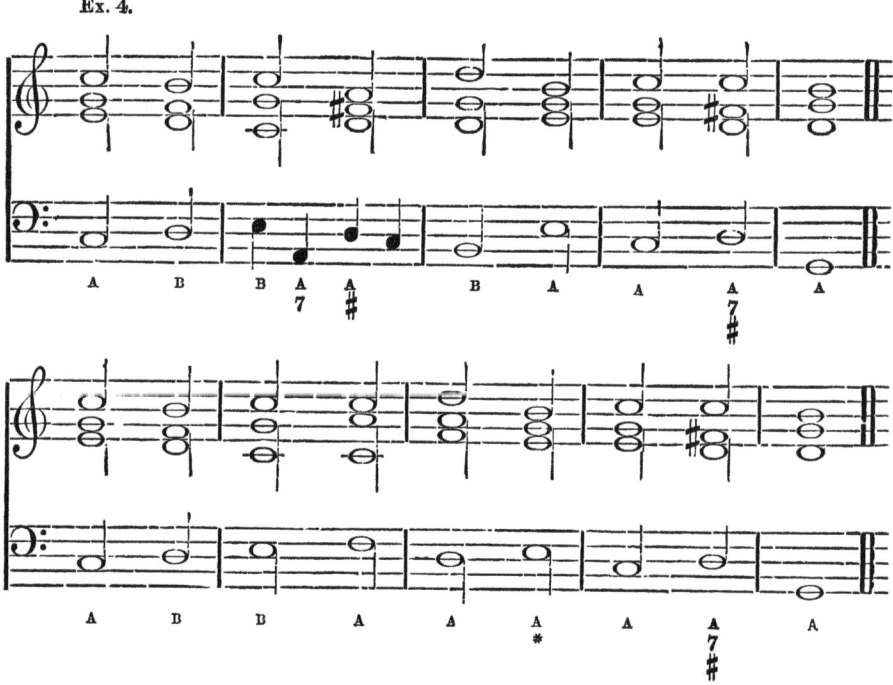

5. In modulating from any minor key to its relative major, if the common chord on the fourth of the minor scale be taken it cannot ever be followed by the common chord of the tonic of the new key or its first inversion. The * marks the bad chord (Chap. IV., sect. 15) (Ex. 5).

Ex. 5.

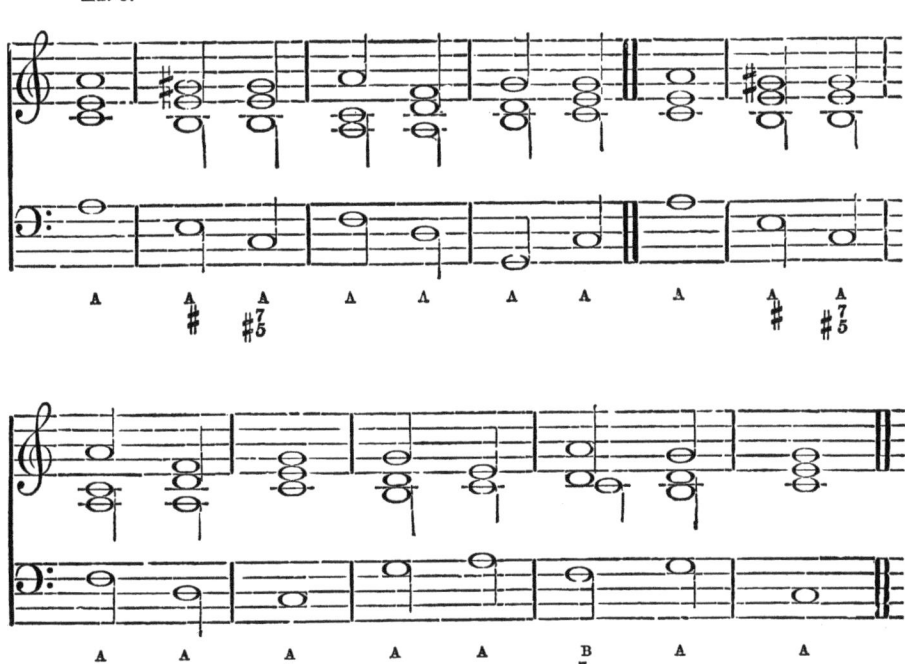

6. The same principle precludes a progression from the chord of the tonic in a minor key, as D, to the chord of a tonic in a major key at a tone below the former, as C (Chap. IV., sect. 15).

PART II.

CHROMATIC HARMONY, OR HARMONY IN THE FREE STYLE.

INTRODUCTION.

THE laws affecting diatonic harmony, however correct and sufficient while such diatonic harmony alone is used, are by no means so when applied to chromatic; the endeavour to force the latter under the same laws which have been found applicable to the former, appears to me the reason why the laws of harmony have been so vague and indeterminate, and so utterly opposed to practice. Diatonic discords require preparation because they are unnatural; chromatic do not, because they may be said to be already prepared by nature. This is practically seen to be true from the comparatively early use which was made of the dominant discords without preparation; these discords in either major or minor key, although diatonic, yet being fundamental chords,* do not require preparation; after these came the supertonic discords; lastly, those of the tonic, of which examples, although as yet comparatively few in number, are to be found in the best modern authors.

I shall not here take the trouble to elaborate the subject of the ratios of vibrations, length of string, order of harmonics, &c., as many persons have already taken that trouble; and in the present state of musical mathematics, without a separate treatise on their application, they would be of little practical utility: the only points where they are of use they are noticed, in a note to Chap. XXI., sect. 18, also in Chap. XXII.†

The harmonics from any given note (without taking the order in which they arise, but their practical use), are, major third, perfect fifth, minor seventh, minor or major ninth, eleventh, and minor or major thirteenth.

The reason why the tonic, dominant, and supertonic are chosen for roots is, because the harmonics in nature rise in the same manner; first the harmonics of any given note, then those of its fifth or dominant, then those of the fifth of that dominant, being the second or supertonic of the original note. The reason why the harmonics of the next fifth are not used is, because that note itself is not a note of the diatonic scale, being a little too sharp (as the fifth of the supertonic), and can only be used as a part of a chromatic chord. (Chap. XXVI., sect. 7.)

The eleventh is only used on the dominant, because its resolution, if taken on either tonic or supertonic, would be out of the key.‡

---

* Appendix R.　　　† Appendix S.　　　‡ Appendix T.

It will most probably be objected to the more extreme chords, as the eleventh with the third, or the thirteenth with the fifth, that they are very harsh: when taken unconnected in the examples, and without any regard to a good position, this may be very true, still it is no reason against their use, as few chords are less pleasant than the chord of the minor ninth, with the root, unconnected with any progression; yet no one doubts its existence or its beauty who has heard the works of the great masters, and no chord can be more extreme than the inversion of the chord of $\flat^{13}_{\substack{9 \\ 8 \\ 3}}$, used in the G minor symphony of Mozart, mentioned in Chap. XV., sect. 6, yet in its place it may very well be borne.

It appears to me that the great thing to be avoided, in a treatise on *practical* as well as theoretical harmony, is making the mathematical part of music of undue importance: were the discords always taken as occurring in nature, in the first place, music would be a succession of fifths and eighths; and in the next, the chords could only be taken in one *position*, and they could never be inverted; even the simple first inversion of a common chord could not be used. The great use of mathematics as applied to music, in the present state of our knowledge on the subject, is to determine whence any chord springs, and to settle any doubtful points of notation in harmony or progression.

CHAPTER XIII.

ON CHROMATIC OR FUNDAMENTAL HARMONY, THE INTERVALS USED
THEREIN, AND CHROMATIC SCALES.

INTRODUCTION.

THE chromatic scale is written in the manner in which it appears in this
chapter for the following reasons.

Every note, whether diatonic or chromatic, must exist before it can be
used.

The key note is assumed; all the rest are generated by it.

One note must be assumed as a groundwork; otherwise, on the principle
" e nihilo nihil fit," there would be no music.

In the diatonic scale of C, no one would think of writing D×, or A♭♭,
because those notes are not parts of any chord in the key, the notes being
E♯, and G♮, the third and fifth of the tonic.

If then in diatonic music no notes are used as parts of the scale but such
as exist as portions of some harmony in the key, why in the chromatic scale
should notes be used which do not exist as a portion of any harmony in the
key? (Chap. XIII., sect. 8.)

The three notes which are taken as the foundation of the chromatic scale
are : I, the tonic; II, the dominant, the first harmonic of the tonic; III, the
supertonic, the first harmonic of the dominant, which is the first harmonic
that is common to both, it being the fifth of the dominant, and the major
ninth of the tonic.

The reasons why these three notes, and these three only, are assigned as
roots are the following :—

1st. All notes which are used in the scale of any given key, should also be
capable of being harmonized in the key.

2nd. No two notes at the distance of a chromatic semitone or any of its
octaves can be sounded together, unless one of them be a passing note.

3rd. When the *enharmonic diesis** (as it is called) takes place, it always
implies a change of key.

4th. Notes of the diatonic scale may be formed from diatonic chords; the
chromatic notes are formed from chromatic chords.

5th. All harmonies being strictly in the key can be taken on either tonic
or dominant pedal, or on the double pedal of both combined; therefore

* The meaning of this word (*diesis*) is division. I have thought it better to use the Greek word,
as being generally understood by musical mathematicians.

If any harmonic, or portion of the chromatic chords, of any note taken as a root of chromatic chords in the key, contradict a diatonic note of either major or minor scale, and form with it the enharmonic diesis, a change of key takes place, and such note therefore cannot be a root in the key; also,

If any harmonic of a root of chromatic chords be a chromatic semitone from either tonic or dominant, such root cannot be a root in the key on account of the false relation.

To prove that no note of the diatonic scale, excepting the first, second, and fifth, as before mentioned, can be taken as a root of chromatic chords, let the double pedal of tonic and dominant in the key of C be taken, and the different notes of the diatonic scale major and minor, with their several harmonics, up to the minor ninth, be taken above them; there is no occasion to carry the harmonics beyond the minor ninth, that being sufficient for the purpose.

Were the minor third (E♭) taken as a root, its minor ninth (F♭) would contradict or form the enharmonic diesis with the major third (E♮). Were the major third used, its major third (G♯) would make false relation with the dominant pedal (G), as would G♭, the minor ninth of the fourth (F), and the minor seventh of the minor sixth (A♭), were either of those notes used. If the major sixth (A♮) were used, its major third (C♯) would make false relation with the tonic pedal (C) (Chap. XXVI., sect. 27). Were the major seventh (B) used, its major third (D♯) would contradict the minor third of the scale (E♭).*

Even the diatonic scales, major and minor, and the use of the common chords in major and minor keys, are in reality dependent on the harmonies of the above three notes and the laws affecting them. The notes of the diatonic major scale are produced in the following manner: C (tonic) produces G its fifth, and E its major third: G produces all the rest, as D its fifth, B its third, F its seventh, and A its major ninth. The minor scale in a similar manner; the E♭, the minor third, is an arbitrary, not a natural third of C, and as part of the common chord of C cannot be used in the major key; G produces A♭ as its minor ninth; this note is a natural harmonic in the key, and it is dependent on this, that the subdominant minor chord can be used in the major key, which the tonic minor chord cannot.

SECTION 1. *Chromatic* or *fundamental harmony* differs from *diatonic*, insomuch as the discords do not require preparation, and the resolution depends on the quality of the intervals and not on the name thereof.

2. Where the note forming the fundamental discord is a diatonic note of the major scale if the passage be in the major key, or of the minor scale if the passage be in the minor key, such discord may be prepared, or resolved, or both, as in diatonic harmony.

----

* Appendix U.

3. This class of harmony is called *chromatic* in contradistinction from *diatonic*, because it admits of notes foreign to the diatonic scales without the key being changed; and *fundamental*, because every harmony springs from some one of three certain roots or fundamentals, and can only be taken on certain notes of the key.

4. By root or fundamental is meant that note, being a diatonic note of the scale, which will amongst its harmonics first produce the notes of which any chord is composed.

5. In addition to the intervals which have been used in diatonic harmony, there are several augmented and diminished intervals which occur in chromatic harmony, and in chromatic harmony only, and which therefore have not hitherto been mentioned. The following is a complete table of all the intervals which can be used in music.*

Ex. 1.

---

* Appendix V.

† This interval should most rarely be used in harmony, but freely in melody.

6. These intervals are all written in the key of C, and are formed from the following chromatic scale :—

Ex. 2.

7. It will be seen that the fourth is the only note of the diatonic major scale which has the note at a semitone above it of its own name; that this note is the only augmented interval reckoning upwards from the key note; and that the key note and fifth are not inflected.

8. In this scale all the imperfect intervals (from the key note), the second, third, sixth, and seventh, are taken both major and minor; the fourth perfect and augmented; the fifth and eighth perfect only.

9. This notation includes both major and minor keys, and in forming the chromatic scale of any key, the notes must stand at the same intervals from the key note, be that note what it may; thus the following are the chromatic scales of F♯ and E♭ :—

Ex. 3.

Ex. 4.

F

CHAPTER XIV.

OF THE PROGRESSION OF PARTS IN CHROMATIC HARMONY.

INTRODUCTION.

THE principal difference between the progression of parts in diatonic and in chromatic harmony is, that in the latter it is allowed to use consecutive fifths, and to come on an octave by similar motion in extreme parts, between certain chords mentioned in the following chapter, whereas in the former these progressions were never allowed.

SECTION 1. As in the diatonic style, no two parts are allowed to move in unison.

2. No two parts are allowed to move to an unison by similar motion.

3. No two parts are allowed to move in octaves by similar motion.

4. The extreme parts may not proceed by similar motion to an octave, except to the octave of the tonic from a chord of the dominant, and to the octave of the subdominant from a chord of the tonic, such octave being the root of the chord, when the top part must move a second (Ex. 1), and except

Ex. 1.

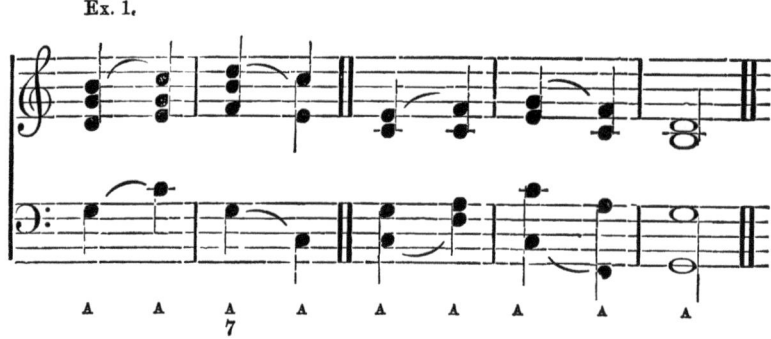

to the octave of the tonic from the chord of the dominant, and to the octave of the dominant from a diatonic or chromatic chord of the supertonic, or from an inversion of the chord of the dominant eleventh, or from the chord of the subdominant, such octave being the fifth of the chord, when the top part may rise or fall a second, or may rise a fourth, or a fifth (Ex. 2); and also, except in passing from discord to discord, when each discord must be derived from dominant, supertonic, or tonic root, the octave being the root or fifth of the chord, and the top part may then move a second or rise a fourth or a fifth when the bass moves a second* (Ex. 3).

5. Octaves by contrary motion in the extreme parts are allowable in the same cases as those in which it is allowable to come on an octave from another interval in the extreme parts by similar motion (Ex. 4).

Ex. 4.

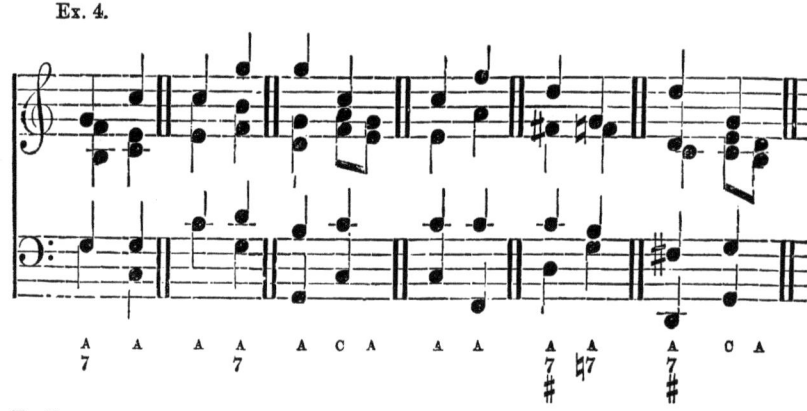

Ex. 5.

The examples (Ex. 5) are bad, because the chords used are not any of those between which octaves, by contrary motion, are allowed to be taken.

6. No part may approach the eighth of a note by similar motion, which note is approached in another part by step of a chromatic semitone downward (Ex. 6).

Ex. 6.

7. No two notes next each other in alphabetical order may ever go to the unison or octave by similar or oblique motion, excepting when the seventh

in a second inversion of a chord of the seventh rises to the third of the
ensuing bass note* (Sect. 15) (Ex. 7).

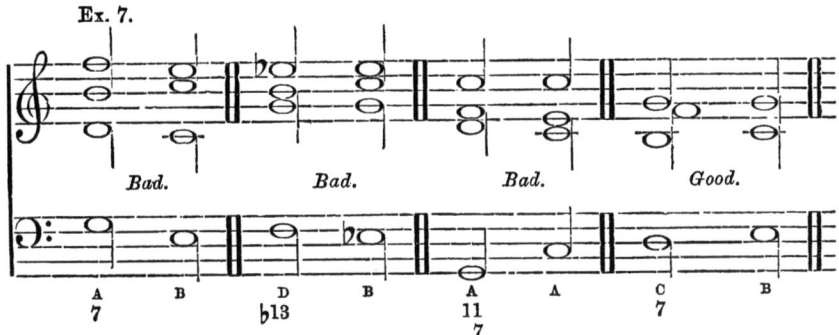

Ex. 7.

8. It is not allowable to proceed by similar motion to the unison or octave
of a note which resolves any discord but a passing-note (Ex. 8).

Ex. 8.   Ex. 10.

Ex. 9.   BEETHOVEN.   WEBER.

9. Fifths by similar motion are generally to be avoided, but they may
(and with better effect in extreme than in inner parts) be used between tonic
and dominant, as in the last two chords of each instance (Ex. 9); or
between tonic and subdominant (Ex. 10).†

10. In the extreme parts it is only allowable to come on a fifth by similar
motion from another interval, when such fifth is the fifth of the common

---

chord of the tonic or dominant, or one of the chords of the fundamental
dominant, supertonic, or tonic, provided that the chord preceding be one of
those chords, or the subdominant major or minor chord; that the top part
move only a second, and that the other rules for the progression of parts be
strictly observed (Ex. 11).

Ex. 11.

11. The following instances are bad; the first, because the chord where
the fifth is taken is not one of the chords mentioned above; the second,
because neither of the chords belongs to those mentioned above; the third,
for the same reason, in addition to which the top part moves more than a
second (Ex. 12).

Ex. 12.   Ex. 13.

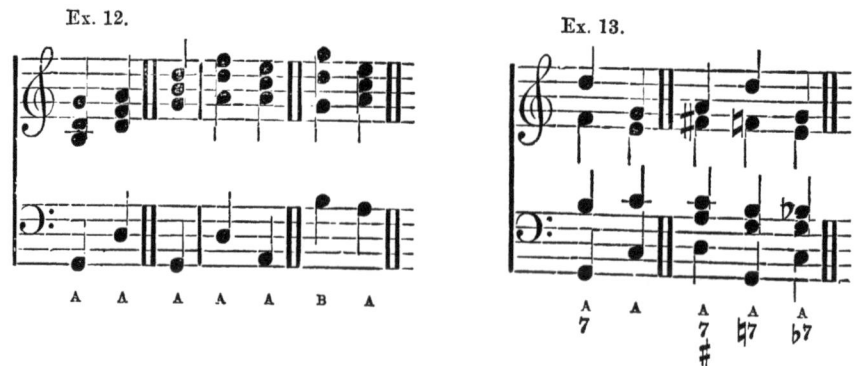

12. Fifths by contrary motion are allowed if either or each of the chords be one of the fundamental sevenths (Ex. 13).*

13. No part may proceed in fourths with the bass (Ex. 14), excepting

Ex. 14.

when the second fourth consists of discordant notes in a fundamental discord (Ex. 15).†

Ex. 15.

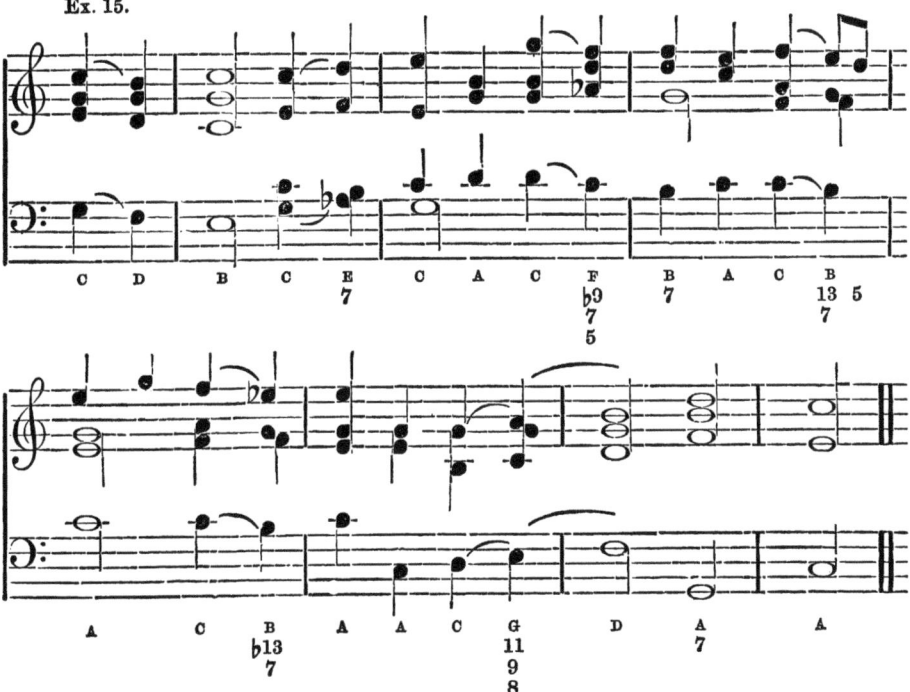

14. No two seconds or sevenths are allowed between the same parts (Ex. 16).

Ex. 16.   Ex. 17.

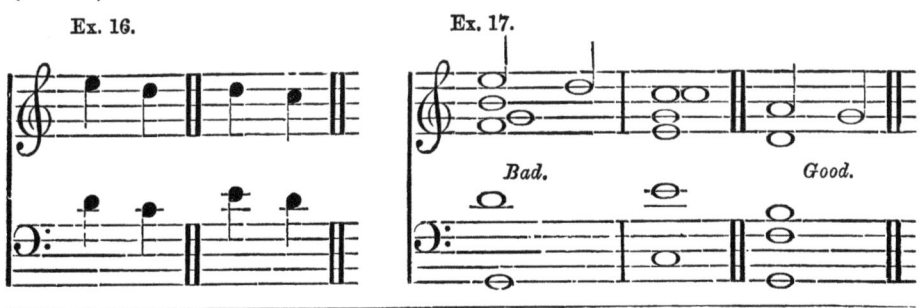

Bad.   Good.

---

* Appendix Y.   † Appendix Z.

15. It is not allowable to take a discord and the note on which it resolves at the same time, excepting the root against the ninth, the root being below the ninth (Ex. 17), and the fifth and thirteenth, the fifth being approached by ascending second in the bass (Sect. 7) (Ex. 18).

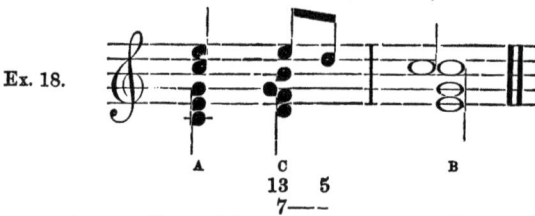

Ex. 18.

16. No two parts are allowed to move to a second by similar motion, excepting (either ascending or descending) in the case of the fundamental sevenths

Ex. 19.

(Ex. 19); or of the minor ninth with the third (Ex. 20); or of the eleventh (Ex. 21): in any of these cases one part must move a second only.

Ex. 20.

Ex. 21.

17. In any other cases than those mentioned in Sect. 16, it is not allowable for the extreme parts to come by similar motion on two notes next to each other in alphabetical order, whatever be their distance from each other, unless such notes, reckoning in the order of their number from the roots of the chords from which they are derived, form the interval of the seventh; as the root and seventh in the first bar; third and ninth in the second; fifth and eleventh in the third; and seventh and thirteenth in the fourth (Ex. 22).

Ex. 22.

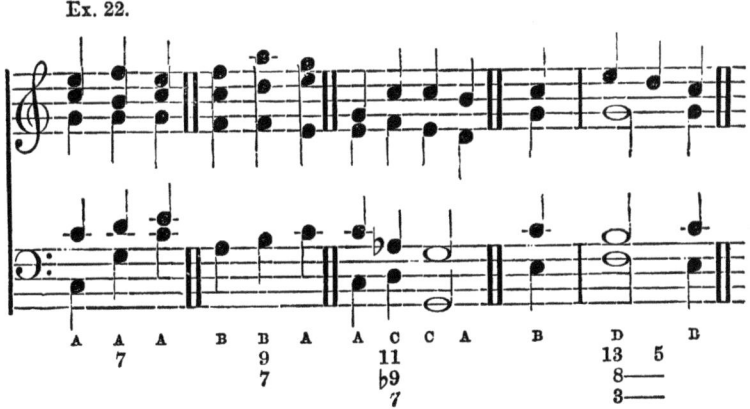

18. In this style it is allowable to change the position of chords, provided the characteristic notes of those chords remain; but in the case of discords, if the discord be taken originally in the bass, it cannot ascend to a note of a lower numbered interval than itself, as from the seventh to the root, third, or fifth; or from ninth to third, as in the first four bars; although it may

Ex. 23.

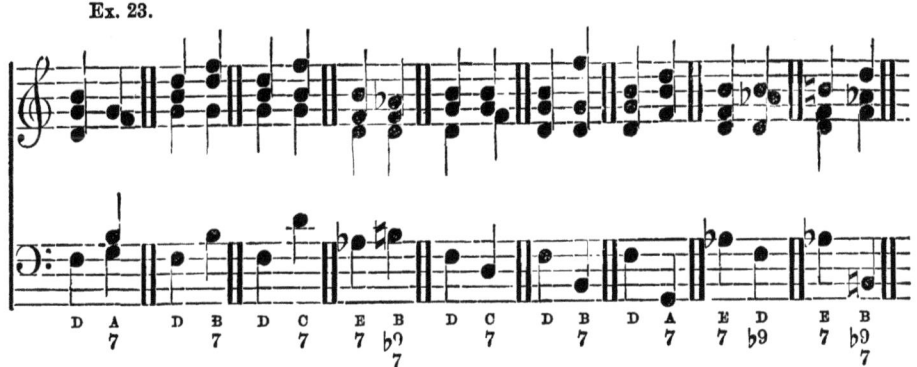

descend to any of them as in the last five; and in these cases all the above rules for the progression of parts may be broken, with the exception of those against direct octaves and coming on an unison by similar motion (Ex. 23).

19. It is not allowable to move from an octave to a seventh by similar motion and by step of a second in either part (Ex. 24).[*]

20. In strict writing it is not allowable to move an augmented interval, and if any part move a diminished interval it must return; this is also the case in free writing, with the exception that in a progression of first inversions in the minor key, it is allowable to move from the minor sixth to the major seventh of the scale, and *vice versâ* (Ex. 25). Another exception occurs in the

Ex. 24.

Ex. 25.

resolution of the minor ninth upon the major third of the same root while the root of the chord remains (Chap. XIX., sect. 12). Augmented intervals are also allowable in an arpeggio of a fundamental discord, or in a change of its position (Ex. 26). Exceptions with regard to passing-notes are explained in Chap. XXV.

Ex. 26.

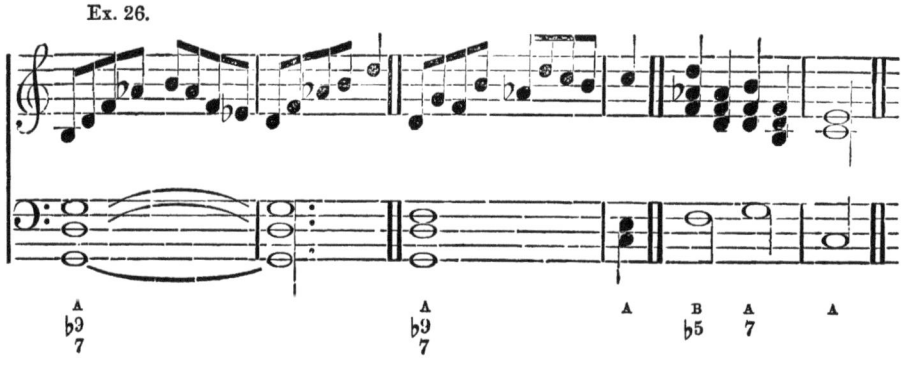

---

[*] Appendix AA.

CHAPTER XV.

OF FALSE RELATION AS REGARDS FUNDAMENTAL HARMONY.

INTRODUCTION.

FALSE relation is here, as in Chapter III., divided into false relation between two notes sounded together, false relation between the first and third chords, and false relation between the first and second chords: in the second will be seen the manner in which chromatic chords derived from the three before-mentioned roots of dominant, supertonic, and tonic, and in the third, how chords related by having certain harmonics in common, are excepted from the general laws relating to false relation; at the same time it must be observed, however, that this is in strict accordance with the practice of the best authors.

SECTION 1. False relation is considered the same as in the First Part of this book, so long as diatonic harmonies alone are used.*

2. In diatonic harmony, it is false relation when two notes of the same name but of a different quality occur in different parts in two chords with one chord intervening, from the obscurity of key caused thereby; because no inflected note can be used in diatonic harmony without the key being changed. But, as in chromatic harmony all the notes of the chromatic scale can be used, the key is not necessarily changed by using inflected notes.

Ex. 1.

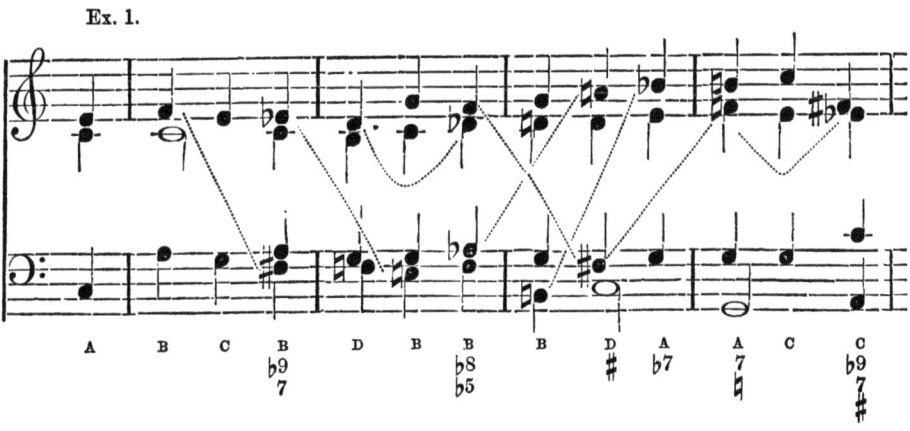

* Appendix BB.

Ex. 1—*continued.*

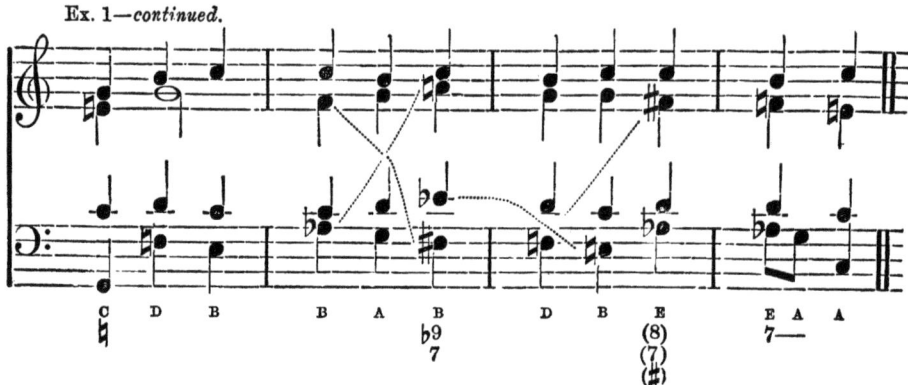

Therefore, it is *not* false relation if the chromatic note belong essentially to any one of the fundamental chromatic harmonies mentioned in this Part, and provided the chromatic note in the first of the three chords be not a thirteenth (Ex. 1).

3. Neither is it false relation if one of the notes be the fifth of a major key, and the other the leading-note of the relative minor (Ex. 2), or if one

Ex. 2.

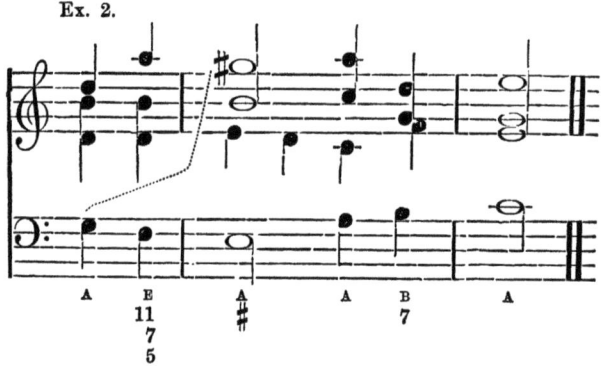

of them be the tonic of a major key, and the other the leading-note of the minor key of the second above (Ex. 3), provided that if the intervening chord contain the second above the dominant of the said minor key, that second must be minor (Ex. 4).

Ex. 3.

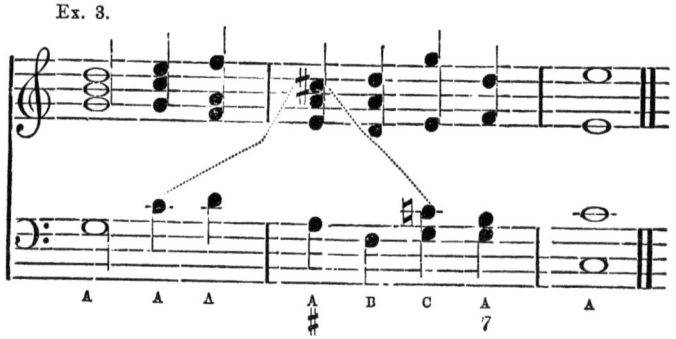

4. In diatonic harmony two notes of the same name, but of a different quality, cannot ever occur in different parts in two consecutive chords, because there is no connexion between those chords, or, in other words, they are falsely related ; but in chromatic

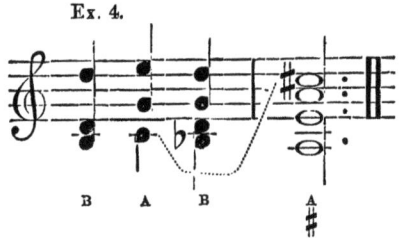

Ex. 4.

harmony if the third of the first chord be the root of the second, the perfect fifth of the first chord and the major third of the second chord may be in different parts, without causing false relation (Ex. 5).

Ex. 5.

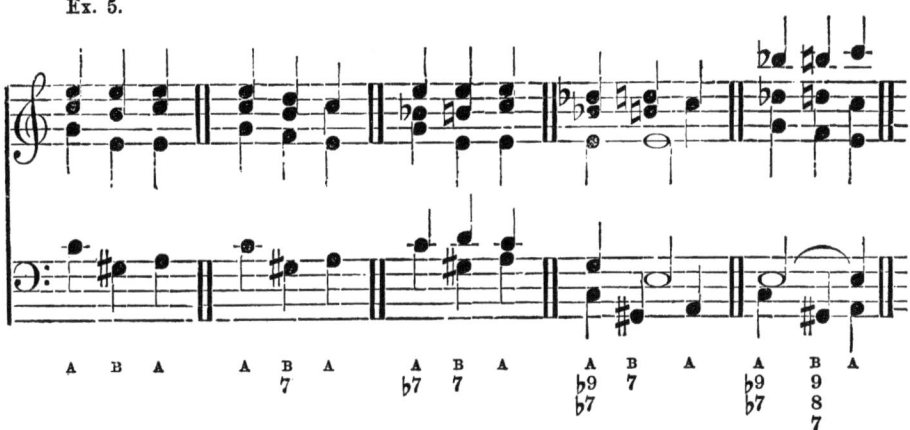

5. Neither is there false relation between the root of the first chord and the major third of the second chord if the third of the first chord be the fifth of the second chord (Ex. 6).

Ex. 6.

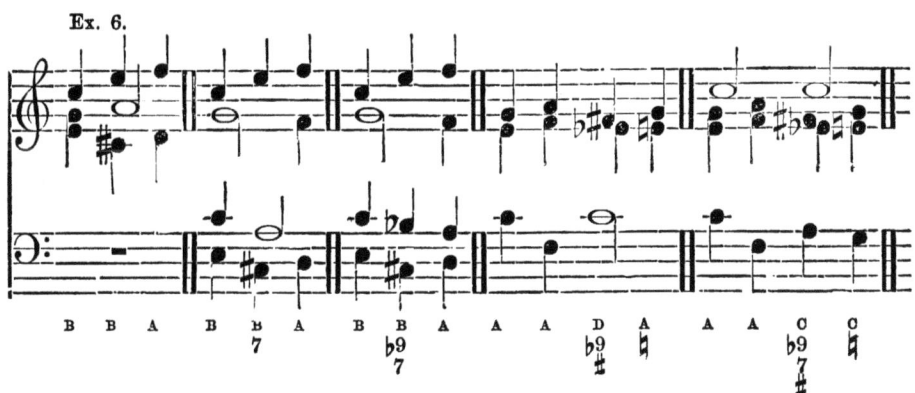

6. In chromatic harmony as in diatonic, it is a rule that no two notes of the same name but of a different quality, can be taken simultaneously in the same chord (Ex. 7); whenever this appears agreeably it will be found a specimen of false notation, as in the following progression from the G minor

symphony of Mozart (Ex. 8), which cannot, as it stands, by any means be rendered into sense; but the notation being altered by the G♯ being written A♭ (Ex. 9), it shows itself to be the progression from the minor ninth and thirteenth of G to the seventh of D.

Ex. 7. Ex. 8. Ex. 9.

7. Beneath is a specimen of the allowable occurrence of two notes of the same name, but of a different quality, in two different parts, in two consecutive chords in the same key, in rather extreme positions (Ex. 10).

Ex. 10.

CHAPTER XVI.

OF COMMON CHORDS AND THEIR FIRST INVERSIONS.

SECTION 1. The same common chords and first inversions are allowed in the chromatic school as in the diatonic. The rules affecting the progression of such common chords are precisely the same, and the same licences are allowed in sequence.

2. The chord of the tonic is major or minor according to the key.*

3. The chord of the sub-dominant *must* be *minor* in the minor key,† with one exception, viz., when the major sixth of the scale, as major third of the subdominant, occurs in the passage from the minor seventh of the scale to the minor sixth (Ex. 1). It *may* be chromatically *minor* in the *major* key (Ex. 2).

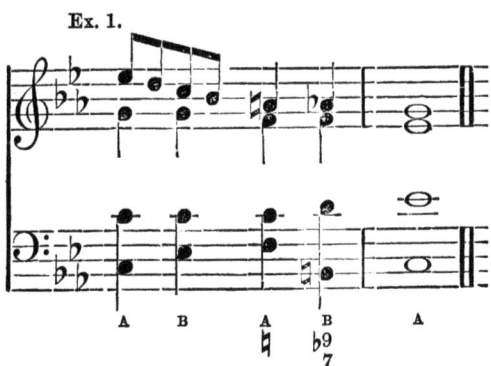

Ex. 1.

Ex. 2.

4. The common chord of the dominant must be in all cases major.‡

5. A chromatic major common chord may be taken on the supertonic, which chord must be followed by the chord of the tonic or some inversion thereof, or some chord comprising the diatonic fourth of the scale; and the third (the augmented fourth of the scale) must rise a minor second or fall to a note of its own name. This chord may be taken with the same intervals

---

* Appendix CC.   † Appendix DD.   ‡ Appendix I.

whether the key be major or minor. Ex. 3 may be read in C major if the signature be cancelled; and, with one exception (Sect. 3) the only instance in which the major sixth can be harmonized in the minor key is when it occurs as the fifth of this chord or of some other derived from the same root.

Ex. 3.

6. A chromatic major common chord may be taken on the minor second of the scale. The first inversion of this chord is the chord usually known by the name of the Neapolitan sixth (Ex. 4).

Ex. 4.

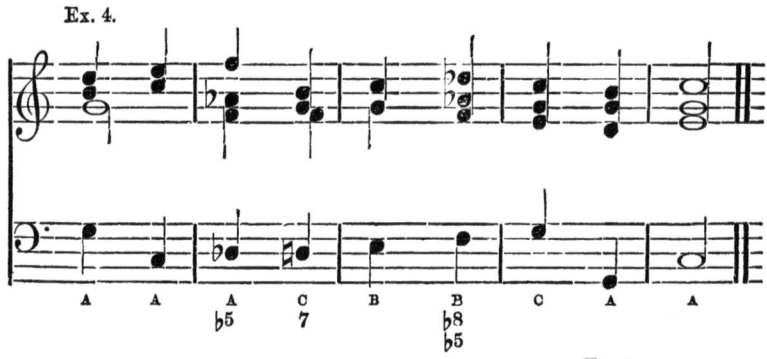

7. A chromatic major common chord may be also taken on the minor sixth of the scale, and these two last chromatic common chords are not otherwise limited in their progression than are other concords (Ex. 5).

Ex. 5.

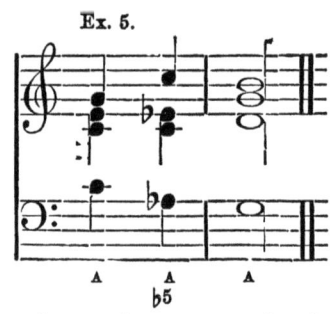

8. The diatonic common chords, and also the chromatic common chords above mentioned, may be taken in their first inversions, as may also the common chord of the third of the major key.*

---

* Appendix EE.

9. With regard to doubling the major third of the diatonic common chords, the rules of the diatonic school are to be strictly observed here also;* more particularly when the third is in the bass. With regard to the major third of the chromatic common chords, the major third of the supertonic chord cannot ever be doubled; the major thirds of the chromatic common chords of the minor second and minor sixth of the scale, are better doubled than not, even when in their first inversion; this is because the third harmonic of the third of the minor second is the key note, and that of the minor sixth is the dominant. The tonic and dominant are both available as pedals, therefore their presence as harmonics is unobjectionable.

* Appendix II.

CHAPTER XVII.

OF THE SECOND INVERSIONS OF CONCORDS.

INTRODUCTION.

THE novelty in this chapter is the legitimatising of the second inversion of the dominant concord, a harmony that is employed with good effect, but has not been mentioned by theorists. Rules for the sequel to a chord in the second inversion are here more completely given, and the freedom of the fourth from the bass is more clearly shown than in some other treatises.

SECTION 1. The second inversion of a chord has the fifth in the bass, which is lettered C. The root and third of the chord are then the fourth and sixth from the bass.

2. The chord of the tonic in the second inversion was the earliest used, that of the subdominant was next in historical order, and that of the dominant was last introduced; all three are available. The second inversions of the tonic and subdominant chords are major or minor according to the key, that of the subdominant may be chromatically minor in the major key, and that of the dominant is always major; in this last chord the sixth from the bass (the leading-note) must rise in proceeding to a chord with another root.*

3. The fourth from the bass, the inverted root of these chords, does not require preparation or resolution (Ex. 1).

Ex. 1.

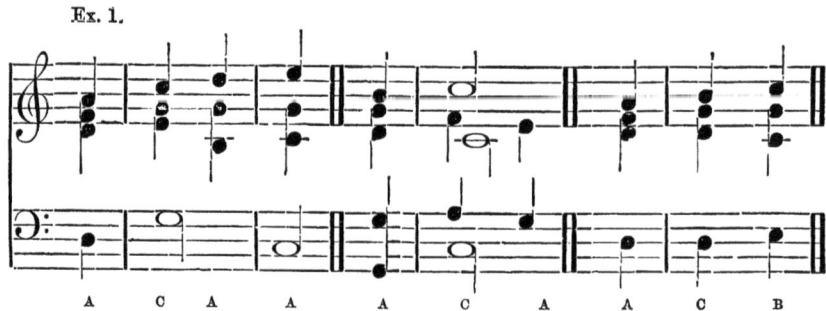

A   C   A   A   A   C   A   A   C   B

4. The bass of a chord in the second inversion cannot be taken by skip, excepting from roots,† as in the first three instances of Ex. 2, or from the third of the chord of which it is an inversion, as in the next three, or (when it is the second inversion of the tonic common chord) from the fifth of the chord of the eleventh, as in the last.‡

---

* Appendix FF.   † Appendix GG.   ‡ Appendix HH.

Ex. 2.

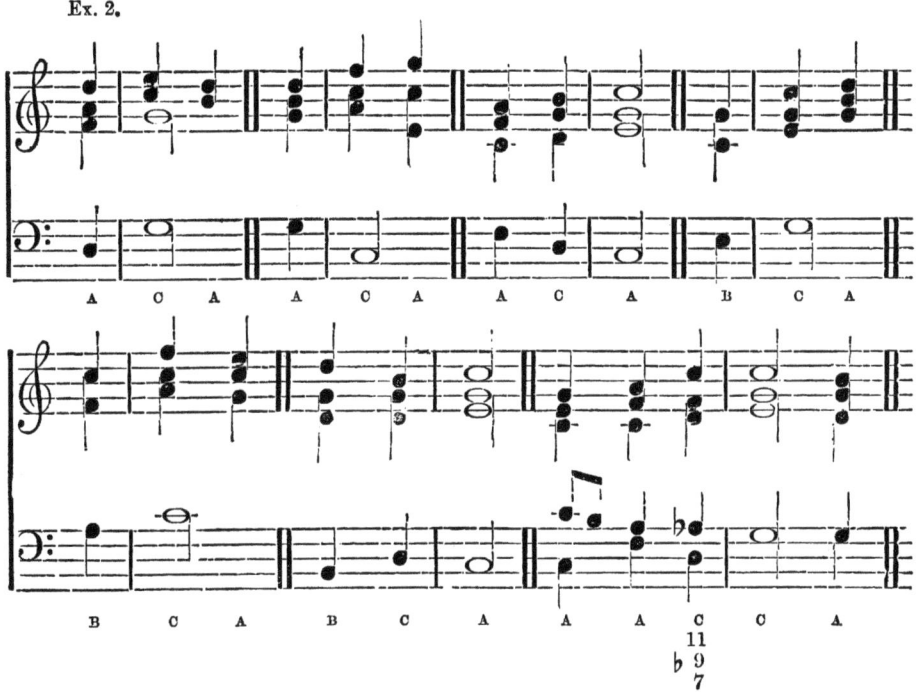

5. A chord in the second inversion must be followed by a chord on the same bass or its octave, or else by a chord on the next note above or below it, which chord and which note may be diatonic or chromatic or enharmonic (Ex. 3).

Ex. 3.

G 2

6. The bass of this inversion may go either to the root or third of the same chord (Ex. 4), or it may proceed by one or more passing-notes

Ex. 4.

(Ex. 5), provided it return to some note to which such bass should progress.

Ex 5.

7. If the second inversion of a common chord be followed by any other chord on the same note, it must be on a stronger accent than the following chord.* This is immaterial if it be followed by any chord on the next note above or below (Ex. 6).

Ex. 6.

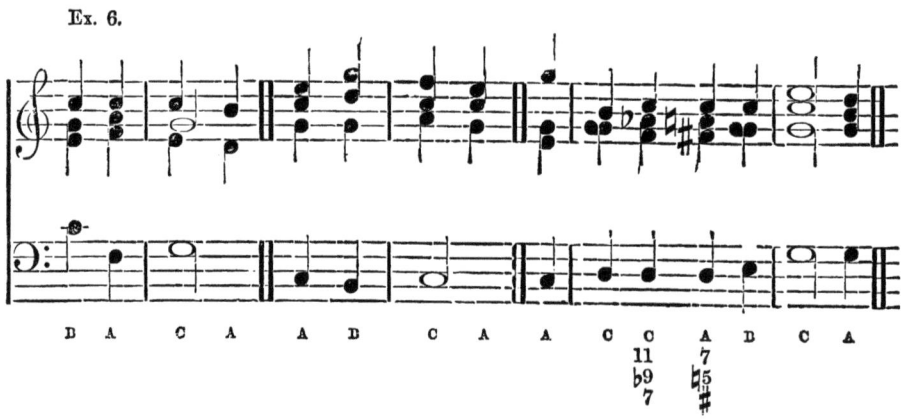

_____

* Appendix II.

Ex. 6—*continued.*

8. The fourth in these chords is not a discord, for even when followed by the common chord on the same note the fourth is not obliged to fall, but may go to any note of the next chord (Ex. 7).

Ex. 7.

9. The second inversion of one common chord can never be followed by the second inversion of another, excepting when the second inversion of the dominant is followed by the second inversion of the subdominant, and this provided no part move in fourths with the bass (Ex. 8); this progression cannot be reversed.

Ex. 8.

10. The common chords on the minor and major seconds, and minor and major sixths of the scale, cannot be used in the second inversion, as the key would be thereby changed, and they would no longer be chords of the second or sixth of the scale.*

---

* Appendix JJ.

CHAPTER XVIII.

OF THE FUNDAMENTAL SEVENTHS OF THE DOMINANT, SUPERTONIC, AND TONIC.

INTRODUCTION.

THE following chords of the seventh, both in their form and their resolution, are perfectly well known; the novelties in this chapter are—I, that the chords which have been generally considered to make modulation, namely, those of the supertonic and tonic, are here treated as strictly belonging to the key, and the proofs of their being so are given; and II, the peculiar resolutions of the sevenths and thirds, the sevenths ascending and the thirds descending, which, although in accordance with the practice of the best modern authors, are now for the first time reduced to rule.

Ex. 1.

SECTION 1. The chord of the fundamental seventh consists of the root, major third, perfect fifth, and minor seventh (Ex. 1).

2. These chords consist of precisely the same intervals whether the key be major or minor; thus, if in C minor the fundamental seventh of the tonic

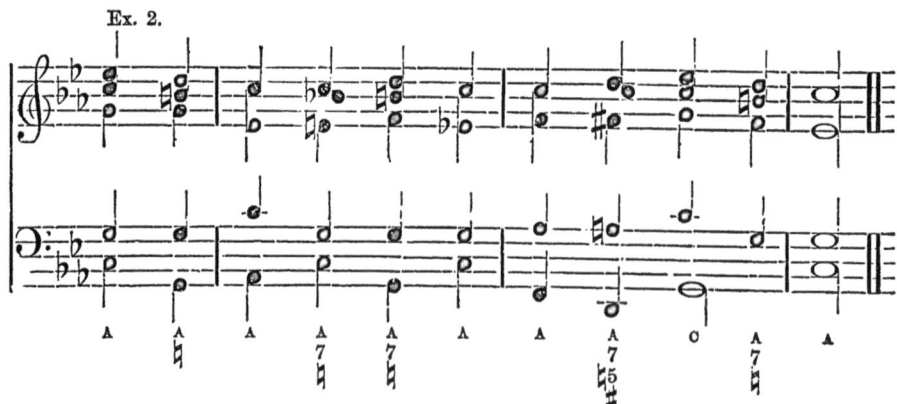

Ex. 2.

be used, the third being major the E will be ♮; or if also in the minor the fundamental seventh of the supertonic be used, the fifth being perfect the A will be ♮ (Ex. 2).

3. Each of these three chords is susceptible of three inversions; the first inversion has the third in the bass, it is lettered B with the figure 7 (Ex 3.)

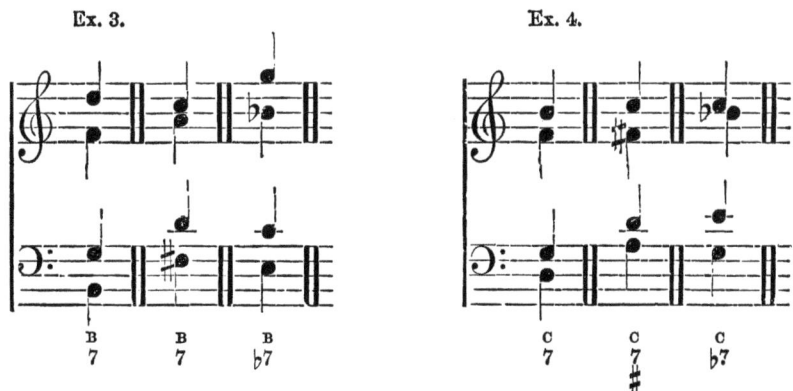

Ex. 3.   Ex. 4.

4. The second inversion has the fifth in the bass; it is lettered C with the necessary figures (Ex. 4).

5. In this inversion the root is frequently omitted, in which case the chord must be lettered B, with figures to show any inflected notes,* (Ex. 5); when this form of the chord occurs as the second inversion of the dominant harmony, it is the chord of the sixth on the second of the scale (Chap. IV., sect. 17).† The incomplete second inversion of the supertonic seventh and that of the tonic seventh are corresponding chords of the sixth, with one or more chromatic notes.

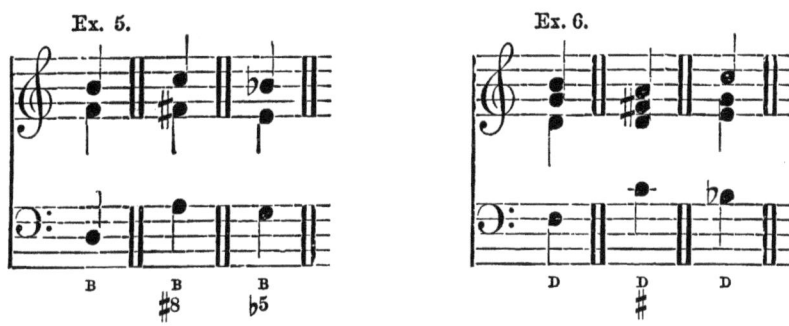

Ex. 5.   Ex. 6.

6. The third inversion has the seventh in the bass; it is lettered D (Ex. 6).

7. The root may be omitted only in the second inversion.

---

* This lettering and figuring is used to identify the chord with that in the diatonic style which corresponds with it.
† Appendix KK.

Ex. 7.

8. The fifth may be omitted at discretion, either in the direct form of the chord or any of its inversions; there is no occasion to indicate the absence of the fifth by any particular figuring (Ex. 7).

9. The third *should* not be omitted.

10. The seventh of course *cannot* be omitted; were it omitted, the chord would be no longer a chord of the seventh.

11. The third can never be doubled.

Ex. 8.

12. The seventh may be doubled when in the second inversion the root is omitted (Sect. 5), or when the seventh remains to be a note of the next chord one of which sevenths is free in its progression (Ex. 8).

13. In these chords of the seventh and their inversions, the third and seventh (which form with each other either a diminished fifth or an augmented fourth) are the only notes the progression of which is limited, excepting the fifth when occurring as the bass; and the same limitations exist whether either of these notes occurs in an upper part or as the bass.

14. The third in these chords must either rise a second, minor or major, or remain, or fall a semitone to a note of its own name (Ex. 9).

Ex. 9.

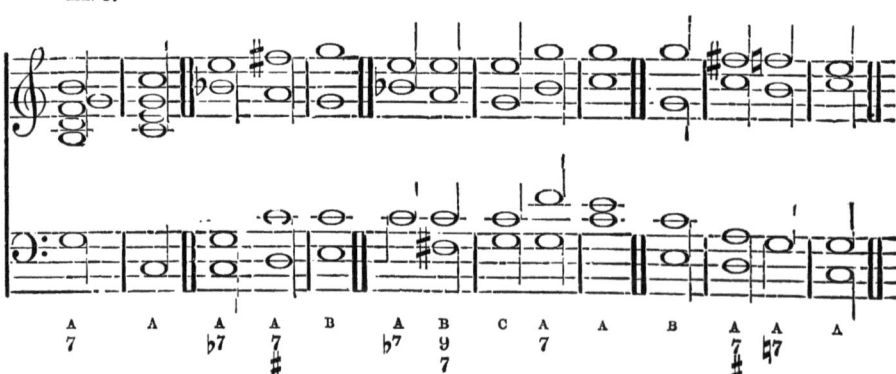

15. The third may fall a major second to the fifth of the next chord (such chord bearing a seventh), provided the seventh rise a semitone to a note of its own name in the following chord (Ex. 10).*

Ex. 10.

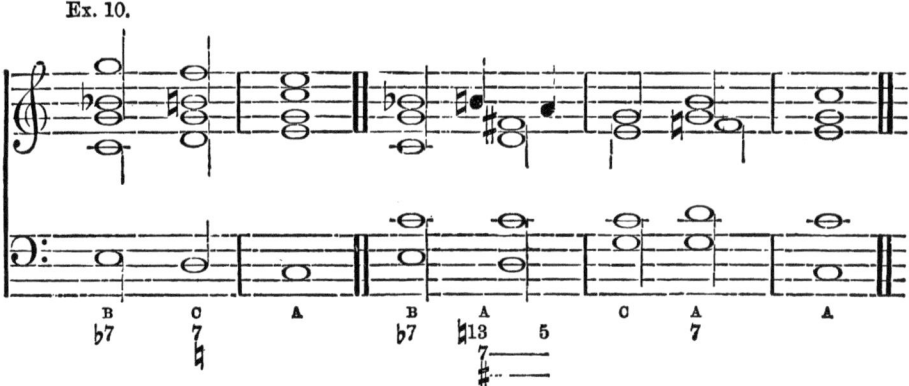

16. The seventh may fall a minor or major second,† or remain, or rise a semitone to a note of its own name (Ex. 11).

Ex. 11.

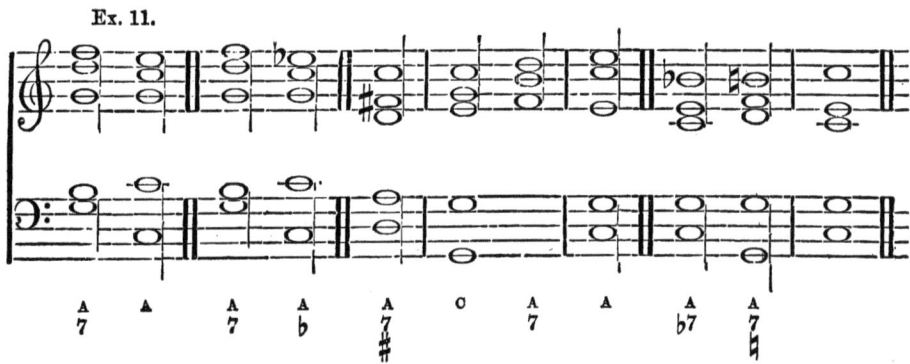

17. Whenever the second inversion of a chord containing a seventh is followed by the first inversion of a chord on the note next above, the seventh

Ex. 12.

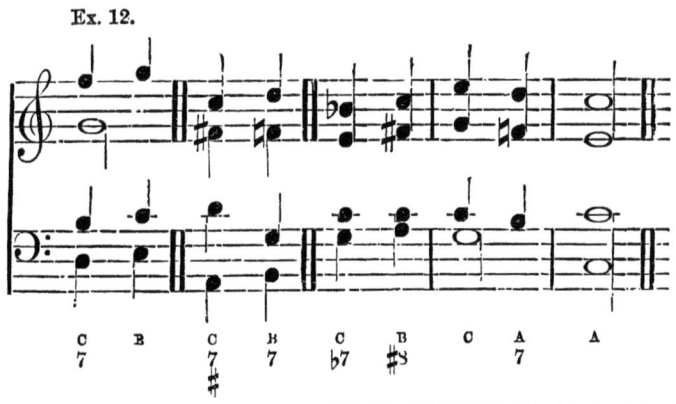

---

* Appendix LL.   † Appendix MM.

is allowed to rise a major second, and in this case the progression from a diminished to a perfect fifth, and that from a seventh to an eighth or a second to an unison by oblique motion, are not objectionable (Ex. 12). In the last instance the absence of the root in the inverted chord of D leaves the harmony consonant, and justifies its treatment as a first inversion (Sect. 5.)

18. The seventh may rise a major second to the fifth of the next chord (such chord bearing a third), provided the third fall a semitone to a note of its own name (Ex. 13).*

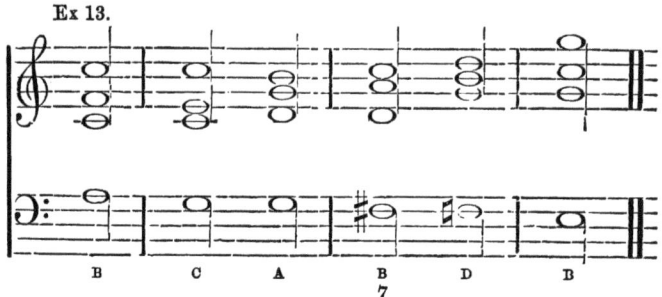

19. The root is not limited in its progression, save by the rules for the progression of parts, viz., that it may not descend a third nor a second, and save also that it may not proceed to any note which may not be doubled in the ensuing chord (Ex. 14).

20. The fifth is free in all cases excepting when in the bass, and then it is governed by the same rule as in the second inversions of concords (Ex. 15). (Chap. XVII.)

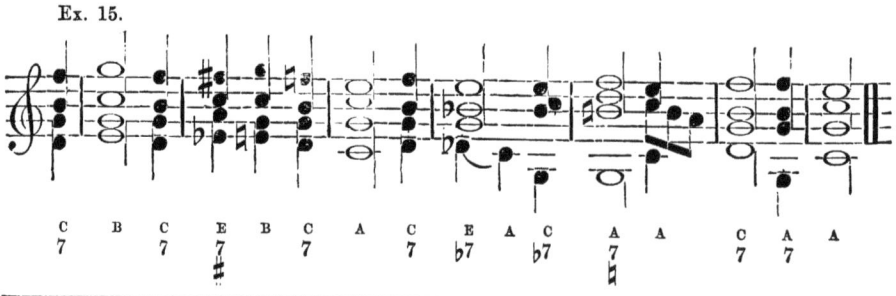

---

* Appendix NN.

21. The natural resolution of the chord of the seventh of the dominant, is to any form of the major or minor common chord of the tonic, or to an inversion of the major or minor common chords of the subdominant (Ex. 16).

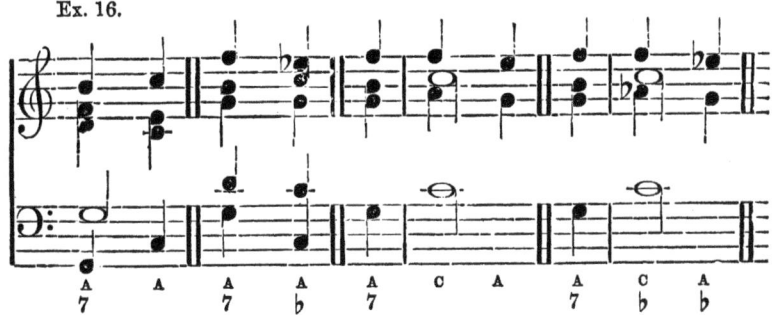

Ex. 16.

22. The natural resolution of the chord of the seventh of the supertonic, is to an inversion of the major or minor* common chord of the tonic, or to a dominant discord.

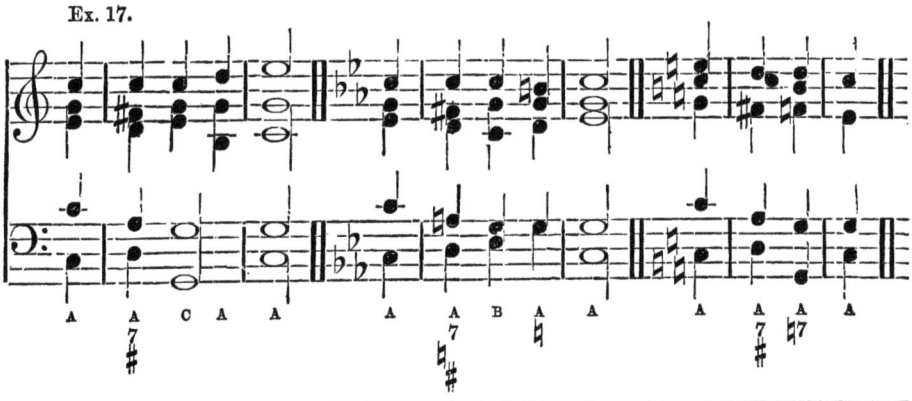

Ex. 17.

---

* This is not a modulation into the dominant as is frequently asserted, the second inversion of the common chord of the tonic being merely a suspension over the common chord on the same bass, because, in the first place, the $\frac{5}{3}$ on the same bass need not follow the second inversion of the tonic; and, in the next place, this may be done on the tonic pedal (C); were the key changed into the dominant (G), the pedal (C) of the example would be the subdominant of the new key, which subdominant is not allowed as a pedal; the key is therefore not changed into that of the dominant (Ex. 18).

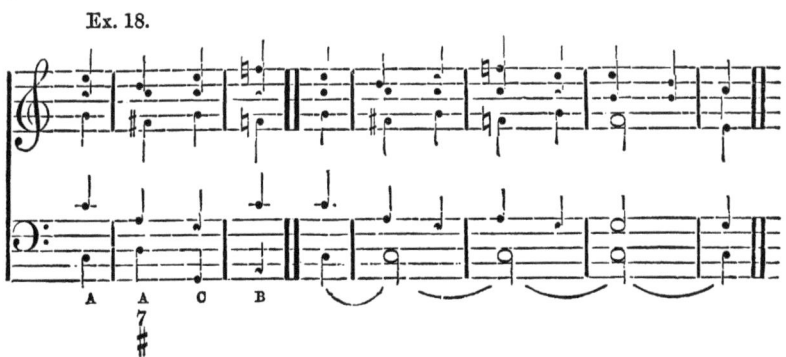

Ex. 18.

23. The natural resolution of the seventh of the tonic is to a dominant or supertonic discord (Ex. 19).

Ex. 19.

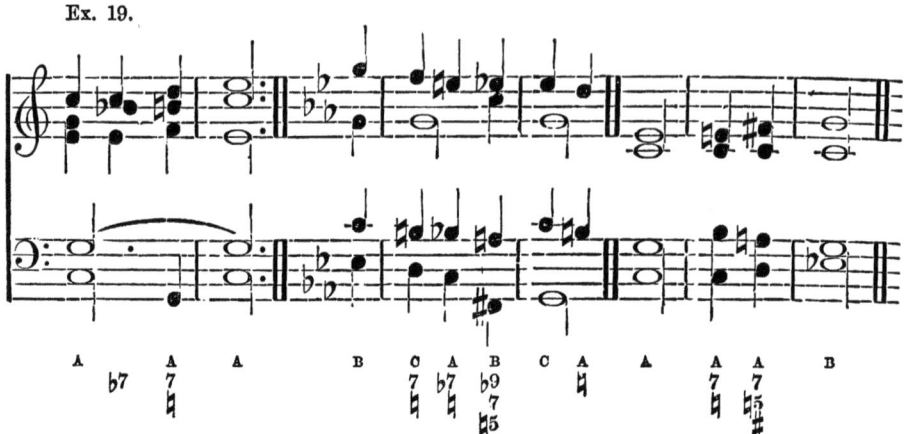

The last instance in Ex. 19 shows the only case in which the third of a fundamental discord may rise a major second.

24. The seventh of the tonic may also be followed by the common chord of the subdominant, either major or minor;* but this must be follcwed by a dominant harmony, or a chromatic harmony of the supertonic (Ex. 20).

Ex. 20.

* This is not a modulation into the subdominant, because this can be done on the dominant pedal; were the key changed into the subdominant, the pedal would be the supertonic of the new key, which supertonic is not allowed as a pedal; the key is therefore not changed into that of the subdominant.

Ex. 21.

CHAPTER XIX.

OF THE FUNDAMENTAL MINOR AND MAJOR NINTHS OF THE DOMINANT, SUPERTONIC, AND TONIC.

INTRODUCTION.

THE following chords of the ninth are very well known in their inversions; they are less familiar in their direct form; it has been therefore thought desirable in the following chapter to take them occasionally with their roots, to show the real nature of the chords; still, be it observed, in this form they should be used but sparingly. Whenever both ninth and eighth are used together, both must be indicated either by the figures or letters, as the case may be.

Ex. 1.

SECTION 1. The fundamental chords of the minor ninth have a minor ninth from the root taken above, or in addition to the three last mentioned chords of the seventh (Ex. 1).

2. These chords of the minor ninth may be used indiscriminately in either the minor or major key.

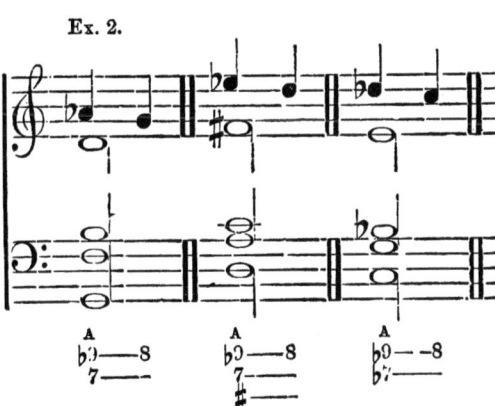

Ex. 2.

3. These chords of the fundamental ninth differ from the chords of the fundamental seventh, insomuch as one of the intervals, the ninth, *may* be resolved, while the rest of the chord continues (Ex. 2).

4. Like the chords of the seventh they may also be resolved on chords derived from another root (Ex. 3).

5. The seventh must be in the chord; the fifth may be omitted.

Ex. 3.

Ex. 4.

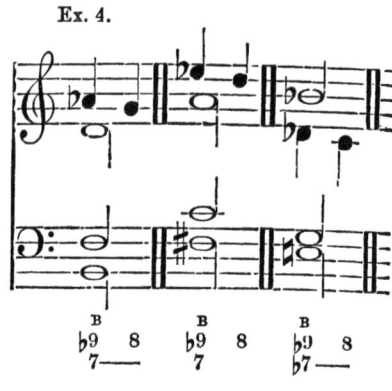

6. The ninth may be resolved on the root, in which case the root cannot exist in the chord, excepting as the bass (Ex. 2).

7. This chord is susceptible of four inversions.

8. The first inversion has the third in the bass (Ex. 4); this is lettered B with the proper figures; it is known as the chord of the diminished seventh, the minor ninth of the chord being at the interval of the diminished seventh from the third.

9. The second inversion has the fifth in the bass; it is lettered C with the necessary figures (Ex. 5).

Ex. 5.

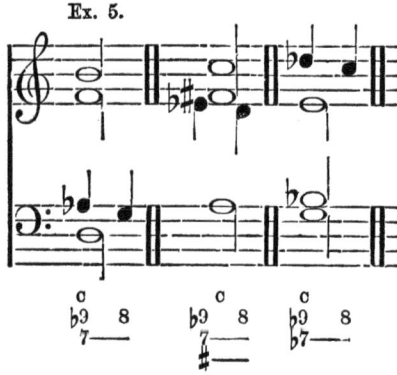

Ex. 6.

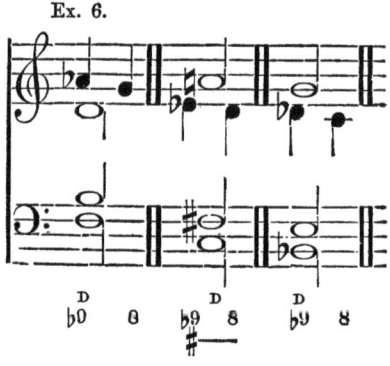

10. The third inversion has the seventh in the bass; it is lettered D, &c (Ex. 6).

11. The fourth inversion has the ninth in the bass; it is lettered E, &c. (Ex. 7).

Ex. 7.

12. When the ninth is resolved on the root the root may be taken in an inner part and retained during the resolution of the ninth, if the root be approached by second upwards; but this extremely harsh form of the chord should be most sparingly used. The root and ninth cannot be taken in the same way on the tonic, because the only way of approaching them is through the doubled leading-note, which is not allowable (Ex. 8).

Ex. 8.

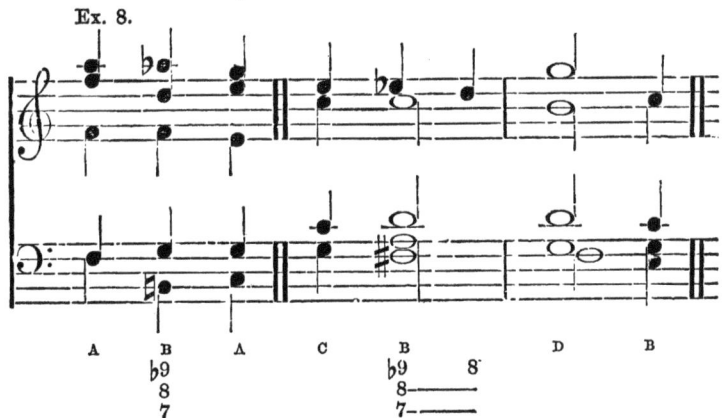

13. Both root and seventh may also be taken in the upper parts if the root have been heard in the preceding chord in the same part; in no case in this form may the root and ninth be at a smaller distance than a ninth from each other. This form of the chord, like that described in sect. 12, should be of rare occurrence (Ex. 9).

Ex. 9.

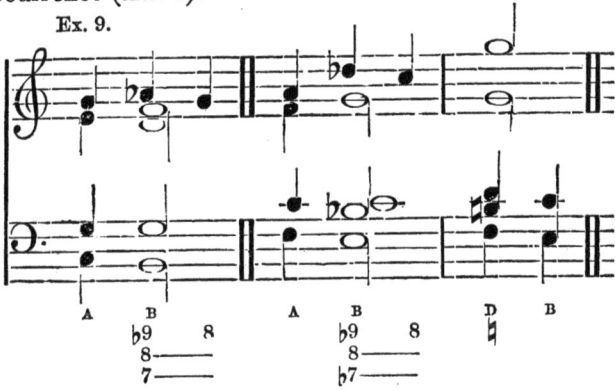

Ex. 10.

14. Instead of proceeding to the root the ninth can be resolved on the third, when the third cannot be sounded with the ninth, but the root must (Ex. 10).

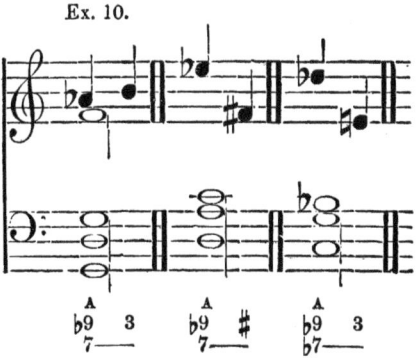

15. The fifth may be omitted, but not the seventh or root (Ex. 11).

16. With the resolution of the ninth on the third, this chord is susceptible of three inversions, the first being unavailable.

17. The second inversion has the fifth in the bass; it is lettered C, &c. (Ex. 12).

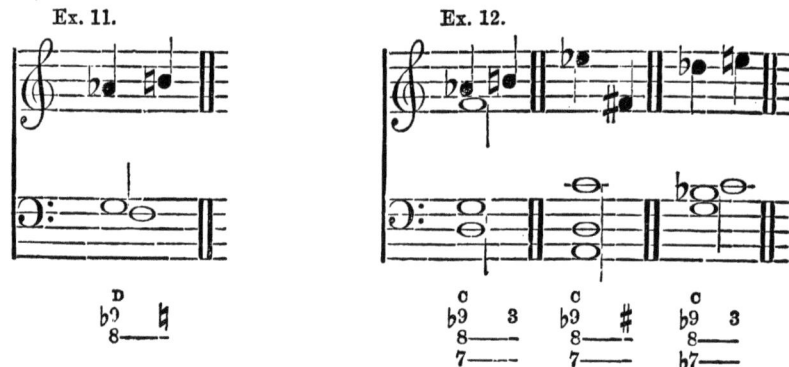

18. The third inversion has the seventh in the bass; it is lettered D, &c. (Ex. 13).

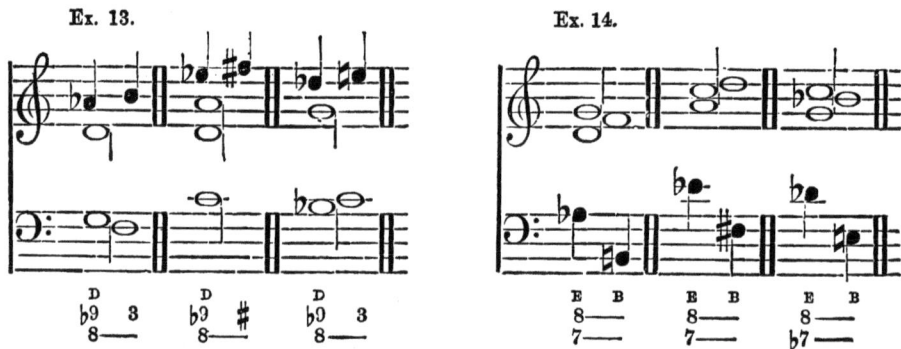

19. The fourth inversion has the ninth in the bass; it is lettered E, &c. (Ex. 14).

20. The root may be taken instead of the seventh, and fall to the seventh, while the ninth remains (Ex. 15).

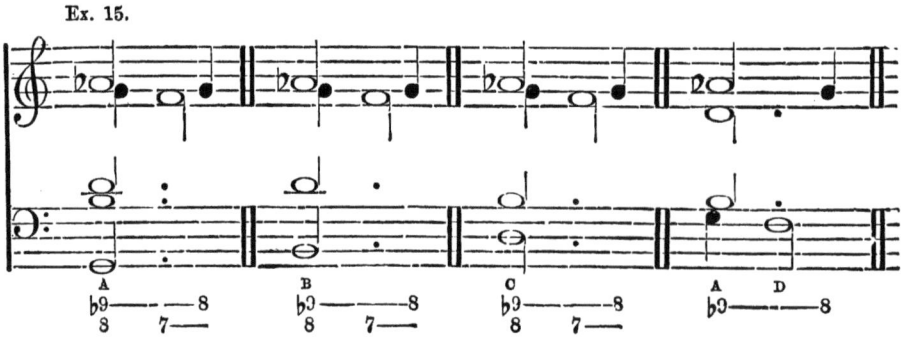

Ex. 15—*continued.*

21. The root may also be taken instead of the seventh, and fall to the seventh while the ninth proceeds to the third (Ex. 16).

Ex. 16.

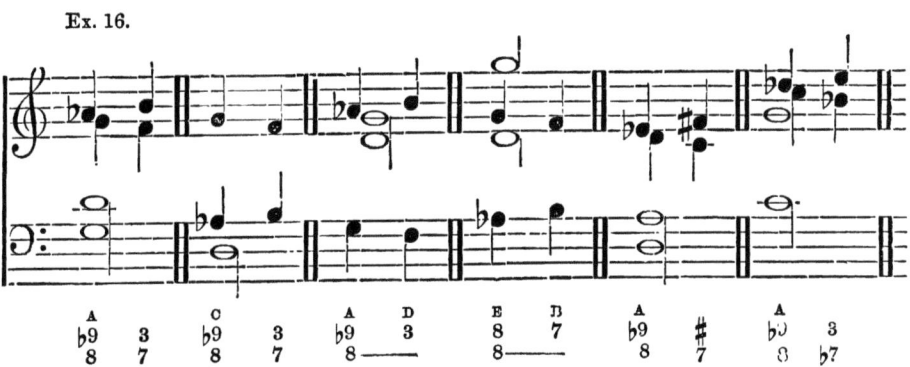

22. The chord of the major ninth with its inversions differs not from the chord of the minor ninth, excepting that the interval of the ninth, is major instead of minor (Ex. 17). The same notes may be omitted. The major ninth is better above than below the third when both are together in the same chord; and therefore the

Ex. 17.

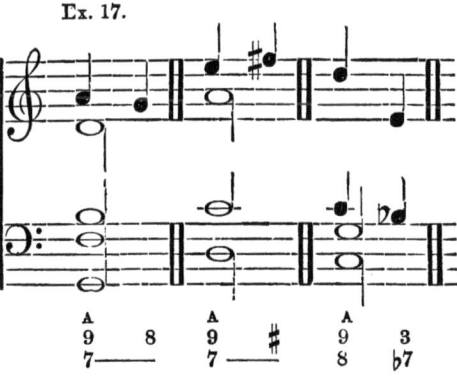

inversion is undesirable with the ninth in the bass resolved on the root.

23. The treatment of the major ninth, when resolving on a chord having the same root, differs in no respect from that of the minor ninth, with the

H

Ex. 18.

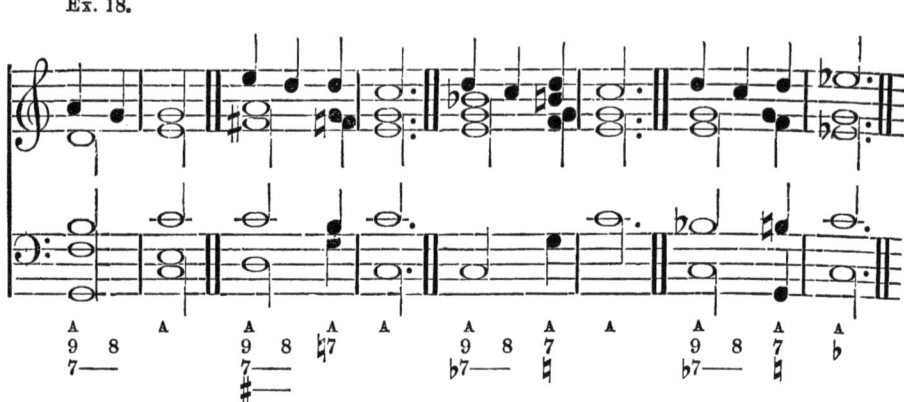

Ex. 19.

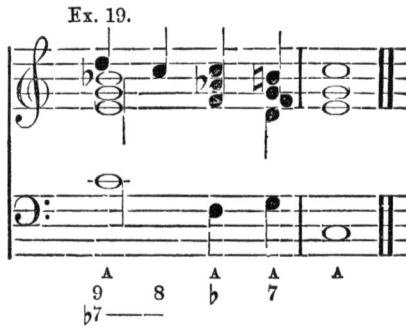

exception that the chords of the major ninth of the dominant and supertonic belong exclusively to the major key. The major ninth of the tonic is common to both major and minor keys (Ex. 18), with this limitation, that when the chord of the major ninth of the tonic is resolved on the same root, if the chord of the subdominant follow, this must have a major third.* Ex. 19 is therefore bad.

24. The minor ninth, in resolving on a chord with another root, may either fall a second, or remain, or rise a chromatic semitone.

25. The progressions of the third and seventh are the same as in the chord of the seventh.

26. This chord, in resolving on a chord having another root, is susceptible of the same inversions as when the ninth is resolved on a note having the same root.

27. In the third inversion, when the seventh is in the bass, the third is frequently omitted, and the chord of the sixth is produced. This inversion is not a discord, because the notes are absent which, if retained, would render the original seventh and ninth (the bass, and third from the bass of this inversion) discords. The augmented fourth in this inversion differs from the same interval in the second inversion of the chord of the seventh, insomuch as in the latter it is formed by the third and seventh from the root, which third may never be doubled; in the former the interval is formed by the fifth and ninth from the root, which fifth is free (Chap. IV., sect. 17; Chap. XVIII., sect. 5).

---

* Appendix OO.

When this inversion occurs without the third it must be lettered B (as if it were the first inversion of a diminished triad of the supertonic), with ♭5 or ♮5 to show the inflection of the apparent fifth, which is the third from the bass* (Ex. 20).

Ex. 20.

28. The natural resolution of the chord of the minor ninth of the dominant is on the major or minor common chord of the tonic, or on the major or minor common chord of the subdominant (Ex. 21).

Ex. 21.

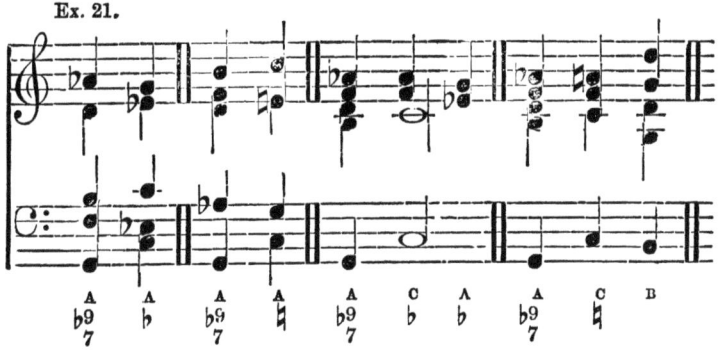

29. The following are the inversions (Ex. 22).

Ex. 22.

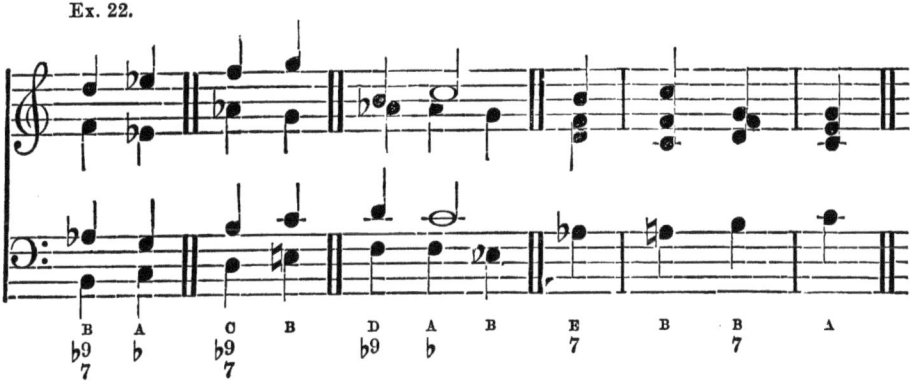

In the second inversion of the ninth, as in the second inversion of the seventh, if the bass rise to the resolution of the seventh, the seventh is allowed to rise a major second to the fifth of the next chord, as in Ex. 22; in this case also, as in that of the seventh, the progression from a diminished to a perfect fifth is not objectionable.

---

* Appendix PP.

30. The natural resolution of the chord of the minor ninth of the super-tonic is either on the major or minor common chord of the tonic, or on a dominant discord (Ex. 23).

Ex. 23.

31. The following are the inversions (Ex. 24)*

Ex. 24.

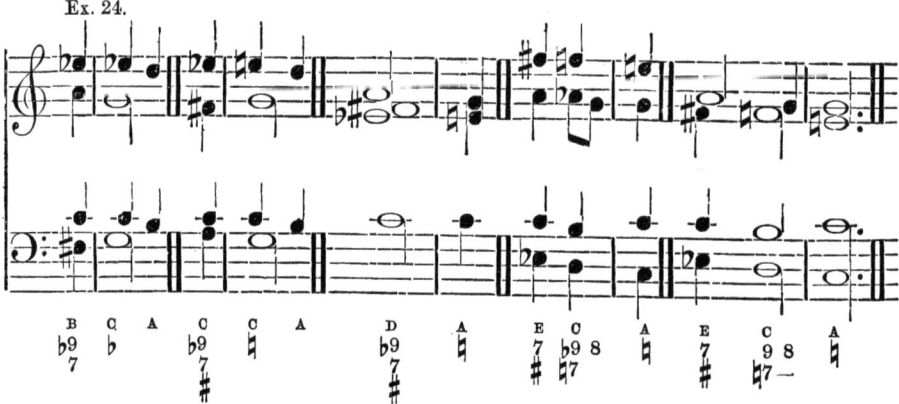

32. The natural resolution of the chord of the minor ninth of the tonic is on a direct or inverted dominant discord, or else on an inversion of a super-tonic discord (Ex. 25).

* Appendix QQ.

Ex. 25.

33. The following are the inversions (Ex. 26).

Ex. 26.

34. The chord of the minor ninth of the tonic, or its inversions, may also (without modulation) resolve on the common chord of the subdominant or its inversions, either minor or major in the major key, or minor in the minor key (Ex. 27). The proof that this is not a modulation into the key of the subdominant is contained in the note to sect. 24, Chap. XVIII.

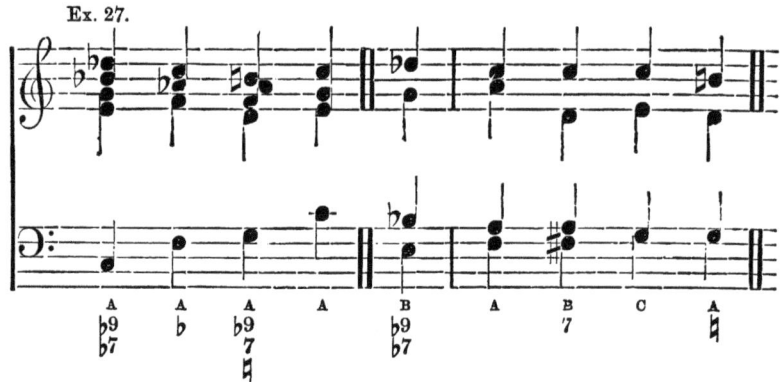

Ex. 27.

35. The roots of these chords of the minor ninth may exist in the upper parts *with* the ninth, either in the direct chord or any of the inversions, in which case the seventh cannot co-exist in the chord; and the inverted root

Ex. 28.

either proceeds to the seventh while the ninth remains, or proceeds to that note in the ensuing chord on which the seventh should have resolved (Ex. 28). As in all other cases where the ninth and root exist in the upper parts, both notes must be indicated by the figures, as in the example.

36. The treatment of the chord of the major ninth, when resolving on a chord having another root, is the same as that of the minor ninth, with the exceptions that where the minor ninth falls a minor second the major ninth falls a major second, and that where the former rises a chromatic semitone the latter remains. As has been before stated, the chords of the major ninth of the dominant and supertonic belong exclusively to the major key, and must be resolved on chords having a major third, and although the chord of the major ninth of the tonic is common to either major or minor key, yet, like the other two, it can only be resolved on a chord having a major third. The major ninth should generally be above the third when they are both in the chord, and therefore the last inversion is most rarely employed.

37. The natural resolutions of the chord of the major ninth of the dominant (Ex. 29).

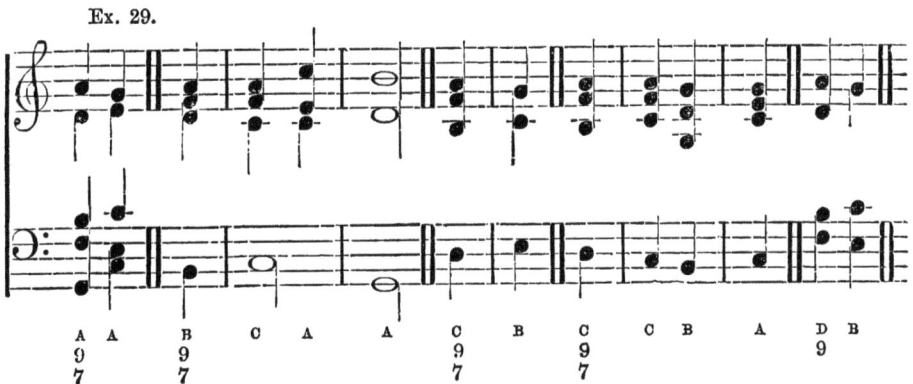

Ex. 29.

38. The natural resolutions of the chord of the major ninth of the supertonic (Ex. 30).

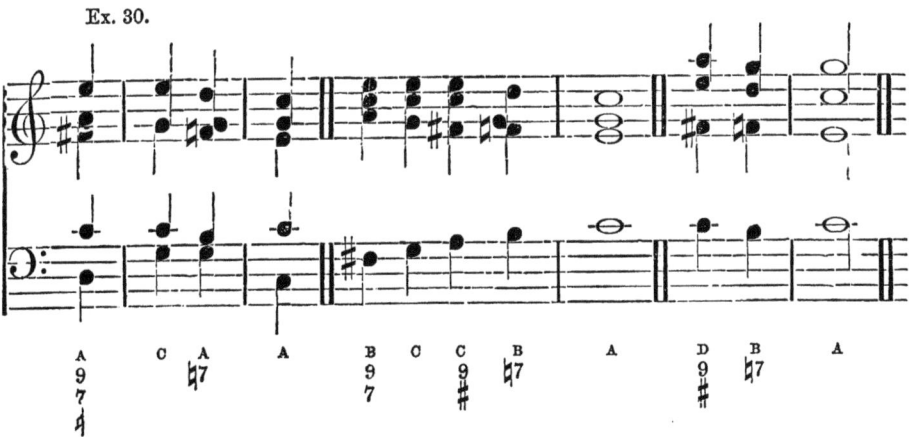

Ex. 30.

39. The natural resolutions of the chord of the major ninth of the tonic (Ex. 31).

Ex. 31.

40. The resolutions of the chords of the major ninth, the root being in an upper part, and the seventh not being present in the chord (Ex. 32).

Ex. 32.

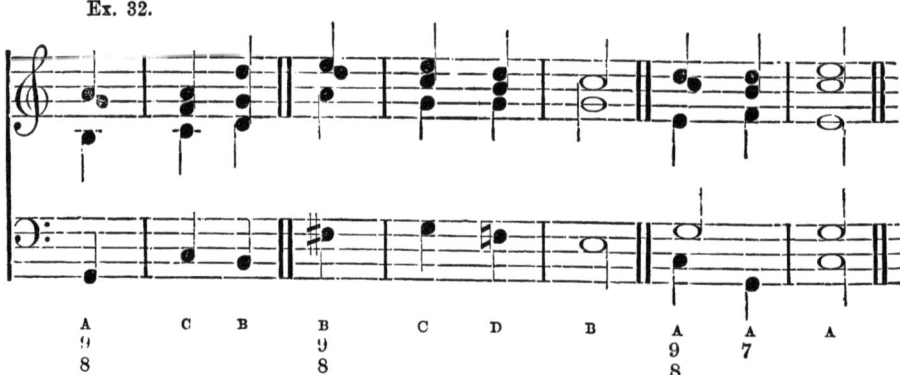

41. The treatment of the inversions of the chords of the major ninth is the same as that of the minor ninth, with the same restrictions as to the key or mode in which they may be used, and the chords on which they may resolve. as in the original position of the chords of the major ninth.

CHAPTER XX.

OF THE CHORD OF THE FUNDAMENTAL ELEVENTH OF THE DOMINANT.

INTRODUCTION.

As the eleventh is fully discussed in this chapter there is no occasion to say anything here on the subject, except that the chord of the eleventh accompanied with the third (as also all chords in which two notes next each other in alphabetical order form with each other the interval of either minor or major ninth, counting from the root, as root and ninth, third and eleventh, fifth and thirteenth), should be used very sparingly. When two notes next each other in alphabetical order form with each other the interval of the seventh, counting from the root, as third and ninth, fifth and eleventh, seventh and thirteenth, there is no occasion for any economy in their use other than is produced by the consideration that their effect is diminished in proportion to the frequency of their repetition.

SECTION 1. The chord of the eleventh, unlike the chords of the seventh and ninth, can only be taken on the dominant.*

2. It can be taken with either a minor or major ninth (Ex. 1).

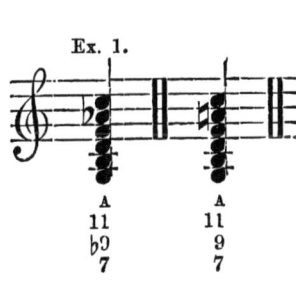

Ex. 1.

Ex. 2.

3. This chord with a minor ninth is an eleventh from the root taken above, or in addition to, the chord of the minor ninth on the dominant.

4. This chord with the minor ninth is common to minor and major keys.

* Appendix T.

5. Like the chords of the ninth, it may either resolve on a chord derived from the same root, or on one derived from another root.

6. In resolving on a chord derived from the same root, the eleventh may fall to the third, in which case the third cannot exist previously in the chord (Ex. 2).

7. In this form the root cannot be taken excepting as the bass.

8. The first inversion is unavailable, the second inversion has the fifth in the bass, the third inversion has the seventh, the fourth has the ninth, and the fifth has the eleventh (Ex. 3).

Ex. 3.

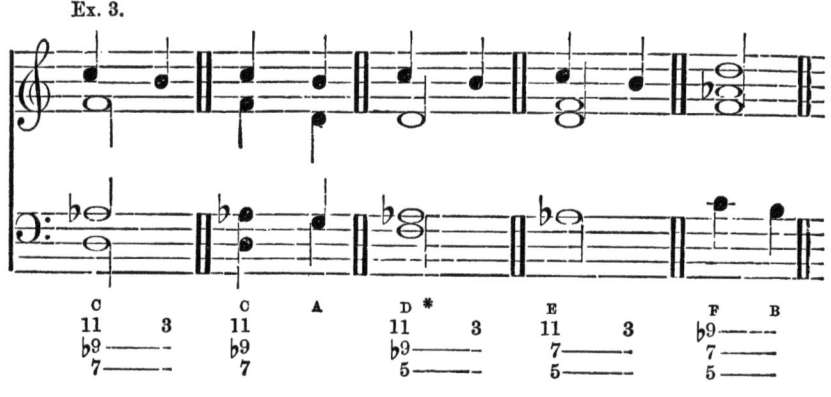

* This inversion is the chord known as the added sixth; it has been much disputed whether the subdominant or supertonic should be assigned as the root. Neither of these notes can be the root. The subdominant cannot, because neither the minor seventh nor ninth to that note can be used with the major third, and the sixth from any given note is never any harmonic but the thirteenth, which in this case it cannot be, as the major thirteenth must be accompanied with either the minor seventh or ninth, or must resolve on the minor seventh, which this cannot. The supertonic cannot be the root as will be seen farther on. It is here assumed that the dominant is the root, and for the following reasons :—

Ex. 4.

It is generally admitted that the unprepared chord of the diminished seventh of the leading note is not a true chord of the seventh, but that the third below the leading note (the dominant) is the real root (Ex. 4). As I am not aware that the reasons for this have yet been given, I shall here state them. It has already been said that the third from any note, such note being the fundamental root of a chord, must be major, the fifth perfect, the seventh minor (excepting in the two cases mentioned in Chap. XXII., where secondary harmonics are involved), the ninth either major or minor, and the eleventh perfect (App. V.) and that eleventh taken only on the dominant; it follows, therefore, that the leading note cannot be the fundamental root of the chord, the third to that note being minor, and the fifth and seventh diminished. The major third below is assigned as the root, because it is the nearest note which produces the different notes of the chord in the order of its harmonics, the apparent root being its third, &c. As on examining the chord it will be found that the third is major, the fifth perfect, and the seventh and ninth minor, and that in all other respects it fulfils the conditions necessary for a root in the key, it follows that the dominant is the root of the chord. By a parity of reasoning it will be seen that the added sixth (as it is called) of the subdominant is an inversion, or a portion, of the chord of the

9. Provided the root, fifth, and seventh be in the chord of the eleventh, the ninth may be omitted (Ex. 11).

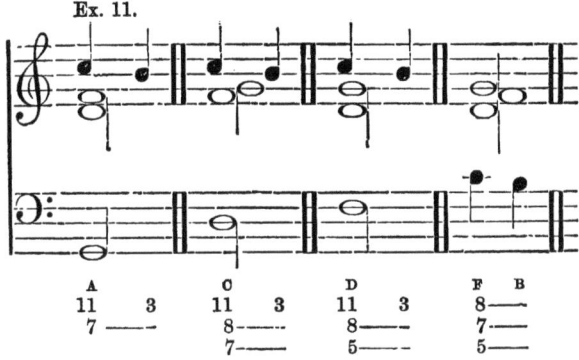

Ex. 11.

A		C		D		F	B
11	3	11	3	11	3	8—	—
7 —	-	8———		8——	-	7——	
		7——		5——	-	5——	

eleventh of the dominant. This chord taken on F, the subdominant, is an apparent inversion of a chord of the seventh, of which D, the supertonic, would be the root (Ex. 5): but as the third is minor, and the fifth diminished, the D cannot be the fundamental root of the chord; the diatonic third below, B♮, is the leading note, and having also a minor third and diminished fifth, it therefore cannot be the root (Ex. 6); the diatonic third below B♮ is G, and G is the note which comprises D numerically earlier in its harmonic column than any other note comprises it, that is, as its fifth

Ex. 5.   Ex. 6.   Ex. 7.

A
11
♭9
7
5

(Ex. 7). There not being any third in the chord does not invalidate the argument, because, as the eleventh must either resolve on the third or on the fifth of the same root, or else be retained as a note of a chord derived from another root, the law that no discord be sounded together with the note on which it resolves (Part I., Chap. VI., sect. 7, &c.), prevents the presence of the third, when the eleventh is to be resolved upon it. The fifth and eleventh are perfect, the seventh and ninth minor, G is the dominant of the key, therefore can bear an eleventh, and in all other respects it fulfils the conditions necessary for a fundamental root in the key; this chord is, therefore, an eleventh, the dominant G of course being the root.

It is not a diatonic seventh of the supertonic: I, because the seventh can be taken unprepared, and the chord may be resolved on chords whose roots are not at a fourth above D, when the seventh

Ex. 8.   Ex. 9.

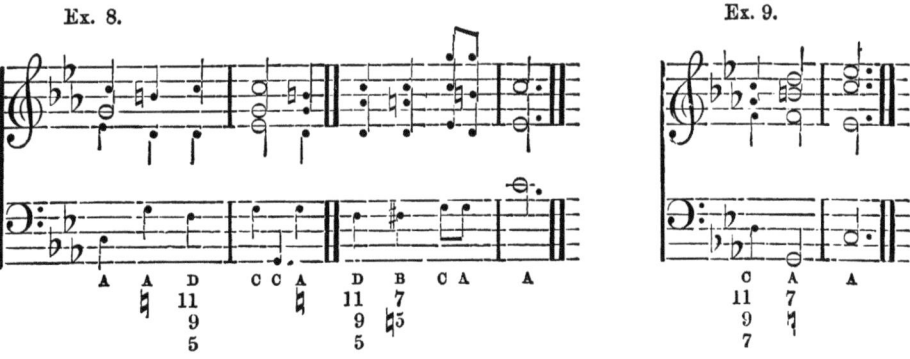

A	A	D		C	C	A		D	B		C	A		A			C	A		A
		11						11	7								11	7		
		9						9	♮5								9	♮		
		5						5									7			

10. The fifth may always be doubled (Ex. 12).

11. The root may be doubled if the ninth be not in the chord (Ex. 13).

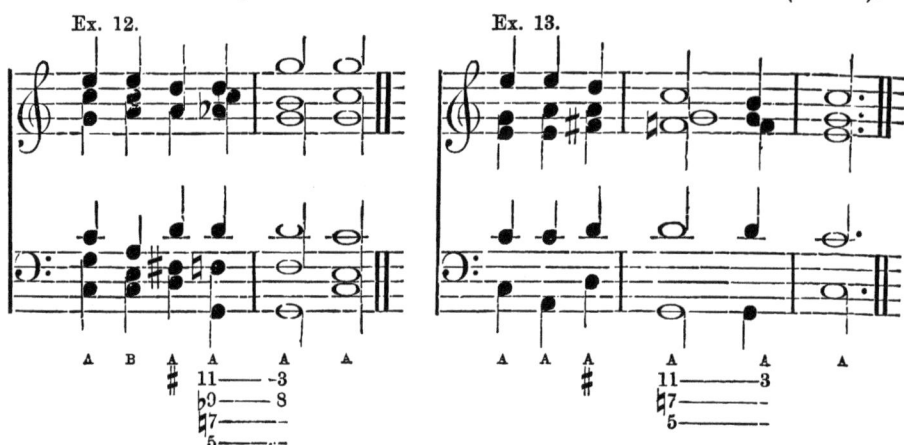

12. If the root be not in the chord, the seventh and ninth may be doubled (Ex. 14).

13. The eleventh may be resolved either with, before, or after the ninth (Ex. 15).

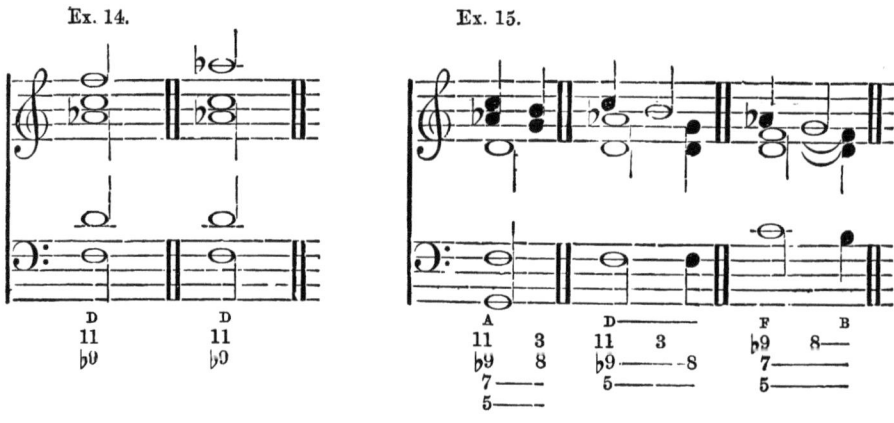

---

does not fall to the third of the ensuing chord (Ex. 8) ; and II, because when the octave of the note on which it resolves is in the bass it may *rise* a second to its resolution if the bass descend a fifth, and the minor ninth of the original chord then proceed to the third from the root (Ex. 9).

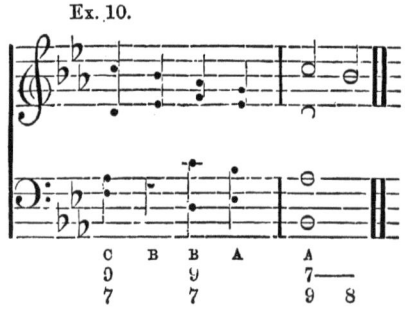

When the same combination of notes occurs in the key of E♭, there has been no difficulty in assign-ing B♭, the dominant, as the root (Ex. 10). Why, when this chord occurs in C, no one has thought of descending a third lower to G, I am at a loss to imagine, unless it be ignorance as to the reason why the first descent of the major third below the bass of the diminished seventh is made.

14. The eleventh may be resolved on the fifth when the ninth is resolved on the third (as in the first instance, Ex. 16), in which case the fifth cannot be in the chord, unless (as in the second instance, Ex. 16) it be in the bass and fall to the root.

Ex. 16.

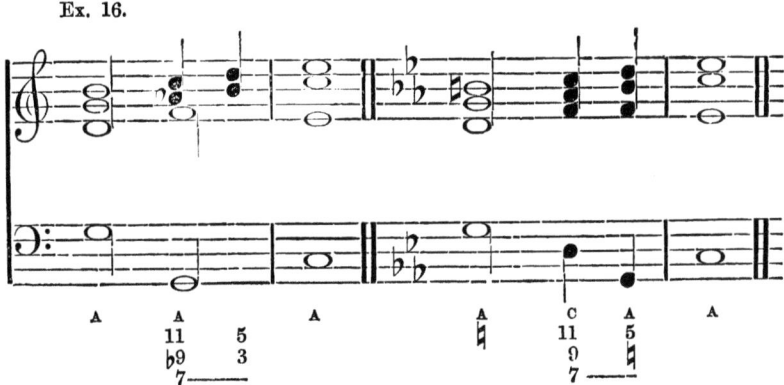

15. When the eleventh is resolved on the fifth, the third may be sounded with it. The first inversion of this chord has the third in the bass, the second inversion is unavailable, the third inversion has the seventh in the bass, the fourth has the ninth, and the fifth has the eleventh (Ex. 17). None of these can be of frequent occurrence, but the last is particularly undesirable.

Ex. 17.

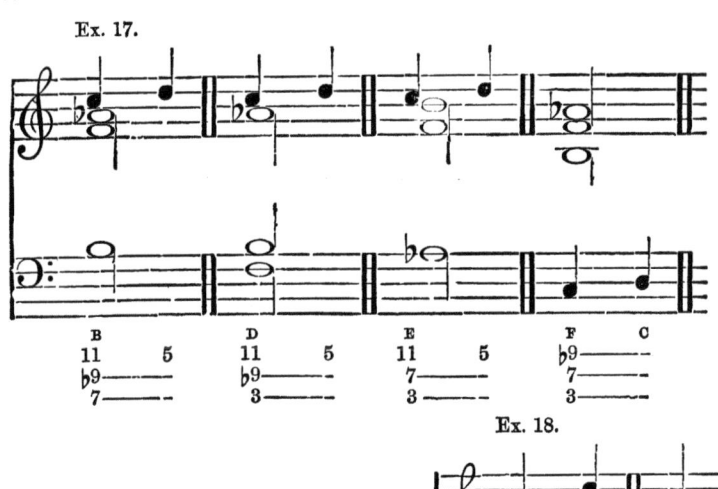

Ex. 18.

16. In the original position or in any of the inversions, the ninth may be omitted (Ex. 18).

17. The root only can be doubled.

18. The eleventh may be resolved either with, before, or after the ninth (Ex. 19).

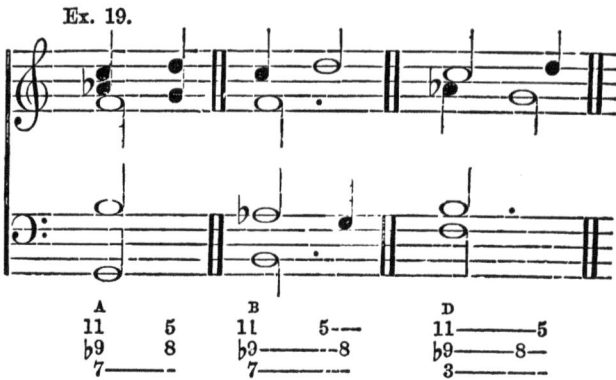

Ex. 19.

A		B		D	
11	5	11	5---	11----5	
♭9	8	♭9-------8		♭9----8---	
7----	-	7-------	---	3-------	---

19. When the eleventh and ninth are to be resolved on the fifth and third, the root may be taken instead of the seventh, and proceed to the seventh at the same time as the resolutions of the eleventh and ninth.* In this case the root may be multiplied to any extent. (Ex. 20, which may also be read in C major if every E be made natural).

Ex. 20.

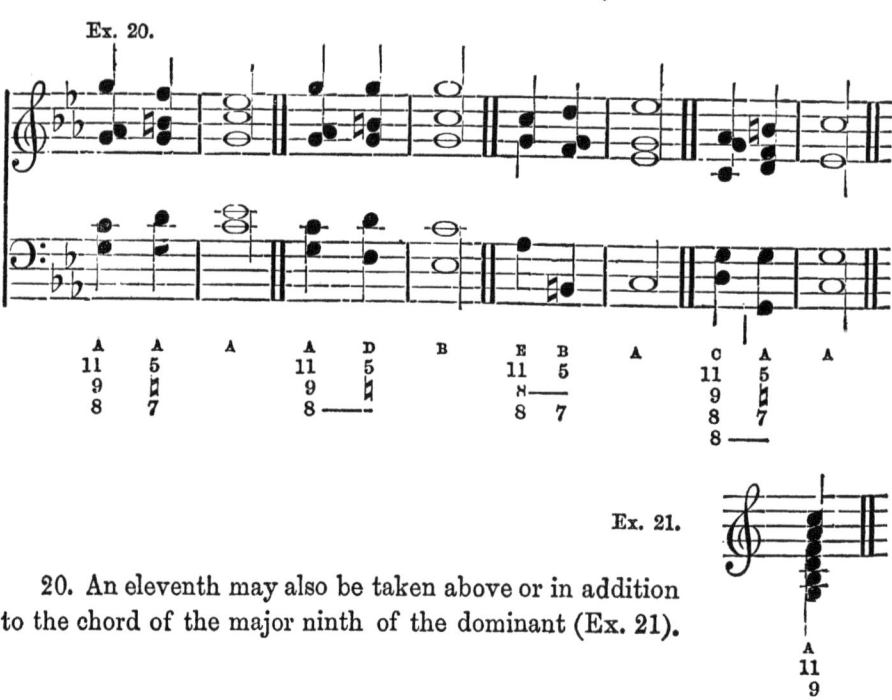

A	A	A	A	D	B	E	B	A	C	A	A
11	5		11	5		11	5		11	5	
9	♮		9	♮		♮			9	♮	
8	7		8 ---			8	7		8	7	
									8 ---		

Ex. 21.

20. An eleventh may also be taken above or in addition to the chord of the major ninth of the dominant (Ex. 21).

A
11
9
7
5
3

* Appendix RR.

21. The eleventh with a major ninth belongs exclusively to the major key, and can be resolved on major chords only.

22. Its treatment is the same as that of the eleventh with a minor ninth, with the exception of the interval of the ninth, the difference being the same as between the chords of the major and minor ninth. In this, as well as in all cases in which the major ninth and third are used simultaneously, the ninth should be above the third.

23. It may, like the chord of the eleventh with a minor ninth, either be resolved on a chord derived from the same root, or on one derived from another root.

24. In resolving on the same root the eleventh may resolve on the third, in which case the third cannot exist previously in the chord (Ex. 22).

Ex. 22.   Ex. 23.

25. In this form, if the ninth proceed to the root, the root cannot be taken except as the bass. The first inversion is unavailable, the second inversion has the fifth in the bass, the third inversion has the seventh,* the fourth has the ninth,† and the fifth has the eleventh (Ex. 23).

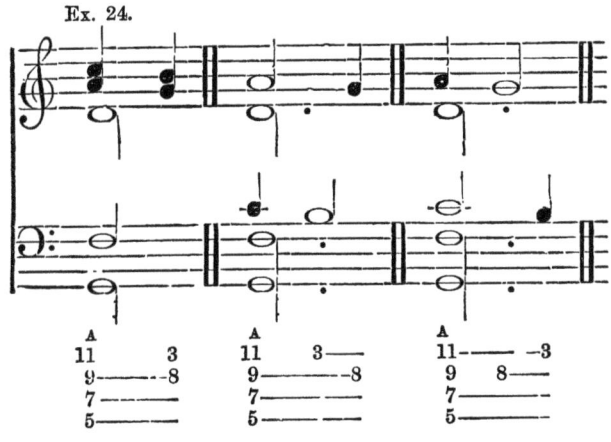

Ex. 24.

---

* The same arguments apply to this chord when taken unprepared as to the third inversion of the eleventh with a minor ninth, the only difference being that in the former chord the ninth from the root is major, and in the latter minor.

† This inversion is undesirable because of the ambiguous character of the perfect fourth above the bass; when it is used, to resolve the eleventh before the ninth is harsh.

26. In the original position the same notes may be omitted and doubled as in the chord of the eleventh with the minor ninth.

27. The eleventh may be resolved either with, before, or after the ninth, unless the ninth be below the eleventh (*vide* sect. 25, note †) (Ex. 24).

28. The eleventh, accompanied with the major ninth, may be resolved on the fifth when the ninth is resolved on the third (Ex. 25), in which case the fifth cannot exist in the chord, unless, as in the second instance of Ex. 25, it be in the bass and fall to the root.

Ex. 25.

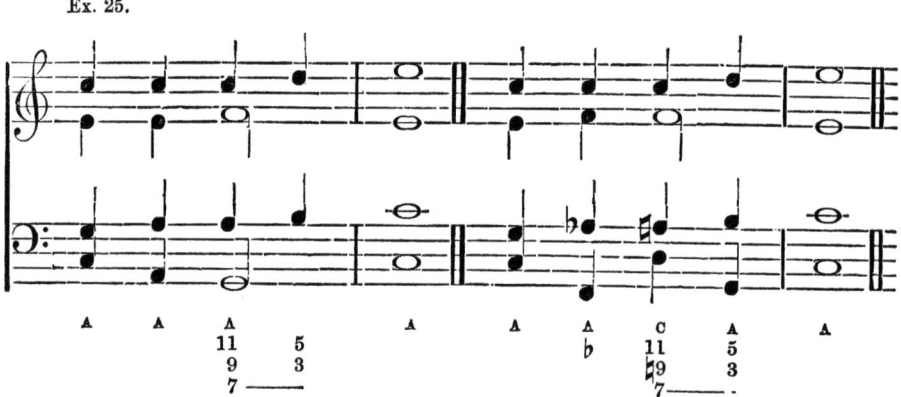

29. When the eleventh is resolved on the fifth, the third may be sounded with it. The first inversion of this chord has the third in the bass, the second inversion is unavailable, the third inversion has the seventh in the bass, the fourth inversion is unavailable, and the fifth has the eleventh in the bass (Ex. 26).

Ex. 26.

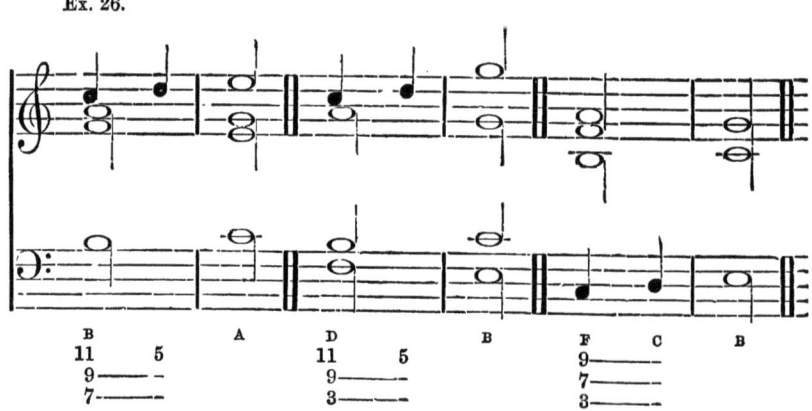

30. The eleventh may resolve either with, before, or after the ninth (Ex. 27).

Ex. 27.

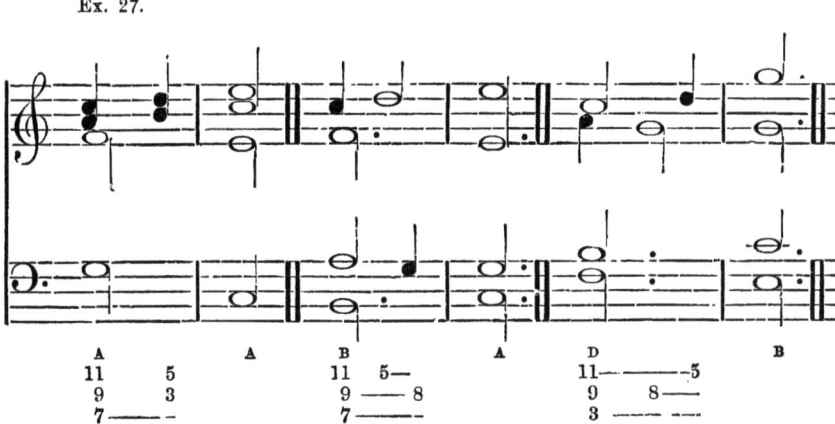

31. In the chord of the eleventh, with the major ninth, the root may be taken instead of the seventh, and treated as described in sect. 19. Ex. 20 may be read in the major key if the signature be withdrawn.*

32. In resolving on a chord having another root, the eleventh, accompanied with either minor or major ninth and seventh and fifth, may be followed by a chord having the tonic for its root when the eleventh remains to be the root of the tonic chord. If neither root nor third be in the chord, the seventh and ninth, as in the chord of the ninth (Chap. XIX., sect. 27), are free notes. The fifth in the chord of the eleventh may not proceed to the root of the tonic chord, but may go to the third or fifth of the tonic chord; and when the latter progression is in the bass it is an exception from the rule against leaping to the bass of a chord in the second inversion from an inversion of another chord (Chap. XVII., sect. 4) (Ex. 28).

Ex. 28.

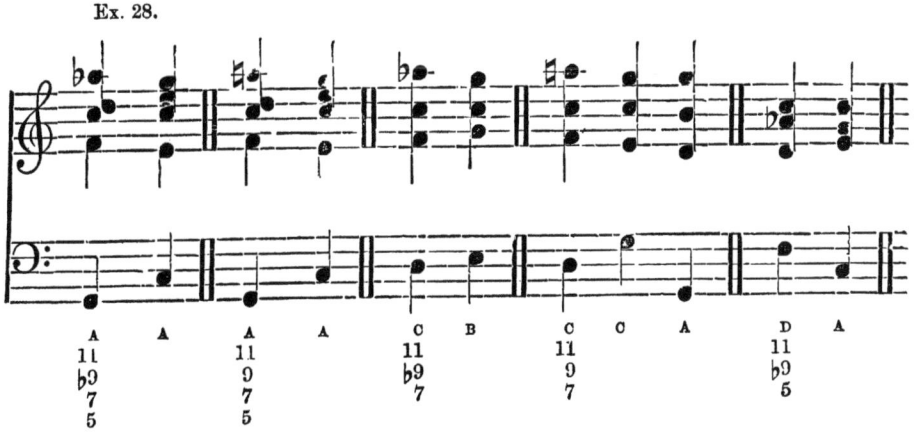

* Appendix RR.

Ex. 28—*continued.*

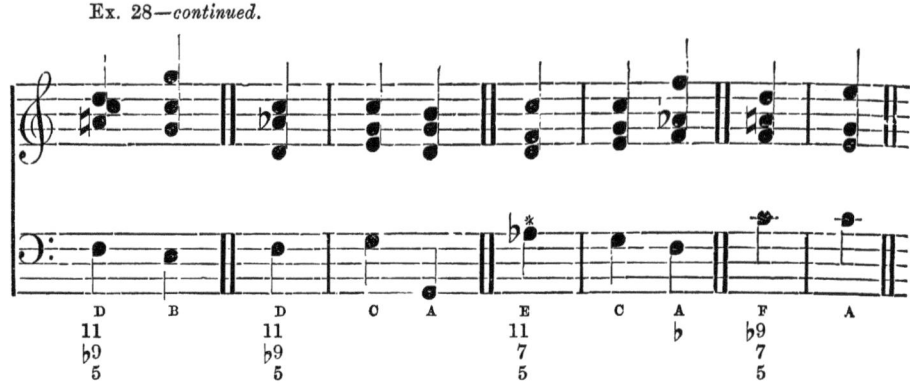

	D	B	D	C	A	E	C	A	F	A
	11		11			11			♭9	
	♭9		♭9			7	♭		7	
	5		5			5			5	

33. The eleventh, seventh and fifth, with either minor or major ninth, may also resolve on a discord having the supertonic for its root, when the eleventh remains to be the seventh in the supertonic chord (Ex. 29).

Ex. 29.

	A	A	A	A	C	A	D	B
	11	7	11	7	11	7	11	♭9
	♭9	♮5	9	♯	♭9	♮5	9	7
	7	♯	7		7	♯	5	
	5		5					

	E	C	F	D	A
	11	♭9	♭9	♭9	♯
	7	7	7	♮5	
	5	♯	5	♯	

---

* The fourth inversion with the major ninth in the bass is undesirable, because of the ambiguous character of the interval of the fourth between the bass-note and the fifth of the chord.

34. In resolving on another chord the root may be taken instead of the seventh, and move to the resolution of the seventh, provided such resolution be to the note of the chromatic scale lying between such root and seventh* (Ex. 30).

Ex. 30.

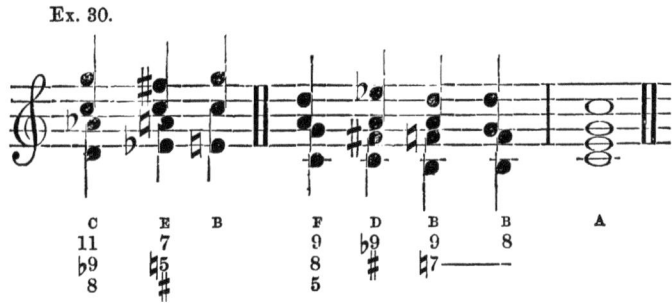

C	E	B		F	D	B	B	A
11	7			9	♭9	9	8	
♭9	♮5			8	♯	♮7		
8	♯			5				

* Appendix SS.

CHAPTER XXI.

OF THE FUNDAMENTAL CHORDS OF THE THIRTEENTH OF DOMINANT, SUPERTONIC, AND TONIC.

INTRODUCTION.

THE chord of the thirteenth, although among the sweetest of all chords when accompanied in its simplest form with the root, third and seventh, yet in some of its more extreme forms may, when taken unconnected in the examples, seem harsh. This is with the fifth, or in any other form in which two notes occur, that, counting from the root, form with each other the interval of the ninth. There are two very remarkable points in which these extreme chords, as allowed in this book, differ from chords which are not allowed. In the former, the more slowly they are played, the more agreeable they sound; they are also more pleasant when, on a pianoforte or any instrument not sustaining the tone, all the chord is struck every time a note is changed. In the latter it is exactly the reverse of this, or, in other words, the less that is heard of the chords the less disagreeable they are.

SECTION 1. A minor thirteenth may be added to either of the above-mentioned fundamental chords of the dominant, supertonic or tonic; that is, to the major common chords, sevenths, minor or major ninths and eleventh; in all which cases the notes composing those chords are treated precisely as though there were no thirteenth present, provided that none of such notes make false progressions with the thirteenth.*

2. The chords of the minor thirteenth may, like the chords of the ninth and eleventh, either be resolved on a chord derived from the same root, or on one derived from another root.

3. In resolving on a chord derived from the same root, of which the supertonic minor thirteenth is not susceptible,† the minor thirteenth of the dominant in the minor key may resolve on the fifth or seventh. When accompanied with the major ninth it can only be used in the major key; it may then resolve on the fifth, or seventh, or major thirteenth. The minor thirteenth of the tonic may be resolved on the fifth, seventh, or major thirteenth.

------

* Appendix TT.   † Appendix UU.

4. If resolved on the fifth, such fifth cannot exist in the chord unless it be in the bass and skip to the root, or unless it be taken according to the diatonic rule by step of a second and in contrary motion, and at the distance of at least an octave from the resolution of the thirteenth.*

5. It may be accompanied with the third and seventh (Ex. 1).

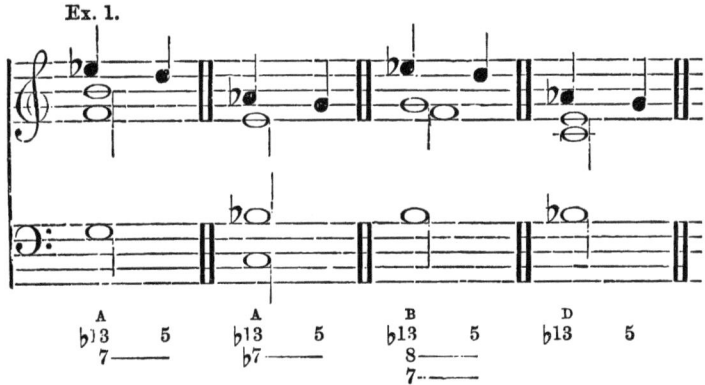

6. It may also be accompanied by the minor ninth; the thirteenth must resolve either before or after the ninth, unless when (the third not being previously in the chord) the ninth rises to the third (Chap. XIX., sect. 14), and also when, being below the ninth. it is accompanied with the eleventh, in which case both thirteenth and ninth may resolve together (Ex. 2).

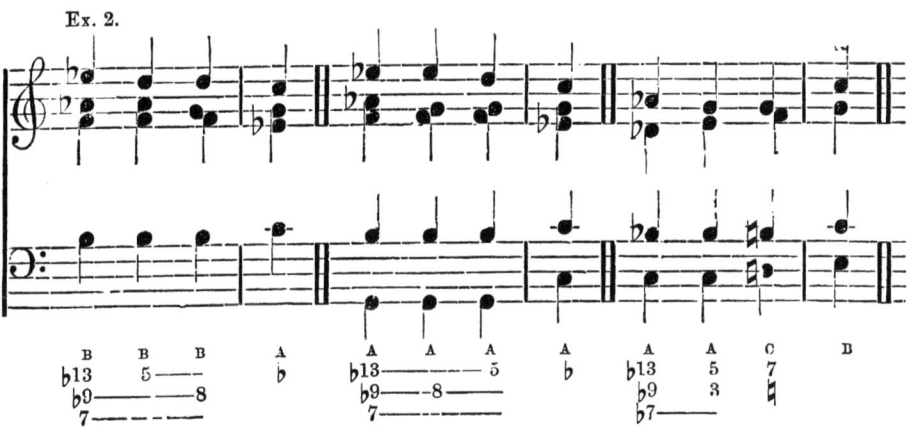

7. It may also be accompanied with the major ninth. In this case either the root or third must be in the chord; the thirteenth must resolve either before or after the ninth, unless the ninth proceed to the third or to the minor ninth (Chap. XIX., sects. 6 and 14). The chord which is produced by the resolution of this minor thirteenth of the dominant on the same root, cannot be followed by the common chord of the tonic or any of its inversions,

---

* Appendix VV.

though it may by a fundamental discord of the tonic. It also, like all other chords of the dominant with a major ninth, can only be used in the major key (Ex. 3).

Ex. 3.

8. When occurring on the dominant, the chord of the minor thirteenth and minor ninth may also be accompanied by the eleventh; in this case, if the root and third be not in the chord the seventh may proceed to the root (Ex. 4).

Ex. 4.

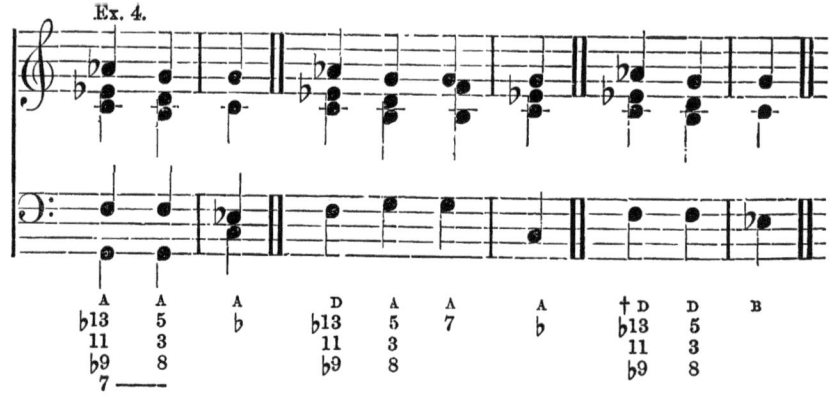

---

* It is not false relation between the E♭ and E♮, as the third chord is a fundamental discord.

† The minor seventh of the subdominant, as will be seen above, is an inversion, or a portion of the ♭13/11/♭9 of the dominant. This seventh and the other inversions of the chord, like the seventh

Ex. 4—*continued*.

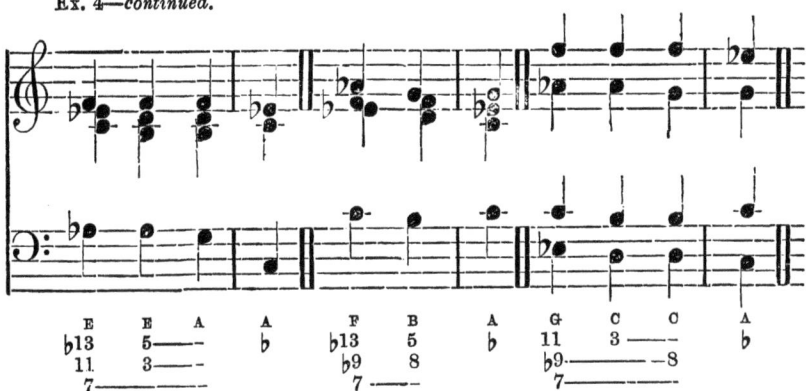

9. The chord of the minor thirteenth and major ninth cannot be accompanied with the eleventh.

---

with a minor third, and either a perfect or diminished fifth of the supertonic and its inversions, can be taken without preparation and by skip.

Although the chord consisting of the subdominant with its sixth, fifth, and minor or major third, has been provided for by calling it an added sixth, and making it an exception to all the rules for the preparation of discords, yet the unprepared chord consisting of the subdominant, with its minor seventh, fifth, and minor third, and that consisting of the supertonic with its minor ninth, seventh, diminished fifth, and minor third have never been explained; therefore, as the laws have hitherto stood, such chords have no right to be used unless prepared or by transition; but now, being shown to be portions of fundamental harmonies, according to the laws given to regulate fundamental harmonies, they can theoretically be used unprepared, as practically they long have been.

Ex. 5.

This chord of the seventh of the subdominant is not a diatonic chord of the seventh, because it can be taken unprepared, and it can resolve on the common chord of the note next above (Ex. 5).

It is not a diatonic $\frac{9}{7}$ of the supertonic, because the ninth, seventh, and diminished fifth can all be taken unprepared, and all three may either fall or rise a second to their resolution (Ex. 6).

Ex. 6.

10. The minor thirteenth may also be resolved on the seventh, in which case the seventh cannot exist previously in the chord, but the fifth may.

11. It may be accompanied with the third and root only, or it may also be accompanied with the fifth (Ex. 7).

Ex. 7.

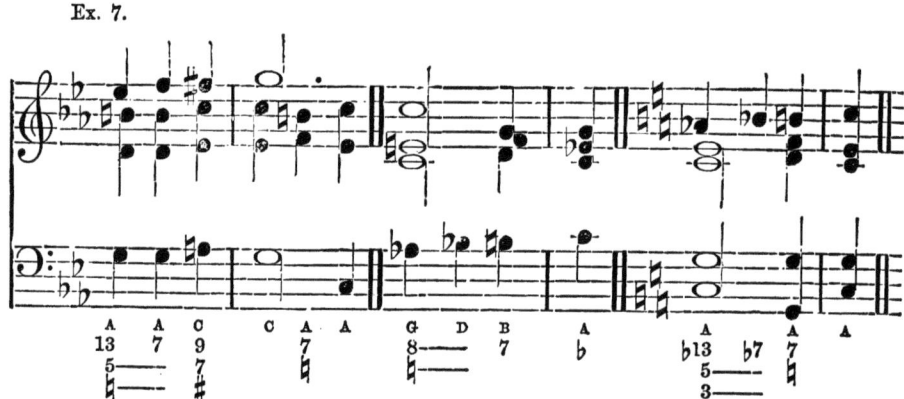

12. It may also be accompanied with the minor ninth, and it may resolve either with, before, or after such minor ninth (Ex. 8).

Ex. 8.

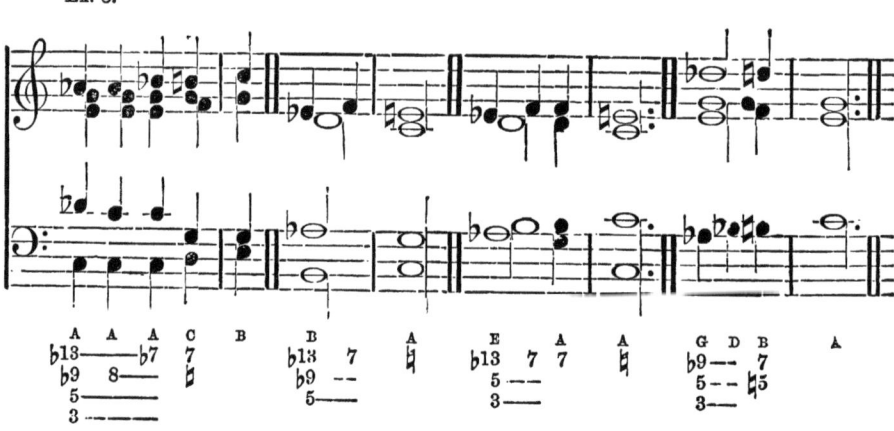

13. It may also, when occurring on the dominant, be accompanied with the eleventh. The thirteenth may resolve either with, before, or after the eleventh (Ex. 9).

It is not a fundamental ninth of the supertonic because the third is minor and the fifth diminished.

The leading note cannot be the root of any fundamental chord, this chord is therefore the $\begin{smallmatrix}13\\11\\9\end{smallmatrix}$ of the dominant; the same arguments apply to the $\begin{smallmatrix}13\\11\\9\end{smallmatrix}$, if both thirteenth and ninth be major or minor.

Ex. 9.

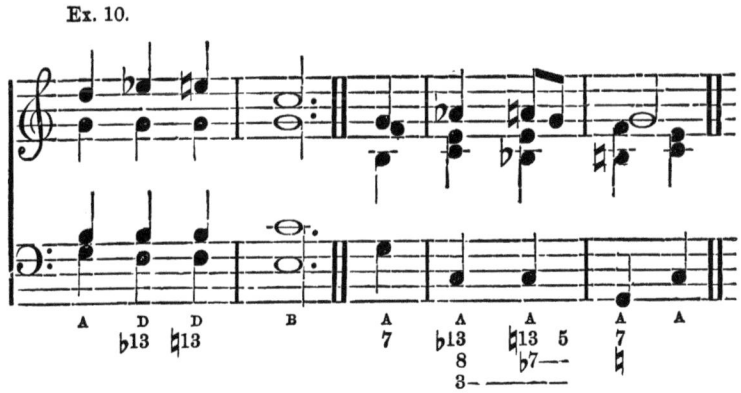

14. The minor thirteenth may, in the major key, however accompanied, resolve on the major thirteenth (Ex. 10).

Ex. 10.

15. In resolving on a chord derived from another root, the following are the natural resolutions.

16. If accompanied with the third and root only, the minor thirteenth may rise a chromatic semitone to the major third of the next chord (Ex. 11).*

* The minor thirteenth in this form is the chord usually known and written as the chord of the sharp or augmented fifth (Ex. 12): that it is not an augmented fifth, but a minor thirteenth, I shall now endeavour to prove.

Ex. 12.

In the first place, this chord when taken in its last inversion in the minor key, as in Ex. 13, is always written as though the original note were a minor sixth and not an augmented fifth : this is probably on account of the extraordinary appearance which the D♯ in one chord, followed by and rising to E♭ in the next, would present (Ex. 14). As the major key in no way differs from the

Ex. 13.   Ex. 14.   Ex. 15.

17. The minor thirteenth of the dominant and tonic may remain to be the minor third or minor ninth, or fall a minor second to the root, or rise a chromatic semitone to the major ninth of the next chord (Ex. 23).

Ex. 23.

minor as regards the second of the scale, but does differ as regards the third, therefore if it be correct in the minor key to write the minor third of the scale, when it remains as the minor third of the tonic common chord, as in Ex. 13, it must be equally correct in the major key to write the minor third of the scale when it rises to the major third of the tonic common chord as in Ex. 15. When this chord is taken in its last inversion as in Ex. 16, or with the root in the bass when coming from the same place, as in Ex. 17, it is always written as though in its original position it were a minor sixth (or thirteenth) : why it should not be written so when coming from other places, as at Ex. 18 and at Ex. 19, I am at a loss to conceive. What possible sense could be made of it were it

Ex. 16.   Ex. 17.   Ex. 18.

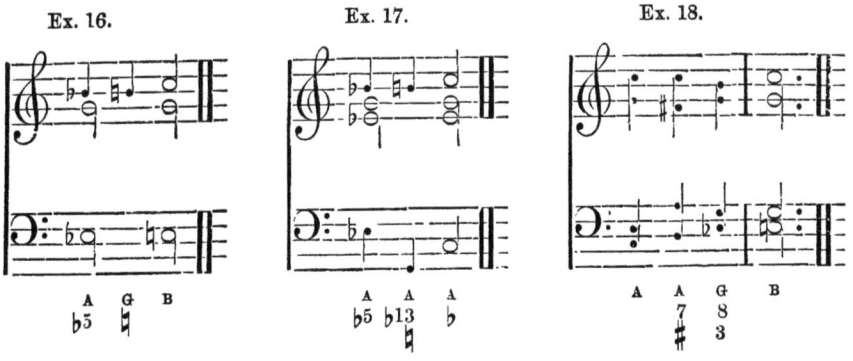

18. The minor thirteenth of the tonic may rise a chromatic semitone to the perfect fifth of the next chord (Ex. 24).

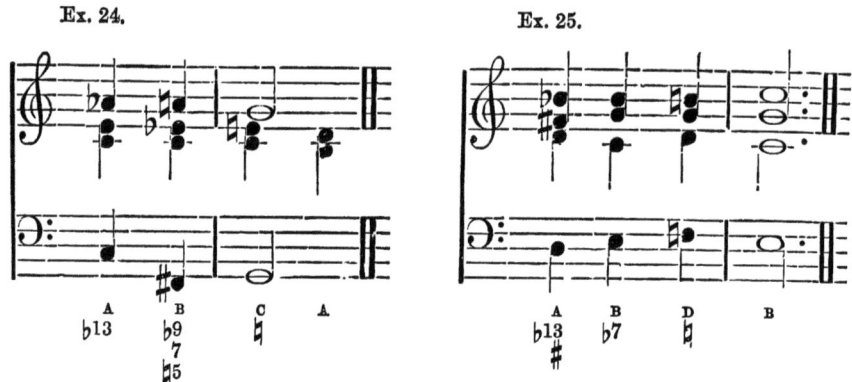

Ex. 24.

A   B   C   A
♭13 ♭9   ♮
     7
     ♮5

Ex. 25.

A   B   D   B
♭13 ♭7   ♮
♯

19. The minor thirteenth of the supertonic may remain to be the minor seventh of the next chord (Ex. 25).

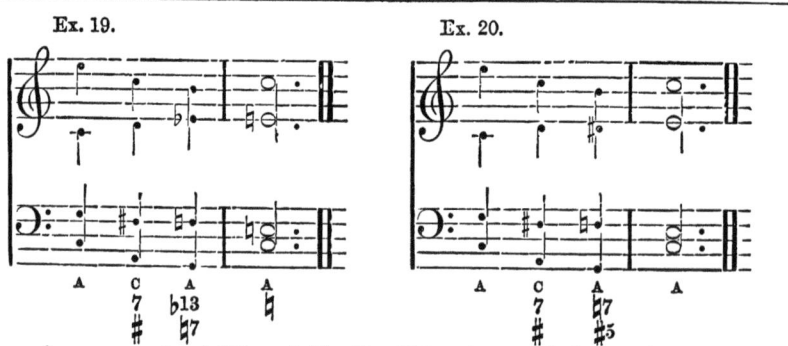

Ex. 19.

A   C   A   A
     7   ♭13   ♮
     ♯# ♮7

Ex. 20.

A   C   A   A
     7   ♯7
     ♯# ♯5

written as a sharp or augmented fifth, as in Ex. 20. It is not generally known that a diatonic semitone is really larger than a chromatic one, therefore E♭ is sharper than D♯, as the following will prove. The ratio of the octave is 2 to 1, and hence that of the seventh octave is 128 to 1 (Ex. 21).

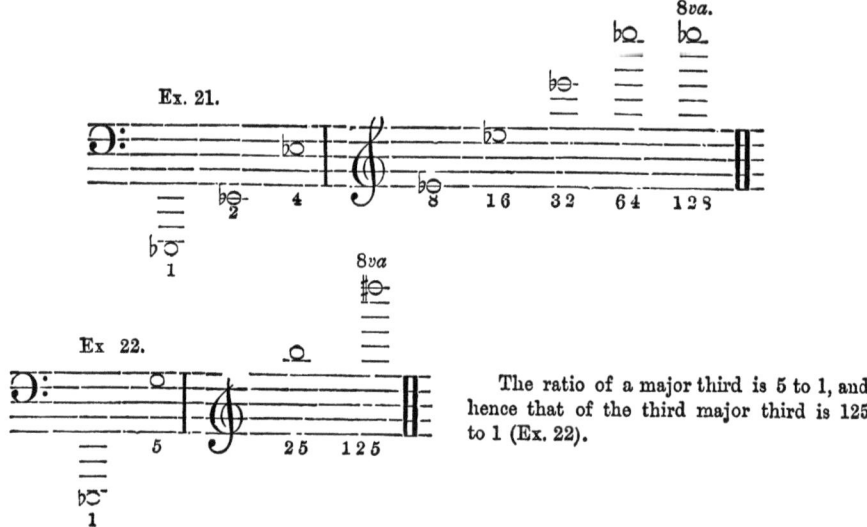

8va.

Ex. 21.

1   2   4   8   16   32   64   128

8va

Ex 22.

5   25   125

The ratio of a major third is 5 to 1, and hence that of the third major third is 125 to 1 (Ex. 22).

Thus E♭ has 128 vibrations to 125 of D♯, or is $\frac{3}{125}$ sharper.

20. If accompanied with the third and fifth the natural resolutions are the same as when accompanied with the third and root only, excepting that the thirteenth cannot fall to the root of the next chord (Ex. 26).

21. When accompanied with the third and seventh, or third, fifth, and seventh, the natural resolutions are the same as when accompanied with the

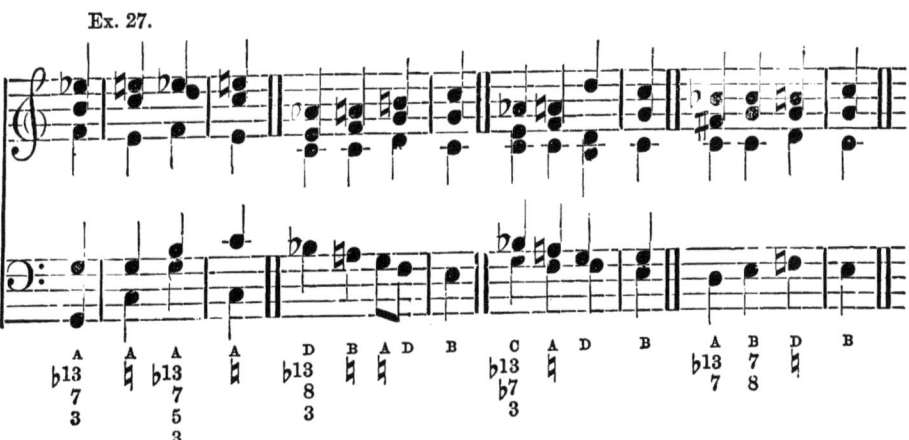

Ex. 27.—*continued.*

third and root only, with the exception that in these, as in all cases where the minor thirteenth and seventh occur together, the thirteenth cannot remain to be the minor third of the next chord, because "No discord, &c." (Chap. VI., sect. 7); nor can it rise a semitone to the major ninth of the next chord on account of the progression of sevenths or seconds between the seventh and thirteenth of the first chord, and the third and ninth of the second; nor can the thirteenth, if accompanied with the fifth, resolve on the root of the next chord (Ex. 27).*

Ex. 28.

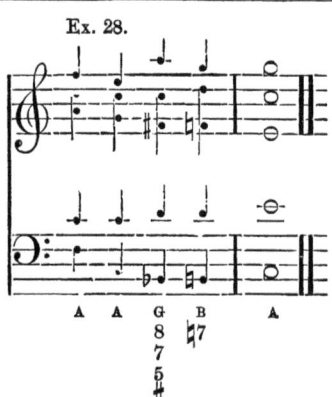

* The minor thirteenth of the supertonic, accompanied with the seventh, can rise to the third of the dominant, in which case, as in the second inversion of the seventh, or $\frac{9}{7}$, the bass taking the resolution of the seventh, the seventh rises a whole tone to the fifth of the next chord (Ex. 28). Other inversions of this resolution are justified by the rule in Chap. XVIII., sect. 18.

Ex. 29.

22. The minor thirteenth accompanied with the seventh, or third and seventh, of dominant and tonic (the fifth not being in the chord), can skip down a third to the root of the next chord (Ex. 29).

23. If accompanied with the third, fifth, seventh, and ninth, or any variety or combination of them including the ninth, the natural resolutions

Ex. 30.

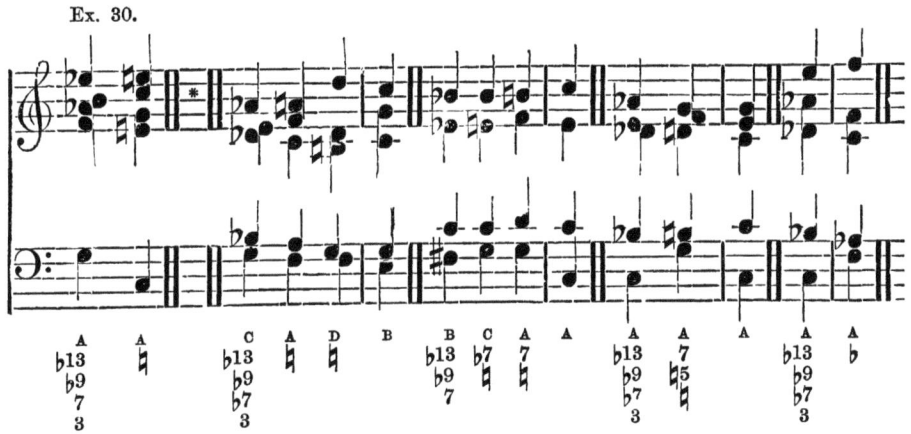

are the same as in similar combinations of those intervals with the thirteenth and without the ninth (Ex. 30).

Ex. 31.

* The chord of the minor thirteenth of the supertonic accompanied with the minor ninth, when resolving on a dominant discord like that which contains the minor thirteenth and seventh without the ninth, may be taken with the thirteenth in the bass (Ex. 31).

24. If accompanied with the eleventh the natural resolutions are either to rise a chromatic semitone to the major third of the next chord, or to remain as the minor ninth, or fall a minor second to the root of the next chord ; the fifth cannot occur excepting as the bass (Ex. 32).

Ex. 32.

25. The major thirteenth may be taken on the same notes as the minor thirteenth, the major thirteenth of dominant and tonic belonging exclusively to the major key, the major thirteenth of the supertonic being common to both major and minor key.

26. It may be resolved either on a chord derived from the same root or on a chord derived from another root.

27. In resolving on the same root the major thirteenth, under the same restrictions with regard to the notes accompanying it as the minor thirteenth, may resolve on either the fifth or seventh.

28. Resolutions of the major thirteenth on the fifth. In the case of the dominant and tonic the major thirteenth is not a discord if accompanied only with the root and third, but a consonant first inversion (Chap. XX.,

* Appendix XX.

but the major thirteenth of the supertonic is restricted in its treatment by the presence of the chromatic major third of the chord (Ex. 33).

Ex. 33.

29. The major thirteenth accompanied with the seventh (Ex. 34).*

Ex. 34.

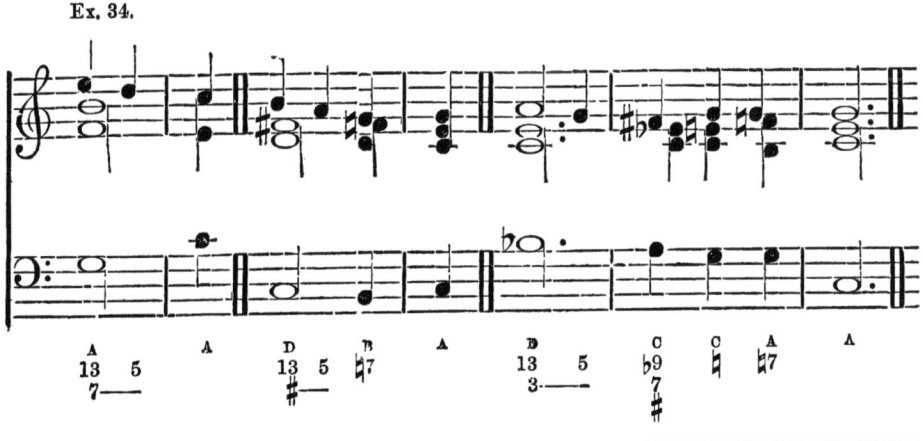

---

* Appendix TT.

K

30. The major thirteenth may also be accompanied with the minor ninth; the thirteenth can only resolve with the ninth when the ninth rises to the third, in which case the third cannot be previously in the chord (Ex. 35).

Ex. 35.

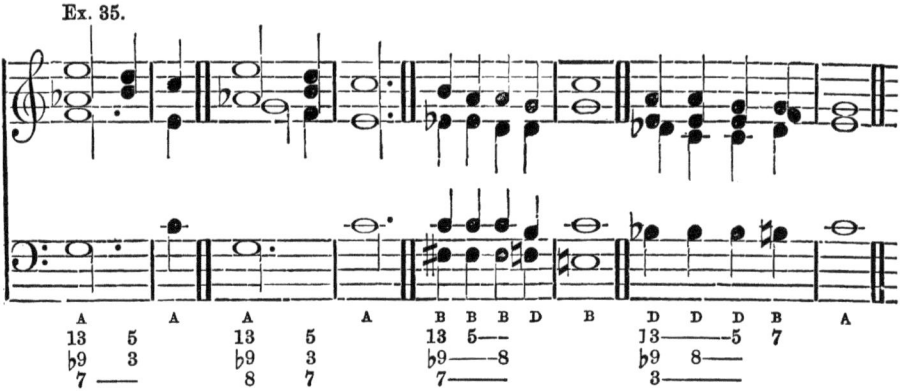

A		A		A		A	B	B	B	D	B	D	D	D	B	A
13	5			13	5			13	5	—	—		13	—	—	—	—5	7
♭9	3			♭9	3			♭9	—	—8			♭9	8	—		
7	—				8	7			7	—				3	—		

31. The major thirteenth of the dominant may also be accompanied with the eleventh; the thirteenth may resolve either with, before, or after the eleventh (Ex. 36).

Ex. 36.

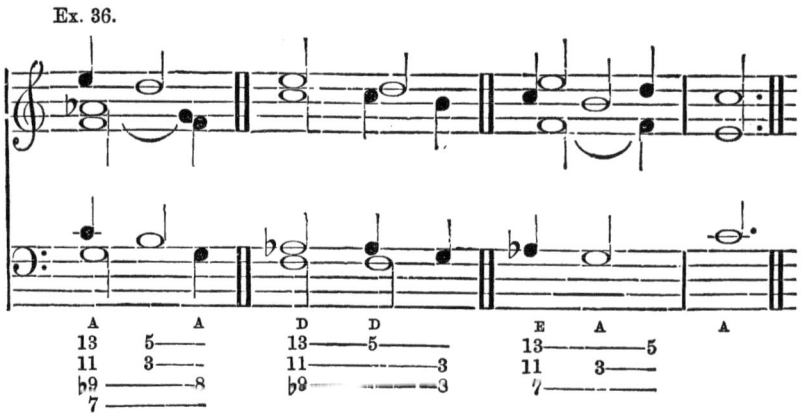

A		A		D		D		E		A		A
13	5—			13—	—5—			13—				
11	3—			11—	—	—3		11	3—			
♭9	—	—8		♭9—	—	—3		7—	—			
7	—											

Ex. 37.

32. The fifth of this chord may exist in the bass if it skip to the root (Ex. 37).

C	A	A	A
13	5	—	
11	3	—	
♭9	—	—8	
7	—		

33. The major thirteenth may be accompanied with the major ninth in place of the minor ninth; the thirteenth can be resolved at the same time as the ninth when the ninth rises to the third, and also when, being below the ninth, it is accompanied with the eleventh (Ex. 38).

Ex. 38.

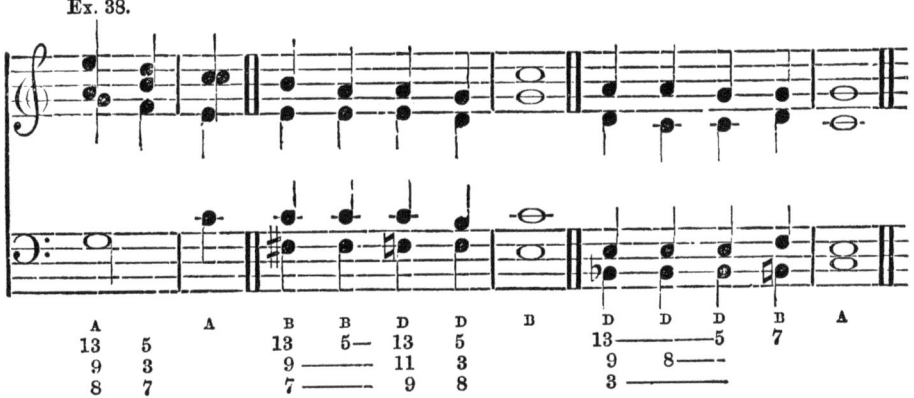

34. The major thirteenth and ninth of the dominant may also be accompanied with the eleventh; the thirteenth may resolve either with, before, or after the eleventh (sect. 8) (Ex. 39).

Ex. 39.

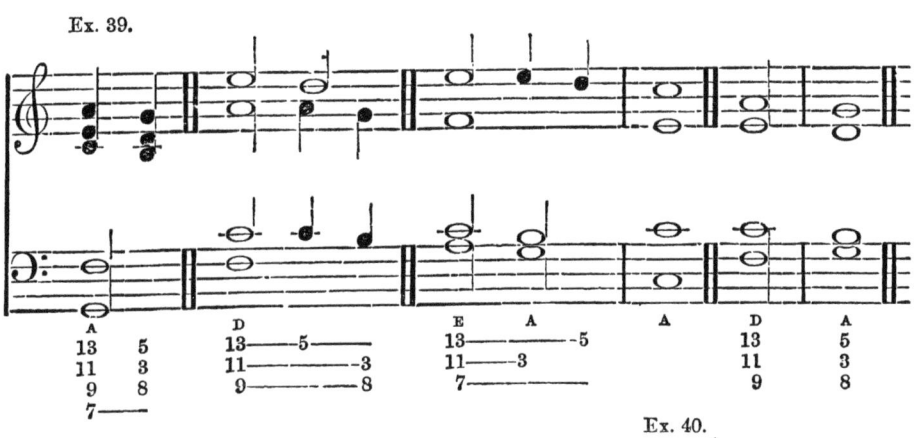

Ex. 40.

35. The fifth of this chord may be used if it be in the bass and skip to the root (Ex. 40).

K 2

36. The major thirteenth may also resolve on the seventh, in which case the seventh may not be in the chord, but the fifth may.

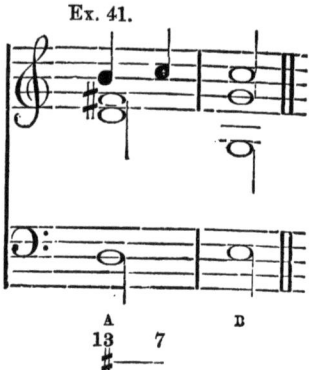

Ex. 41.

37. The major thirteenth of the supertonic may be accompanied with the third only (Ex. 41).

38. The major thirteenth of dominant, supertonic, and tonic, may be accompanied with the third and fifth (Ex. 42).

Ex. 42.

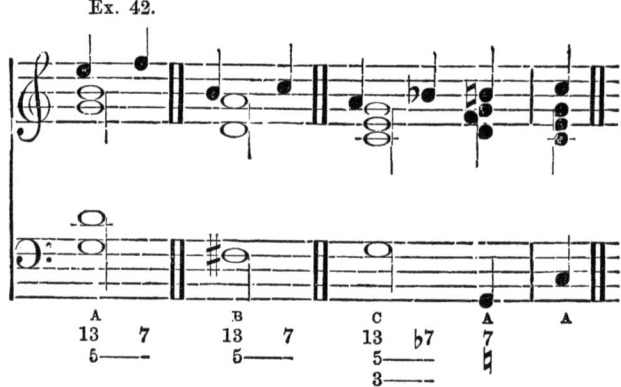

39. The fifth of this chord when taken in the bass may skip to the root at the same time as, or before, the thirteenth resolves on the seventh; this is perhaps the most agreeable form of the chord. In Ex. 43 are all three

Ex. 43.

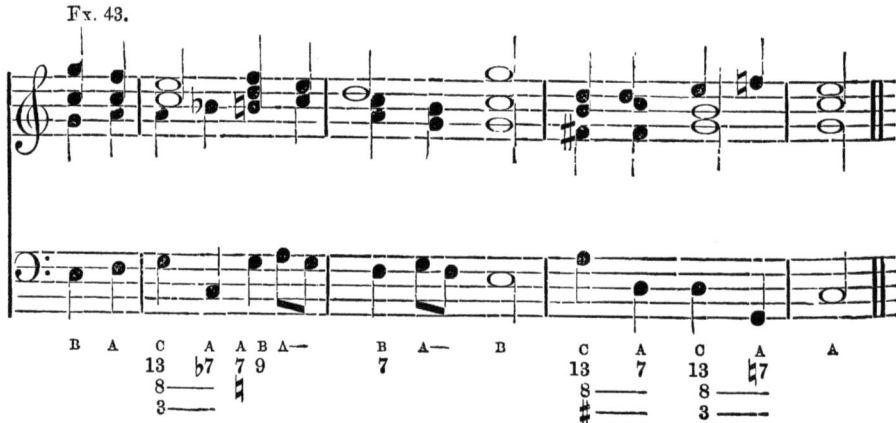

thirteenths with the fifth in the bass skipping to the root: at the first full bar the tonic $1\frac{3}{5}$, at the third the supertonic and the dominant.

40. The major thirteenth may also be accompanied with the minor ninth, and it may resolve either with, before, or after the ninth (Ex. 44).

Ex. 44.

41. It may also be accompanied with the eleventh; if the eleventh resolve on the third, the third cannot be in the chord; if it resolve on the fifth, the fifth cannot be in the chord, excepting as the bass, when it must fall to the root, and the ninth and seventh from such fifth (the thirteenth and eleventh of the chord) may rise a second to their resolutions (Ex. 45).

Ex. 45.

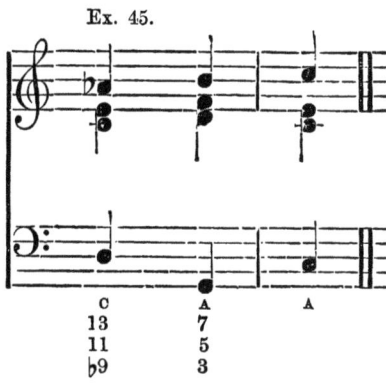

42. The thirteenth may resolve either with, before, or after the ninth, which, when the eleventh resolves on the fifth, may rise to the third, the third not being previously in the chord (Ex. 46).

Ex. 46.

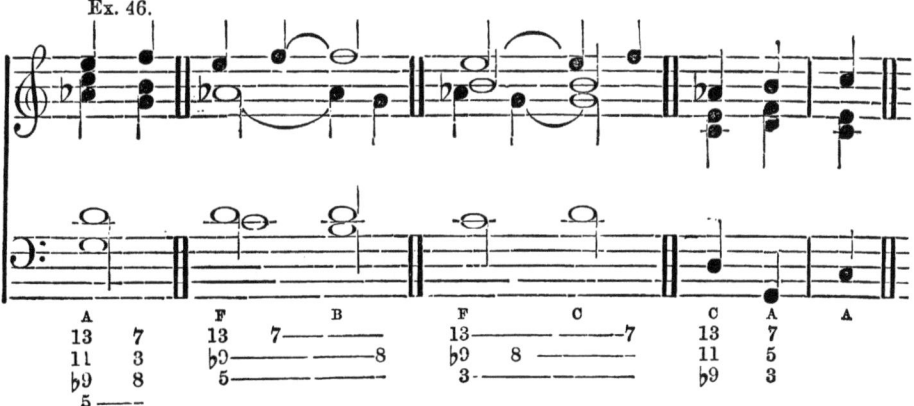

43. The major thirteenth with this resolution may also be accompanied with the major ninth in place of the minor ninth; the thirteenth may be resolved either with, before, or after the ninth (Ex. 47).

Ex. 47.

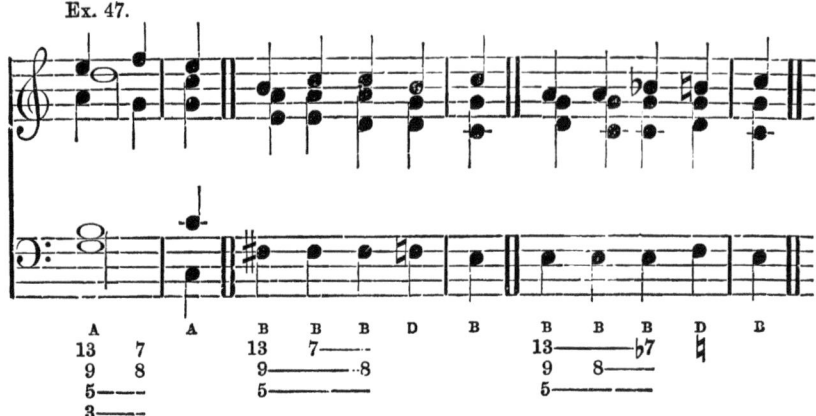

A	A	B	B	B	D	B	B	B	B	D	B
13	7	13	7——-				13——	——b7			
9	8	9——		—8			9	8——			
5——-		5——		——			5——	——			
3——											

44. It may also be accompanied with the eleventh in addition to the major ninth (Ex. 48).

Ex. 48.

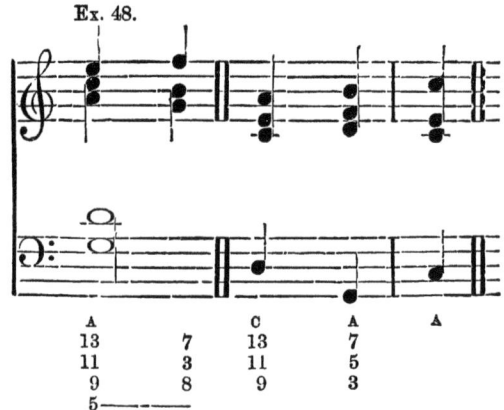

A		C	A	A
13	7	13	7	
11	3	11	5	
9	8	9	3	
5——				

45. The thirteenth may resolve either with, before, or after the eleventh, and the eleventh either with, before, or after the ninth (Ex. 49).

Ex. 49.

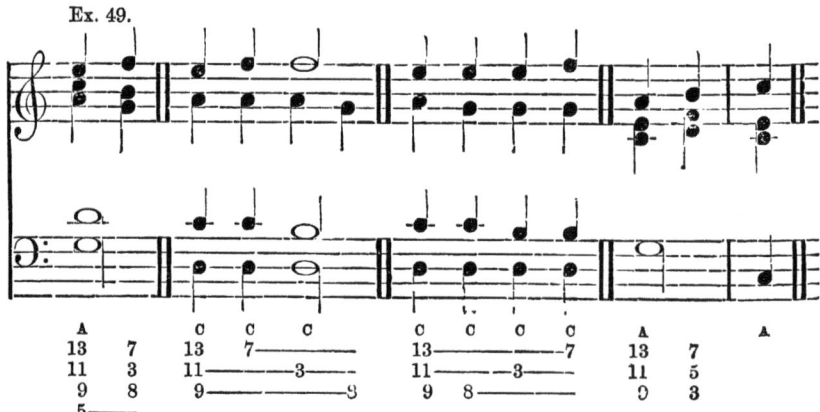

A		C	C	C	C	C	C	C	A	A
13	7	13	7——		13——		——7		13	7
11	3	11——	——3——		11——	——3——			11	5
9	8	9——	——	—3	9	8——	——		9	3
5——										

46. In resolving on a chord derived from another root, the major thirteenth of the supertonic if accompanied with the third, or with the third and fifth, may remain to be the third of a dominant discord (Ex. 50).

Ex. 50.

47. If accompanied with the seventh, or third and seventh, the major thirteenth of the dominant and tonic may remain to be the major ninth of the next chord, or fall a chromatic semitone to the minor ninth, or fall a major second to the root (Ex. 51).

Ex. 51.

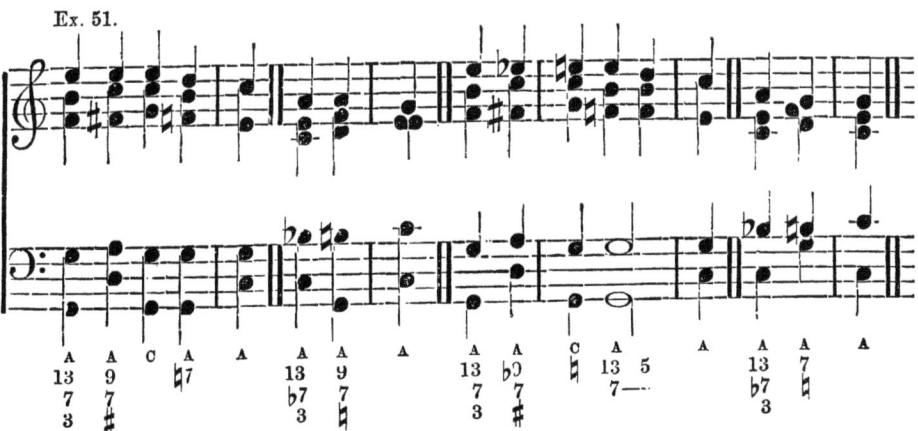

Ex. 52.

48. The major thirteenth of the supertonic may fall a chromatic semitone to
the minor seventh of the tonic (Ex. 52).

49. The major thirteenth of all three roots may fall a third to the root of
the next chord, the fifth on no consideration being taken with the thirteenth
(Ex. 53).

Ex. 53.

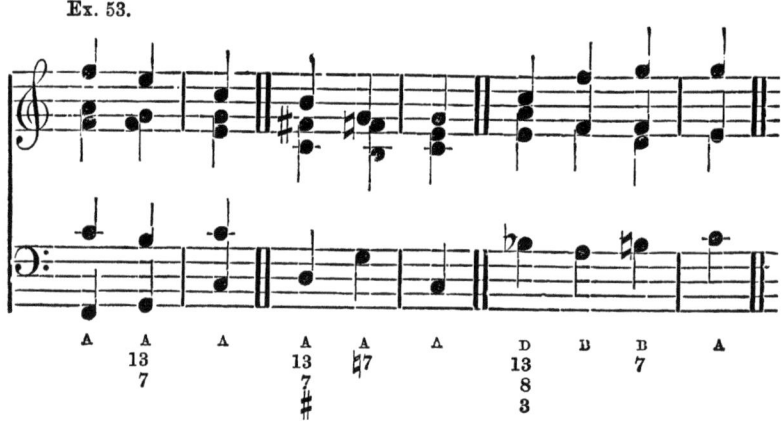

50. The major thirteenth of the dominant and supertonic may fall a
major third to the fifth of the next chord, but cannot be used in those
inversions which have either the fifth or thirteenth in the bass (Ex. 54).

Ex. 54.

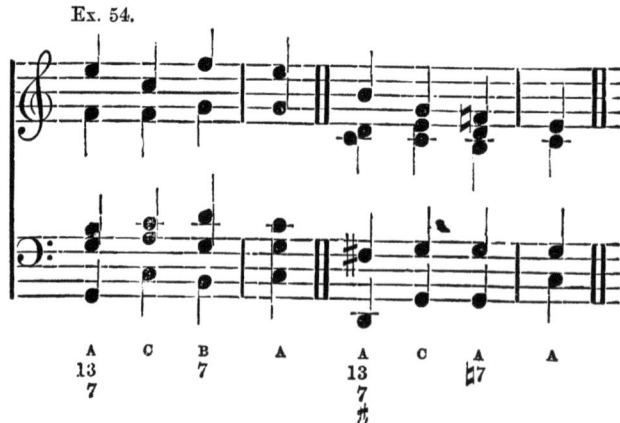

Ex. 55.

51. The major thirteenth of the tonic may fall a minor third to the third of the super-tonic (Ex. 55).

52. If accompanied with the minor ninth the foregoing resolutions of all three major thirteenths are available (Ex. 56).

Ex. 56.

53. If the seventh be omitted the thirteenth may remain as the major third of the next chord, which it would not were the seventh used, as the thirteenth could not remain to be the third of the next chord at the same time as the seventh fell to it (Ex. 57), because no discord, &c. (Chap. VI., sect. 7).

Ex. 57.

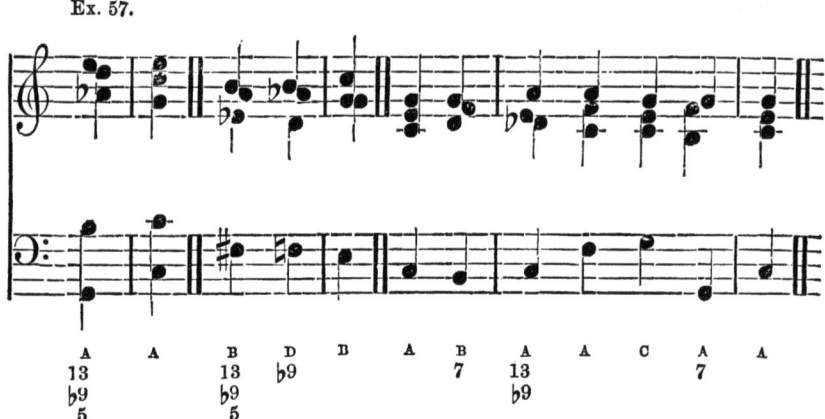

54. If the seventh be omitted, the major thirteenth of the tonic may also remain to be the perfect fifth of the next chord (Ex. 58). In this case both roots cannot be in the bass.

Ex. 58.

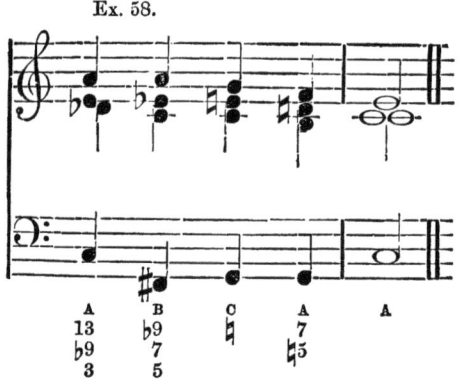

55. With the major ninth, the resolutions are the same as with the minor (Ex. 59).

Ex. 59.

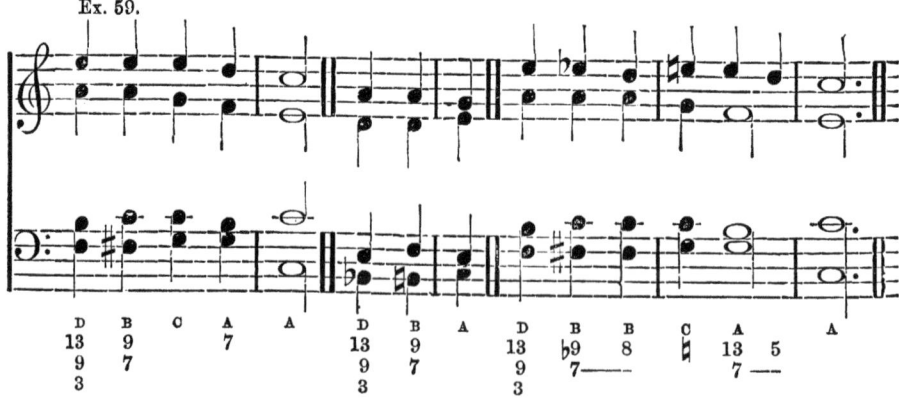

Ex. 59—*continued.*

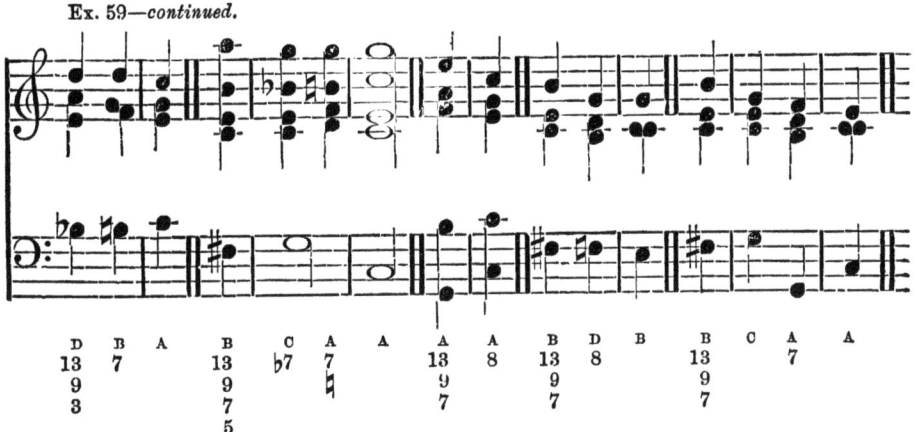

D	B	A	B	C	A	A	A	A	B	D	B	B	C	A	A
13	7		13	♭7	7		13	8	13	8		13		7	
9			9		♮		9		9			9			
3			7				7		7			7			
			5												

56. The seventh being omitted, the thirteenth, accompanied with the major ninth, may remain either as the major third, or perfect fifth of the next chord; in the latter case, as with the minor ninth, both roots cannot be in the bass (Ex. 60).

Ex. 60.

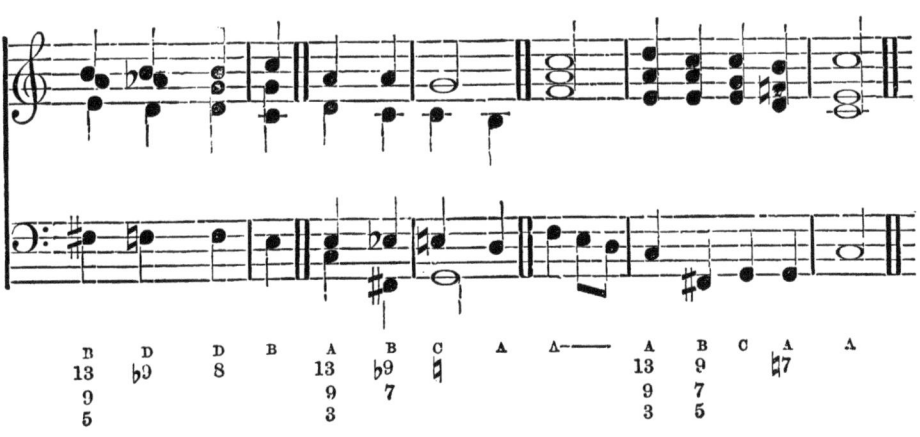

D	D	D	B	A	B	C	A	A——	A	B	C	A	A
13	♭9	8		13	♭9	♮			13	9		♮7	
9				9	7				9	7			
5				3					3	5			

Ex. 61.

57. The major thirteenth and minor ninth and seventh of the dominant, may be accompanied also with the eleventh; in this case the third cannot be in the chord, nor can the fifth, excepting as the bass (Ex. 61).

C	C	A	A
13		7	
11			
♭9			
7			

58. The natural resolutions are for the thirteenth to remain as the major third or major ninth of the next chord, or fall a chromatic semitone to the minor ninth, or fall a major second to the root of the next chord. It is also susceptible of the same resolutions with the fifth in the bass (Ex. 62).

Ex. 62.

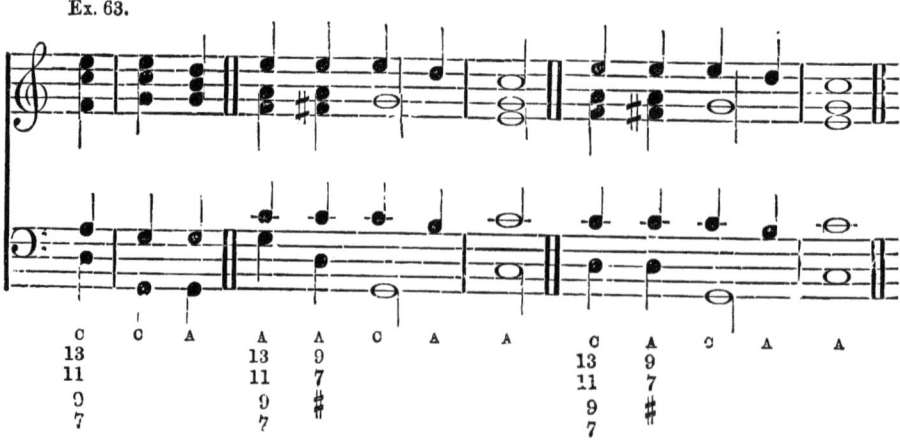

59. The treatment of the major thirteenth and eleventh with the major ninth is the same as with the minor ninth (Ex. 65).

Ex. 63.

60. However accompanied (except with a seventh), in resolving on the same root, the root of the chord of the thirteenth may, as in the chords of the ninth and eleventh, be taken instead of the seventh, and fall to the seventh (Ex. 64).

Ex. 64.

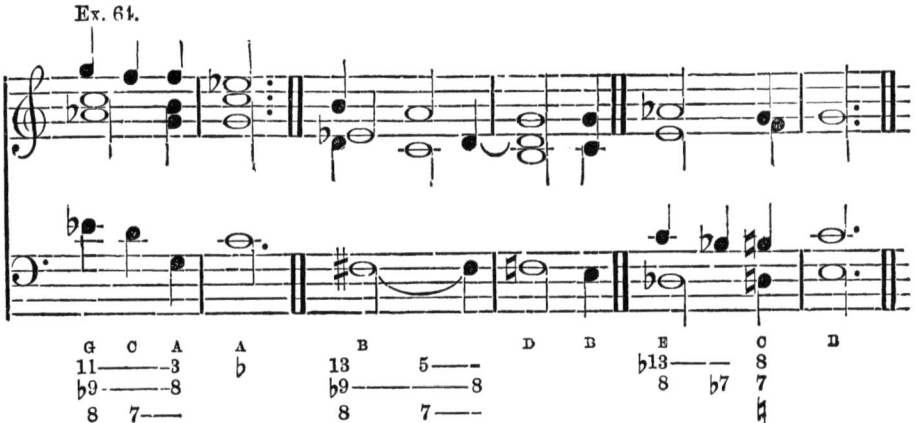

61. In resolving on a chord having another root, the root of the chord of the thirteenth may be taken instead of the seventh and fall to the resolution of the seventh, provided the resolution of such seventh be on the note lying between the root and seventh (Ex. 65).*

Ex. 65.

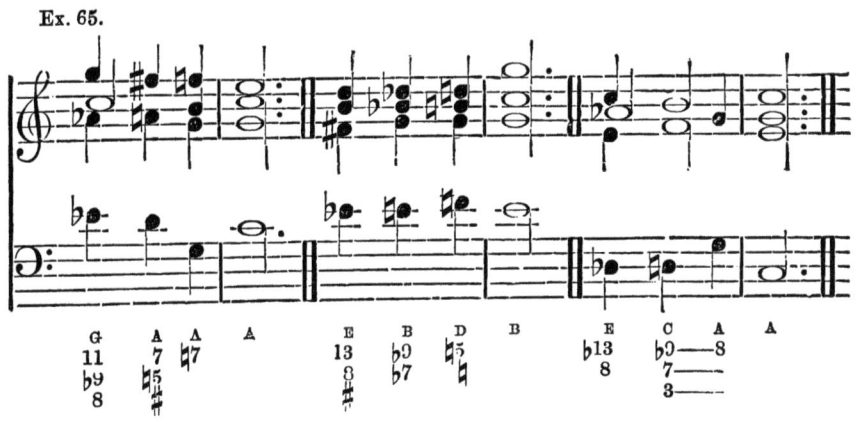

---

* Appendix YY.

CHAPTER XXII.

OF THE CHORDS OF THE AUGMENTED SIXTH.

INTRODUCTION.

ALL the chords which have hitherto been described as derived from the scale of harmonics, comprise only the primary harmonics arising from any given root; of course each of those harmonics would in turn give out a fresh series, which I will call secondary harmonics, and the note whence they spring, the secondary root.*

The harmonics which arise from the fifth are naturally more prominent than any other, as they arise next to those from the primary root, and they are practically the only secondary harmonics which are available for the purposes of harmony; the application of this series of harmonics accounts for the chords of the augmented sixth.

SECTION 1. The three notes which have been assigned as the only roots to chromatic chords, are still the only notes which can be allowed as either primary or secondary roots; therefore these augmented sixths can be taken as springing from the dominant and tonic only, and not from the supertonic, because the perfect fifth to such supertonic, namely, the major sixth of the scale, is not allowed as a root.

Ex. 1.

2. The interval of the augmented sixth is formed between the minor ninth of the primary root, and the major third of the secondary root (Ex. 1).

3. The only interval which in the figuring is reckoned as belonging to the primary root, is the lower note of the interval of the augmented sixth (the primary ninth); the other notes are reckoned from the secondary root, and figured accordingly. The notes belonging to the primary root (that is, either the primary root or ninth), whether in the bass or otherwise are

---

* Appendix ZZ.

marked as in all other instances; the notes belonging to the secondary root are marked each within brackets (Ex. 2); the figures referring to the primary root are below those referring to the secondary root.

Ex. 2.

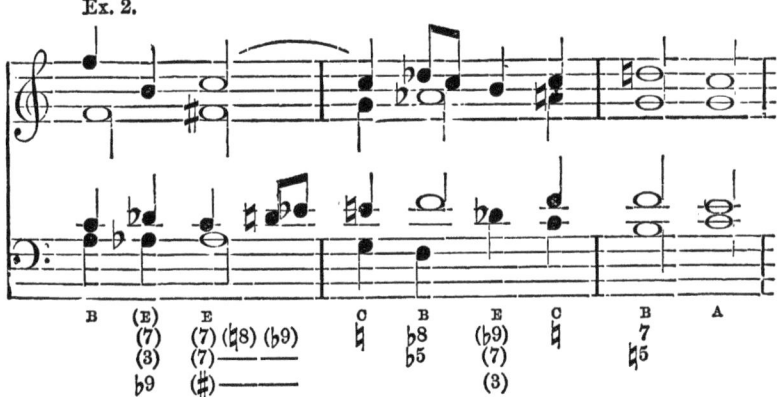

4. The augmented sixth springing from the dominant occurs on the minor sixth of the scale, and that from the tonic on the minor second (Ex. 3).

Ex. 3.   Ex. 4.

5. The interval of the augmented sixth should not be inverted and become a diminished third, but the other notes of the chord may stand in any position with relation to each other.*

6. This interval may be accompanied with the third, which is the seventh of the secondary root (Ex. 4).

Ex. 5.   Ex. 6.

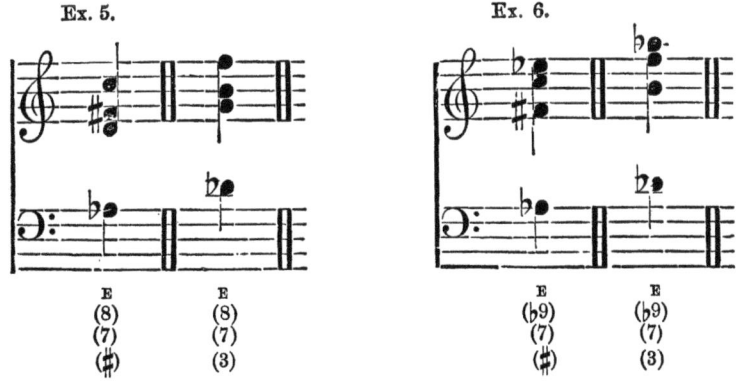

---

* Appendix AAA.

7. It may be accompanied with the third and fourth, which fourth is the secondary root itself (Ex. 5).

8. It may be accompanied with the third and perfect fifth, which fifth is the minor ninth of the secondary root (Ex. 6).

9. If in the resolution both notes forming the augmented sixth move, the lower one must fall, and the upper one rise a minor second to a note which is either the root or fifth of the next chord (Ex. 7).

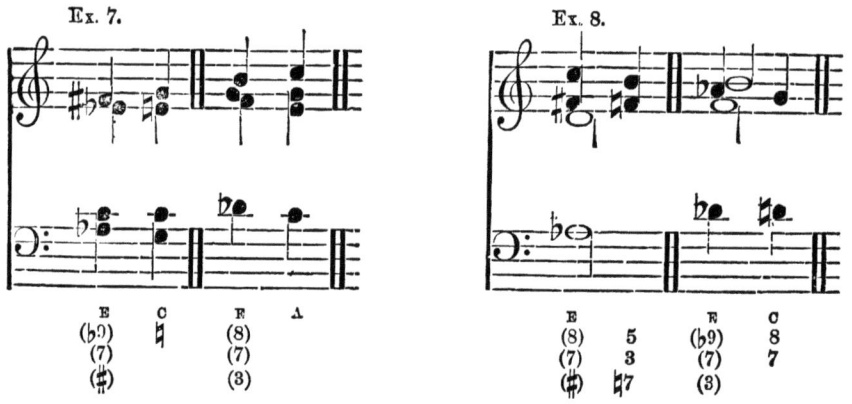

10. If one note remain, the other may approach it by moving a chromatic semitone (Ex. 8).

11. The third and fifth to the bass are to be treated as the seventh and minor ninth of the secondary root, and as though the minor ninth of the primary root were not in the chord, provided they make no false progressions with such primary ninth; thus, the third (the seventh of the secondary root) either remains or falls, or, if doubled, one of the two is free in its progression. The fourth (the secondary root) is independent in its motion, provided it make no false progression with the other parts. The fifth (the ninth of the secondary root) may either remain or fall a minor second, or rise a chromatic semitone.

12. These chords and their inversions may either be resolved on the common chord of the primary root, which chord must in all cases be major, or on the second inversion of the major or minor common chord of the fourth above the primary root, or on the minor ninth of the primary root, or on the seventh or ninth of the secondary root, or on their inversions (Ex. 9).

* This progression is sometimes used, but by no means recommended, although when the chord is resolved on the common chord of the primary root, the consecutive fifths are perhaps less objectionable than in most other places.

13. It has been already mentioned that the interval of the augmented sixth should not be inverted; but this law does not affect the other intervals of the chord. If accompanied with the secondary seventh only, the one inversion has this seventh in the bass (Ex. 10).

14. If accompanied with the secondary root and seventh, it is susceptible of two inversions; the first inversion is with the secondary root in the bass; the second inversion is with the secondary seventh in the bass (Ex. 11).

Ex. 11.

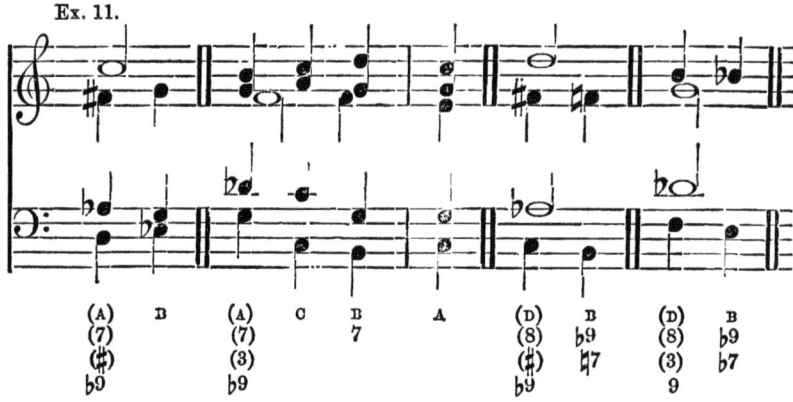

15. When accompanied with the secondary seventh and ninth it is also susceptible of two inversions. The first inversion has the secondary seventh in the bass; the second inversion has the secondary ninth in the bass (Ex. 12).

Ex. 12.

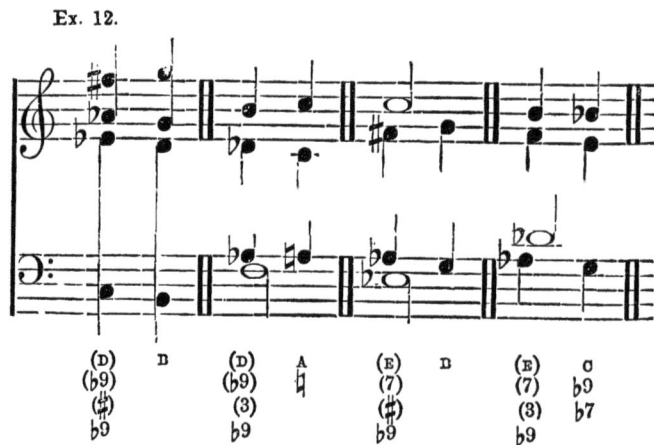

16. The secondary root may also exist in this chord (as the bass) with the secondary seventh and ninth above it (Ex. 13)*

17. The secondary root of either of these chords of the augmented sixth may be taken instead of the secondary seventh, and fall either to the

---

* Appendix BBB.

Ex. 13.

secondary seventh itself, or to the resolution of such seventh, provided the resolution be on the note lying between the secondary root and seventh (Ex. 14).

Ex. 14.

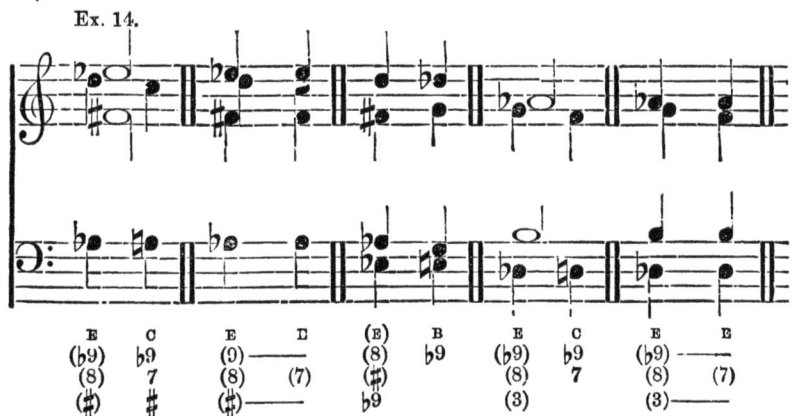

18. Whenever it can be done compatibly with the rules for the progression of parts, either of these chords or its inversions may be followed by the other of them or its inversions (Ex. 15).

Ex. 15.

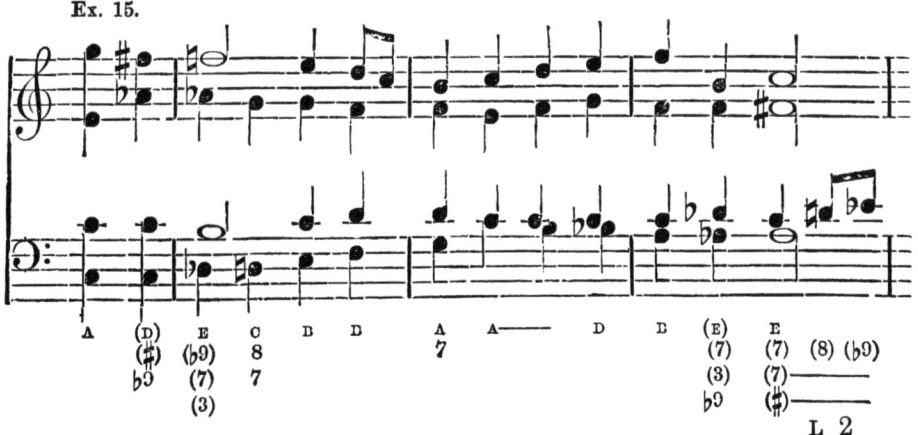

Ex. 15—*continued.*

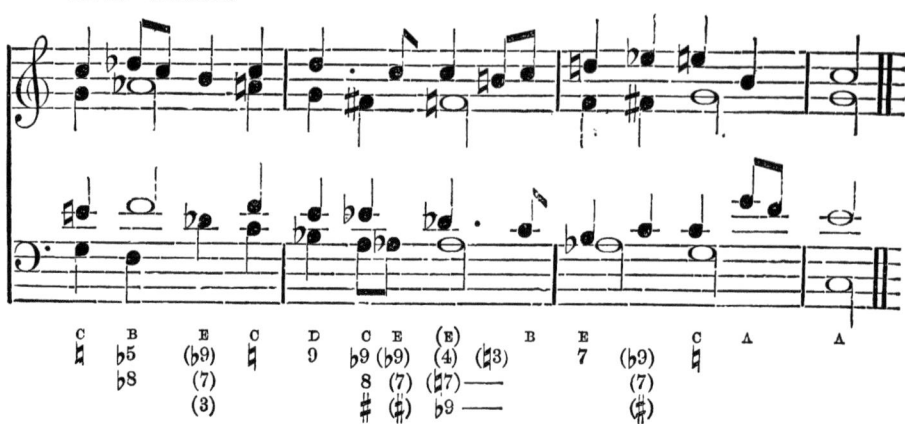

C	B	E	C	D	C	E	(E)	B	E	C	A	A
♮	♭5	(♭9)	♮	9	♭9	(♭9)	(4)	(♮3)	7	(♭9)	♮	
	♭8	(7)			8	(7)	(♮7)			(7)		
		(3)			♯	(♮)	♭9			(♯)		

CHAPTER XXIII.

OF THE SUSPENSION OF FUNDAMENTAL CHORDS.

INTRODUCTION.

THIS Chapter contains only the laws affecting suspensions of fundamental chords. As, however, all the fundamental chords which can be used have already been described, it may here be opportune to observe that although the *natural* resolutions of those chords have been given, there are many more resolutions left than have been detailed. The general rule for all is, that any one of these chords or its inversions may go to any other of them or its inversions, provided that the laws for the progression of parts generally, those for the progression of particular intervals of fundamental chords, and those against false relation are observed.

SECTION 1. Either the minor seventh, minor or major ninth, or minor or major thirteenth, in resolving on the next chord, may, like diatonic discords of the second species (Chap. VIII), be suspended over the root of the resolution, or over the bass of the first inversion, provided the root of the resolution be the fourth above that of the suspended chord (Ex. 1).*

Ex. 1.

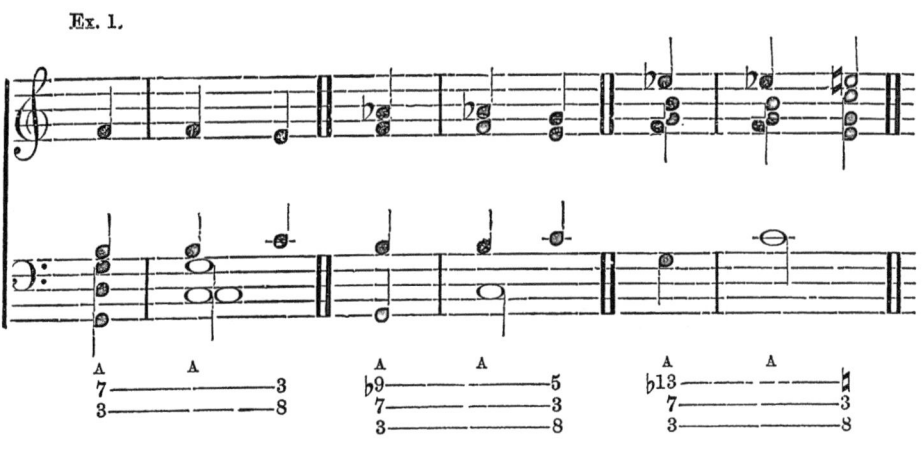

---

* Appendix CCC.

Ex. 1—*continued.*

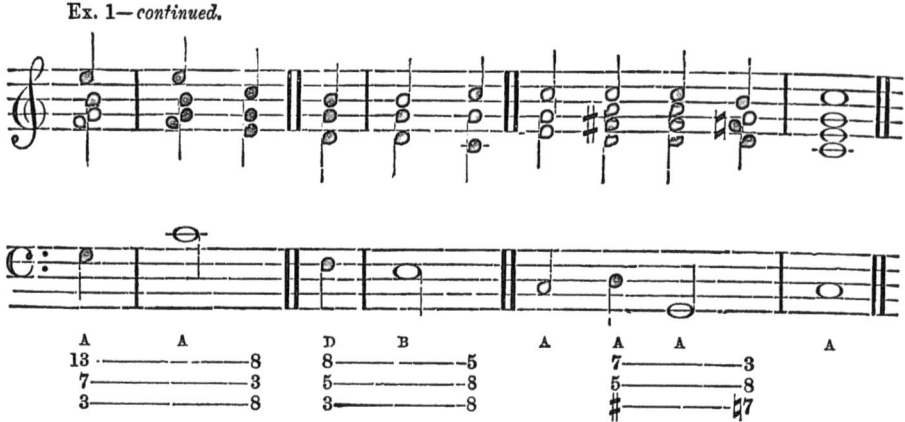

2. The chords of the augmented sixth may also be suspended over the root of the resolution, or the bass of the first inversion, if the root of the resolution be a fourth above the secondary root of the augmented sixth (Ex. 2).

Ex. 2.

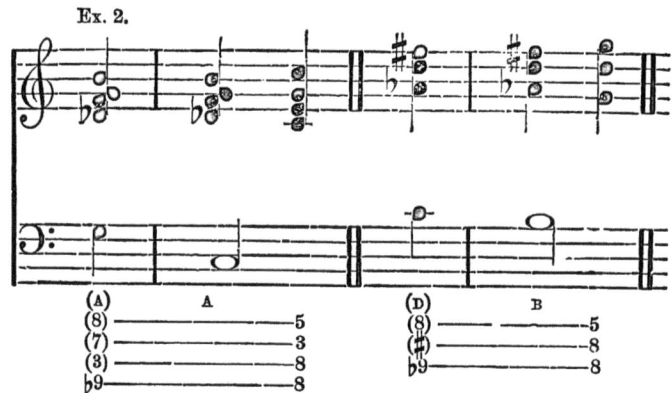

3. The supertonic discords may also be suspended over the bass of the second inversion of the tonic chords (Ex. 3).

Ex. 3.

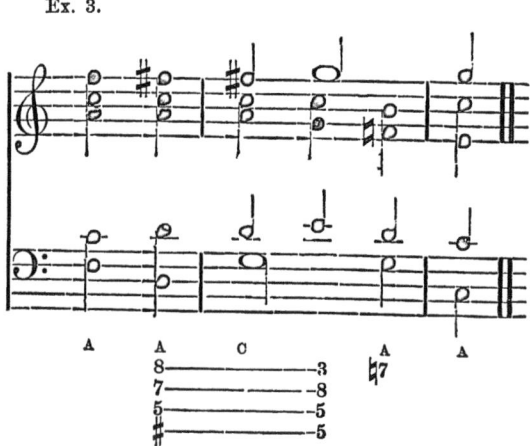

4. In the General Introduction to the Second Part of this book, it is stated that the chromatic discords are already prepared in nature ; therefore if *any* chord of any of the three notes assigned as roots of chromatic discords be taken, any of the fundamental discords derived from that note are *understood.* On this principle, if *any* chord of one of these three notes be taken, *not only that particular chord,* but *any fundamental discord of the same root* may be suspended over the resolution. Where the notes so suspended have not been sounded in the previous chord, of course there will not be any figure indicating that interval to continue into the next chord ; it will be better, therefore, to draw a line from the place where such figure *would* occur in the previous chord, were it sounded there, to the figure itself, which should be marked where the note is actually struck, the figuring being that of the previous chord, and not of that over which it is suspended. There is no necessity to figure such concords in the first chord as are concords in the second (Ex. 4).

Ex. 4.

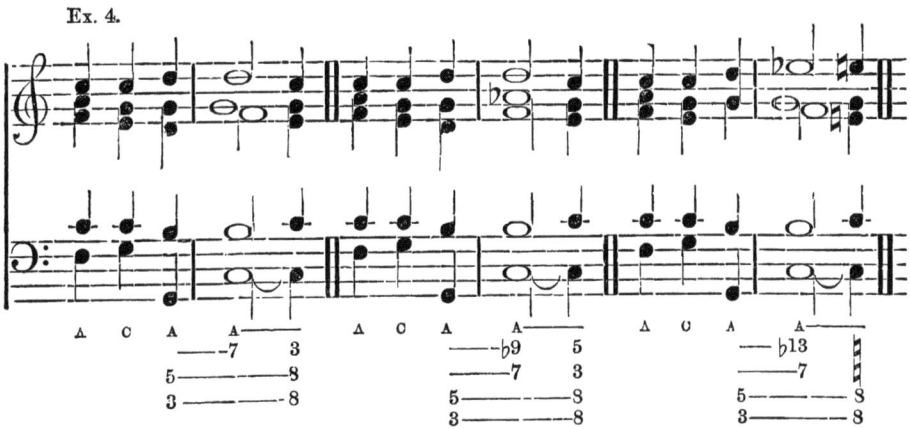

5. No false progressions must be made in any of the above cases ; the suspension must always be on a stronger accent than its resolution, and the chord when suspended must be clearly made out, free from any obscurity.

Chapter XXIV.

OF MIXTURE OF THE DIATONIC AND CHROMATIC STYLES.

Section 1. Analogous to the first species of discords, the diatonic fourth may be suspended over the third of any chromatic chord, even over the third of the secondary root of the augmented sixths; and the same in the inversions, provided always that the fourth and third be not ever sounded together (Ex. 1).

Ex. 1.

2. A major ninth may be suspended over the eighth on the minor second of the scale, where also may be suspended together the ninth and fourth; the same also in the inversions (Ex. 2).

Ex. 2.

3. Analogous to the second species of discords, a prepared diatonic seventh may be taken on the minor second, or minor sixth, of the scale, and the resolution is on a chord having for its root the fourth above or fifth below. That of the minor sixth must be resolved either on the chromatic chord of the minor second of the key, or else on some chromatic chord of which the supertonic is the root (Ex. 3).

Ex. 3.

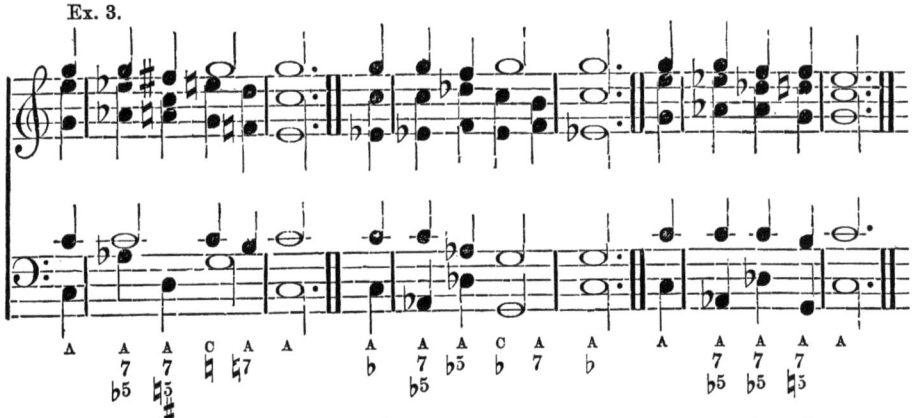

4. A diatonic suspended ninth or fourth, or both, in the minor key, may be taken on the minor or major second of the scale, either without or in

Ex. 4.

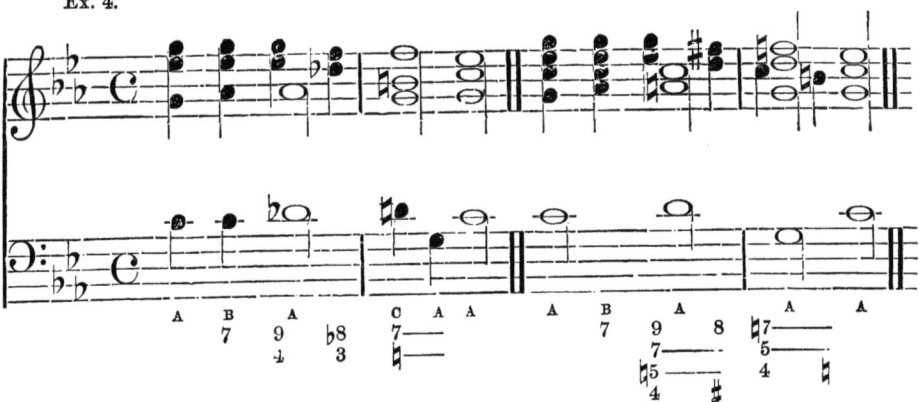

addition to the prepared seventh. The resolution is on the eighth and third of the same chord (Ex. 4).

5. Either part or the whole of any of the chords mentioned in section 3 may be suspended over the bass of its resolution. These, like all other suspensions, must be taken on a stronger accent than their resolution (Ex. 5).

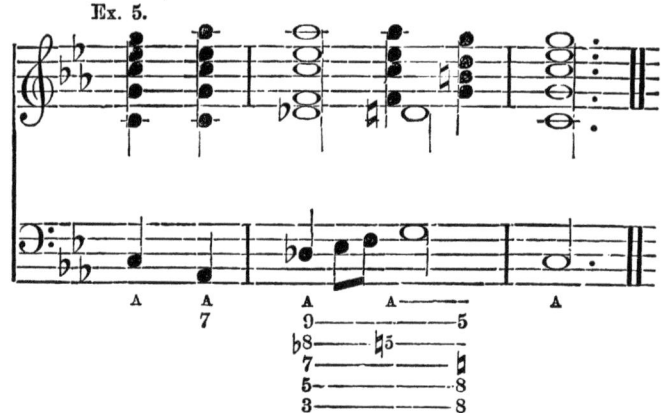

6. The augmented fifth on the minor second of the scale, moving to the dominant harmony, and the augmented fifth on the minor sixth of the scale, moving to a chord of which either the minor or major second of the scale is the root, may be used, provided the augmented fifth be prepared (Ex. 6).

CHAPTER XXV.

OF DIATONIC AND CHROMATIC PASSING NOTES IN THE FREE STYLE, AND ARPEGGIOS.

INTRODUCTION.

IN this Chapter are contained the laws affecting that part of music which has hitherto been the most difficult because the most uncertain, namely, that comprehending chromatic passing notes and arpeggios. The laws affecting double chromatic passing notes and chromatic passing notes in contrary motion are given, not because either the one or the other is recommended,—far from it (as the utter impossibility of rendering either of them very agreeable cannot be too much impressed on the student), but because they may not be rendered unnecessarily disagreeable. The extreme limits to which they may be allowed to go are set down, and those limits should not be passed.

SECTION 1. Free passing notes differ from diatonic or strict passing notes, insomuch as they may be taken on any part of the bar, and they may be either accented or unaccented (Ex. 1).

Ex. 1.

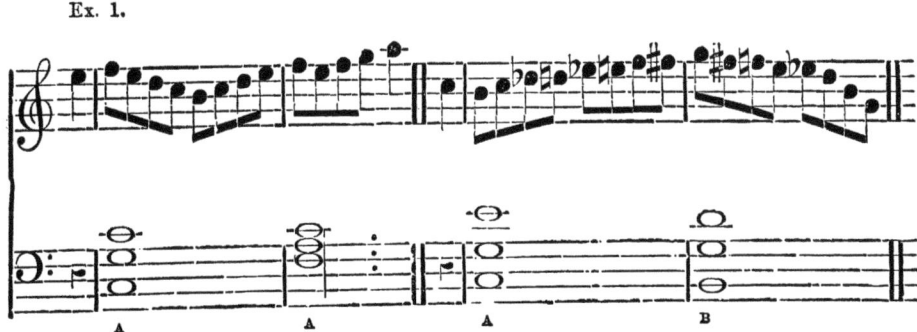

2. They also differ from diatonic, as they may be taken by skip, although like them they cannot be quitted by skip (Ex. 2).

Ex. 2.

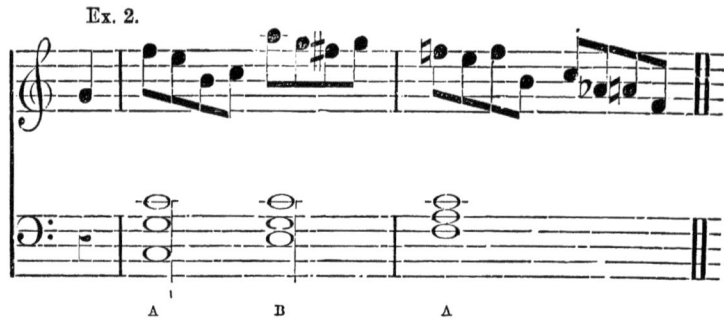

A   B   A

3. They differ also from diatonic, as they can be taken not merely as passing notes from concord to concord, but also from any note of a chord whether consonant or dissonant (if the discord be a fundamental discord), to any other note of the same chord, or to any note of any other chord to which such note might proceed (Ex. 3).*

Ex. 3.

4. It is a commonly received opinion that a chromatic passing note should be at a minor second and not at a chromatic semitone below or above the note to which it proceeds. This is to a certain extent the truth, but not entirely. Where the same chord continues, the chromatic scale, as written

---

* Appendix DDD.

in Chap. XIII., sect. 6, is to be observed so long as the passing notes are on the chords of the tonic, subdominant, minor second or minor sixth of the scale; if any other chord be used, the chromatic notes are to have reference to the root of the chord as a new tonic (Ex. 4).

Ex. 4.

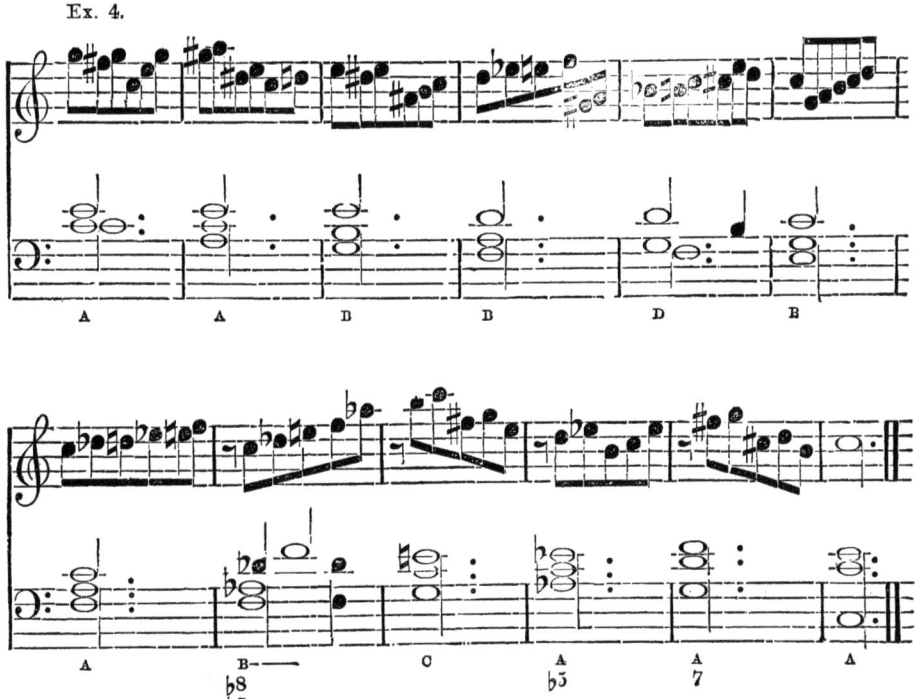

5. If a chromatic passing note lie between a note of one chord and a note of another chord, such chromatic passing note has reference to the second chord and not to the first. A chromatic passing note will thus be written two ways when occurring between the same notes; for example, if the key note (say C), being part of the tonic harmony, be followed by the second of the scale, being part of the dominant or supertonic harmony, the chromatic passing note *may* be C♯*; if the progression be reversed, in passing from D to C the passing note *must* be D♭, and the same with other note similarly situated. Also when the fifth of the scale, being part of the dominant or tonic harmony, is followed by the major sixth of the scale, being part of the supertonic harmony, and *vice versâ*, in the former case the passing note *may* be G♯†, and in the latter it *must* be A♭. It will, from this and sect. 4, appear that the old system is about as often wrong as right (Ex. 5).

---

* This may also be D♭, an essential note of the chord of the minor ninth of the tonic.

† This may also be an A♭ if coming from the dominant chord.

Ex. 5.

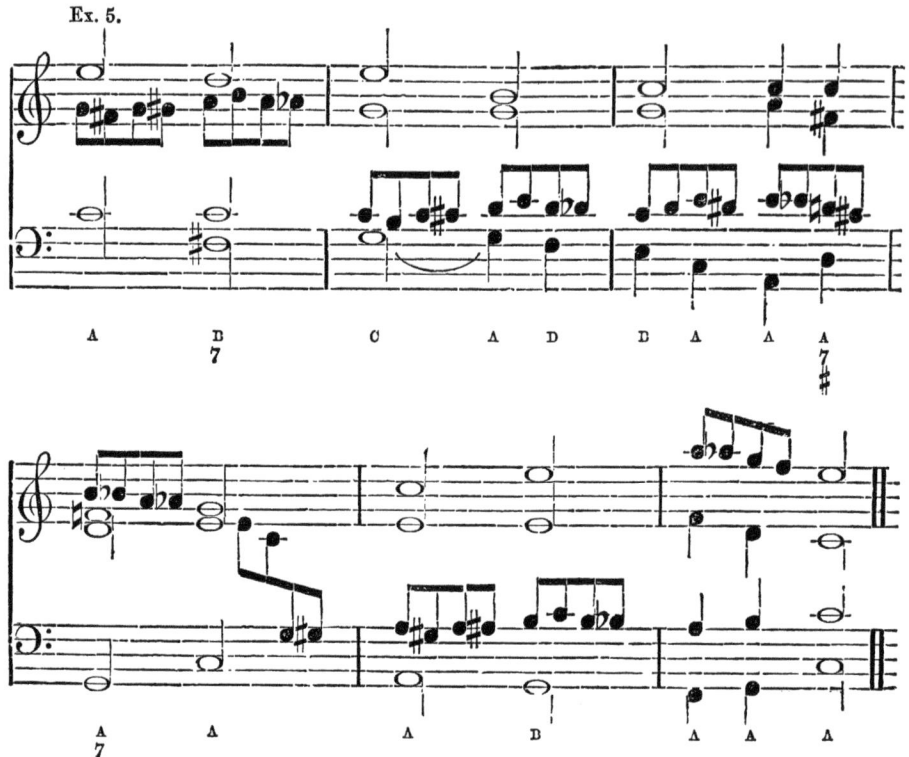

6. It is allowable to skip to a note at a diatonic or chromatic semitone below any note of a chord, or to the diatonic note below the major third of a chord. Should the passing note below any given note be at a diatonic semitone from any note of the chord, it is not in false relation to that harmony note.

Ex. 9.

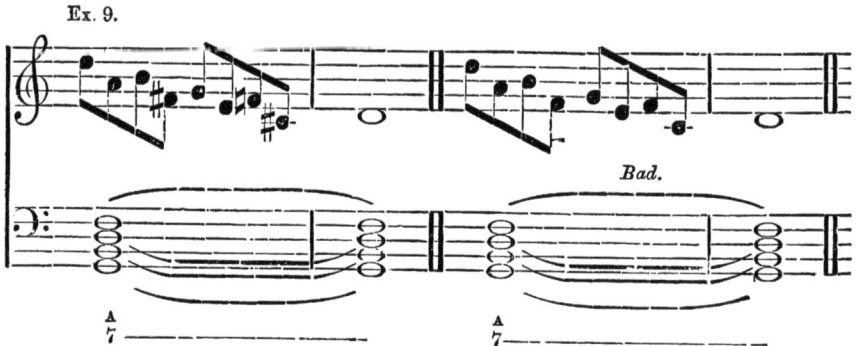

Bad.

7. It is allowable to skip to the note at a diatonic major or minor second above any note of a chord, to that at a major second above the root of the common chord of the minor sixth of the scale, or above the third of the sub-dominant minor chord, or above the fifth of the common chord of the minor

second of the scale ; and to the note at a major second above the root of the common chord of the minor second of the scale.   It is allowable also to skip to the note at a minor second above the root and fifth of the chromatic chords, or of the tonic and dominant common chords, or above the third and fifth of the subdominant major chord, such minor second being in all cases a note belonging to the chromatic scale of the key (Ex. 10).

Ex. 10.

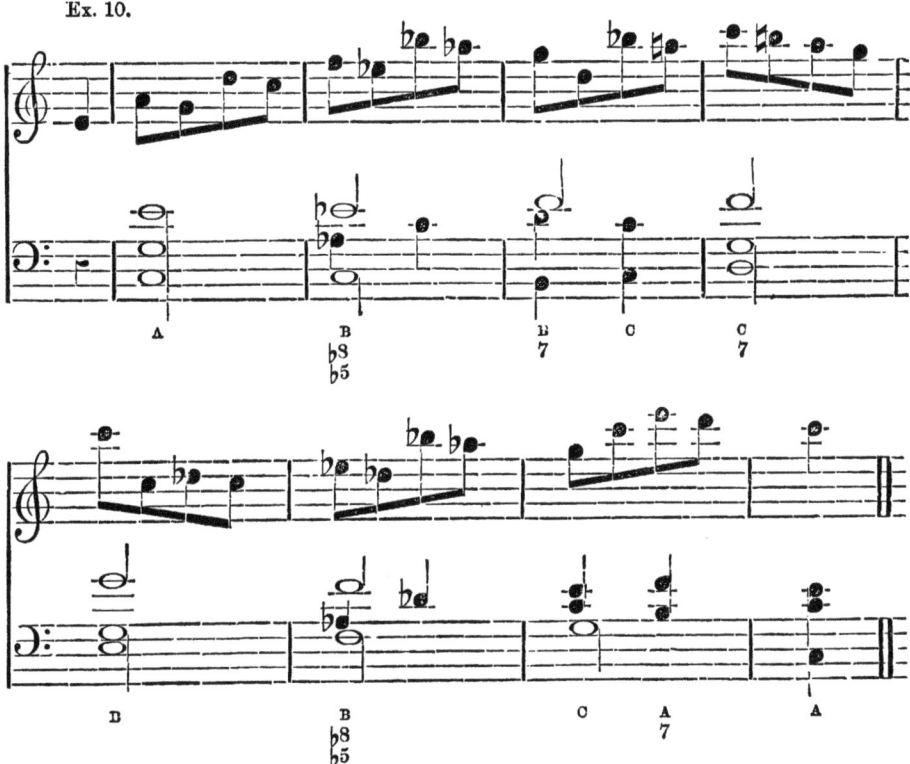

8. A passing note that is to be resolved on the harmony note at a chromatic semitone below it, must be approached by semitone from above (Ex. 11).

Ex. 11.

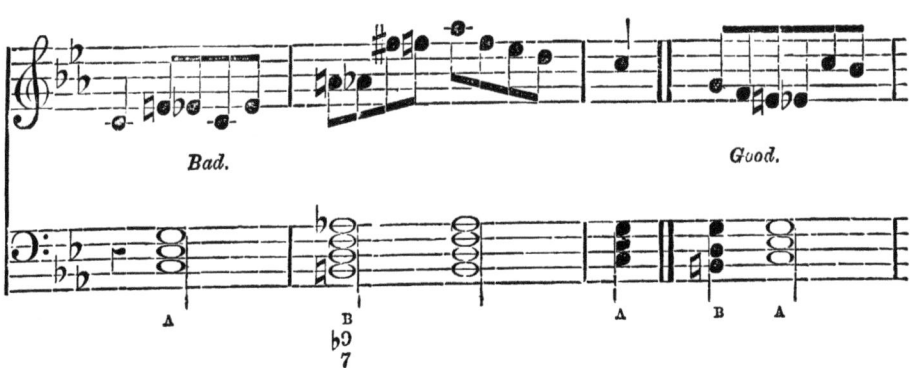

Ex. 11—*continued.*

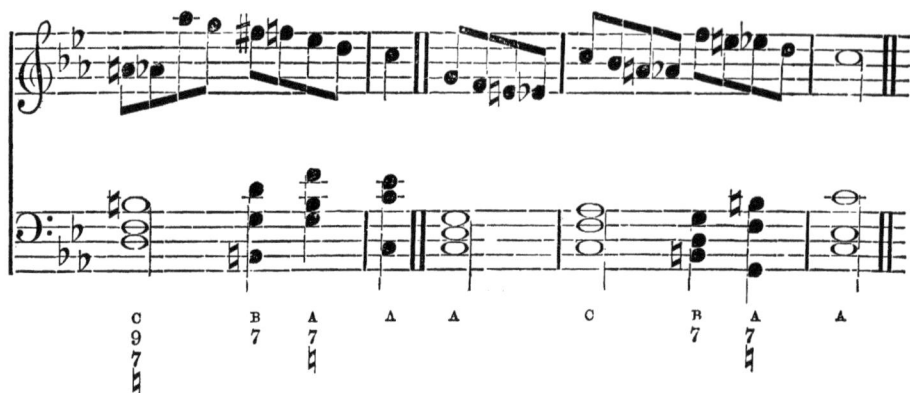

9. A passing note at a tone above a fundamental minor ninth is available in rare cases, and is not in false relation to the third of the same chord (Ex. 12).

Ex. 12.

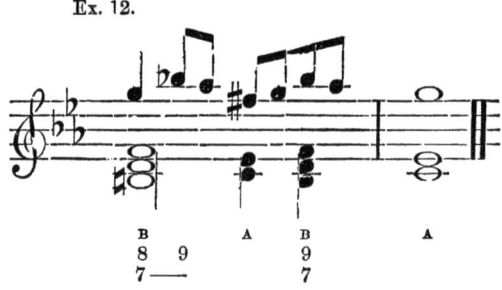

10. It is also allowable to skip from a passing note above to a passing note below, or *vice versâ,* before proceeding to the note of the chord lying between, which, however, *must* follow the second of these passing notes (Ex. 13).

Ex. 13.

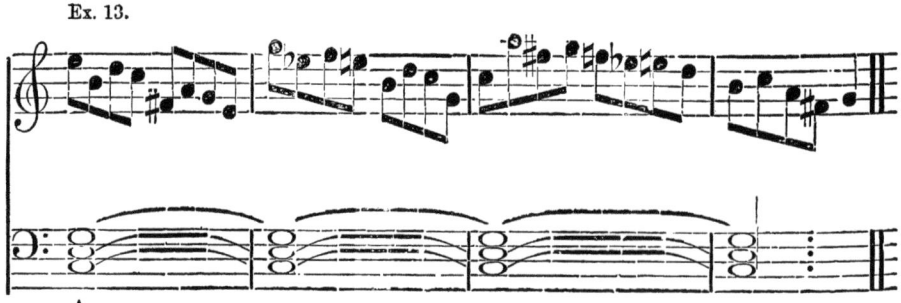

11. When any passing note may be taken by skip, or by step of a second, it is also allowable to take it as an apparent suspension from a previous chord (Ex. 14); that these notes when taken thus, are passing notes, and not suspensions, is proved by Ex. 15, in which the F is not allowable, being the major second below the fifth of the chord.

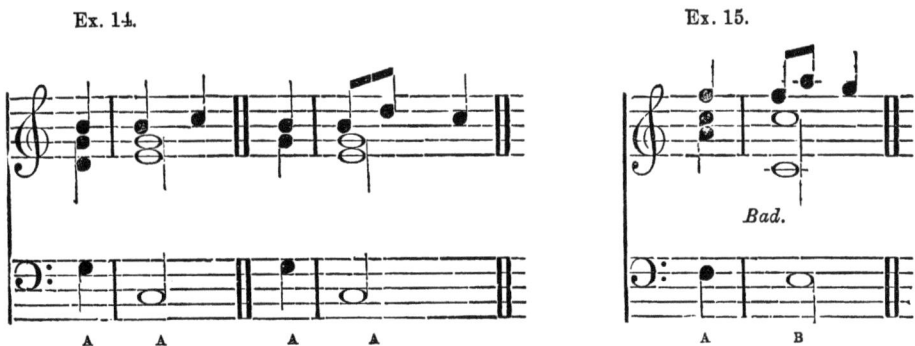

Ex. 14.   Ex. 15.

12. If a part move by semitone to a chromatic note not belonging to the chord, it must proceed by semitones in the same direction to a note of the same or another chord, or, when within a semitone of this note, may skip to the allowable note above or below it, if the part return immediately to the intervening harmony note (Ex. 16). If a note approached by semitones be

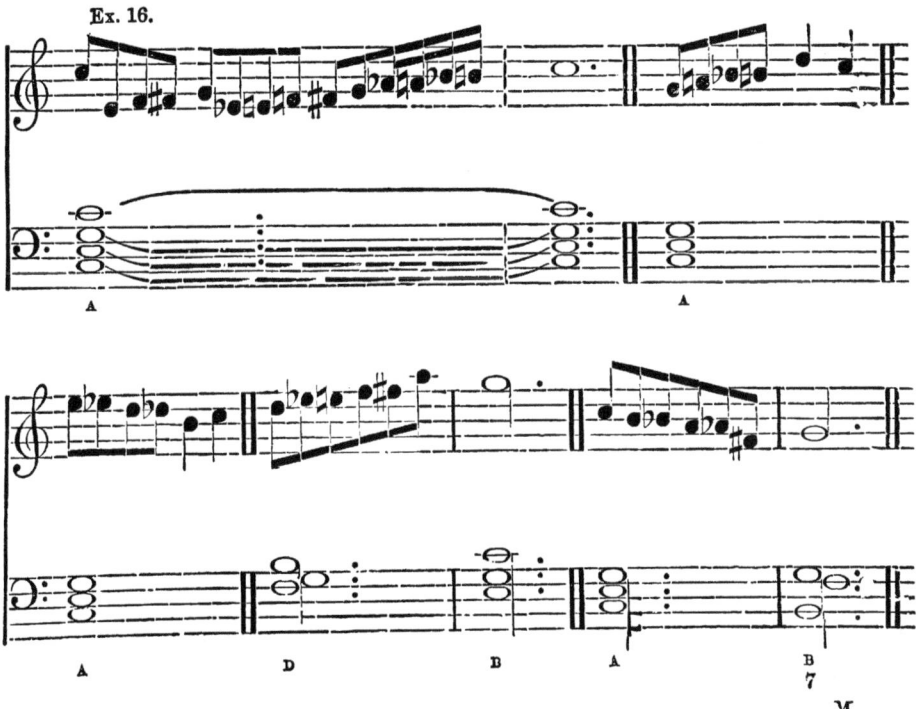

Ex. 16.

M

a discord derived from the same root as the prevailing harmony, even though it be not previously sounded in the chord, it may be the last note of the progression by semitones (Ex. 17). Example 18 is good because the major

Ex. 17.

ninth may be a harmony note in the major key. Example 19 is bad because the major ninth may not be a harmony note in a minor key. Example 20 is bad because in each instance the progression by semitones ends before reaching a harmony note.

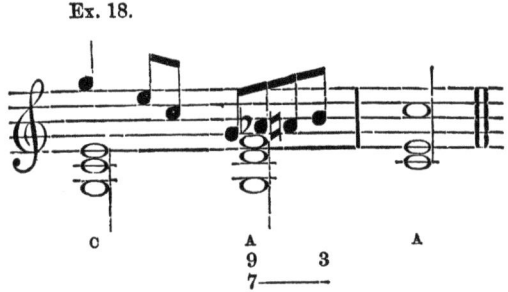

Ex. 18.

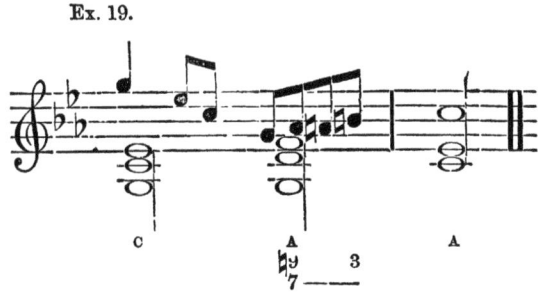

Ex. 19.

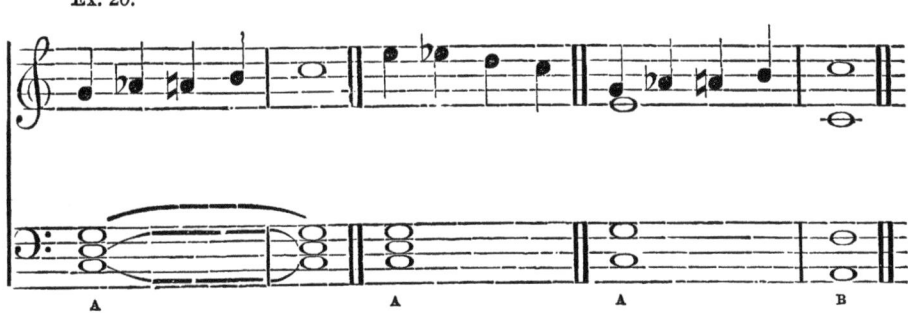

Ex. 20.

13. Simultaneous free passing notes in two or more parts are divided into two kinds.

14. The first kind has all the passing notes moving in the same direction.

15. The second kind has the passing notes in contrary motion.

16. The first kind bears the same relation to chromatic or free music as does the third species of diatonic discords to diatonic or strict music, and the second kind as does the fourth species.

17. As regards the progression of free passing notes with each other in similar motion, the augmented fifth or diminished fourth formed between the minor seventh and augmented fourth of the scale can only be used in ascending, and not in descending: it is anything but agreeable at any time (Ex. 21).

Ex. 21.

18. Passing notes may be double, triple, or even quadruple, if the laws affecting the passage of a single part in its relation to the harmony notes, and the laws affecting the progression with each other of parts moving in the same direction, be observed (Ex. 22).*

Ex. 22.

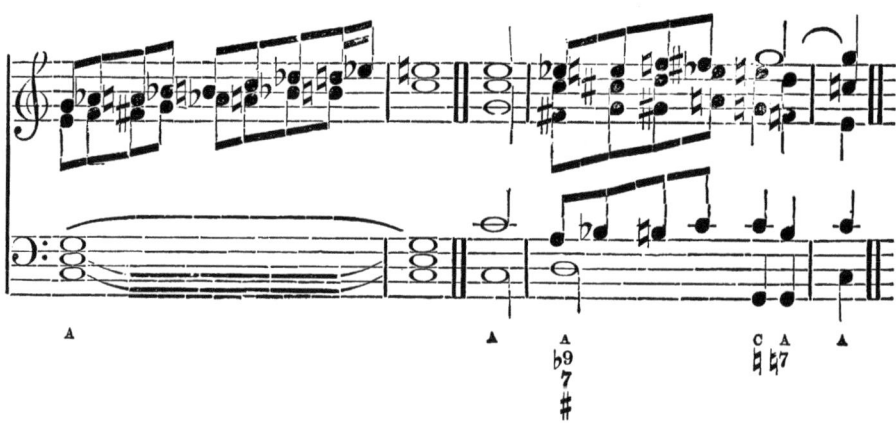

19. In passing notes in the free style in contrary motion, the laws for progression of parts generally, also the particular laws given in this chapter for parts moving the same way, are to be observed.

20. It is essential that the parts in contrary motion should each be in the same key as the others.

21. It is desirable that not more than two parts move by semitones in contrary motion at the same time. Chromatic passing notes follow the diatonic law, that, provided they reach their proper places at last, they may be hurried or protracted at pleasure (Ex. 23).

---

* Appendix EEE.

Ex. 23.

22. It can scarcely be said that any progression by semitones in contrary motion is agreeable, but it will be less disagreeable in proportion to the number of concords, and intervals being part of harmonies in the key, formed by the moving parts.   Among the least disagreeable places to start from are the major third and its inversion, and the diminished fifth and its inversion (Ex. 24).

Ex. 24.

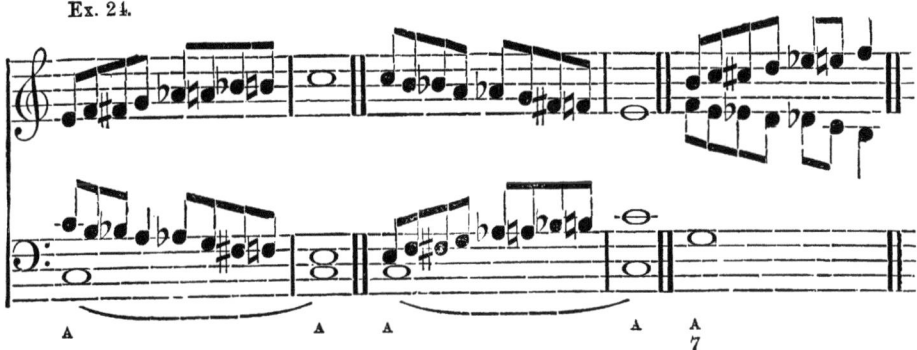

23. In free passing notes, all the chromatic notes in the ascending parts are reckoned as discords; also, as in diatonic discords, all the descending parts; it is therefore allowable, whether the chromatic notes be in the ascending or descending parts or both, to bring up the ascending part or parts to concords with the descending, and then to treat them as any other concords (Ex. 25);

Ex. 25.

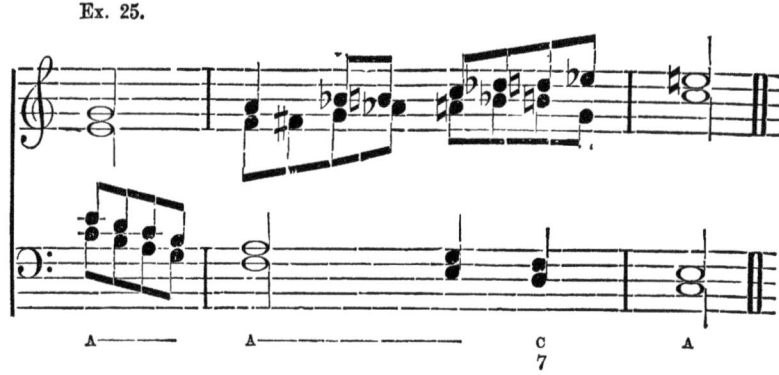

24. Or the descending part or parts may fall to the concord (Ex. 26);

Ex. 26.

25. Or the parts may proceed by contrary motion to a concord (Ex. 27);

Ex. 27.

26. Or else, when the ascending parts rise to a fundamental discord with the descending, it may be treated as though produced in any other way (Ex. 28).

Ex. 28.

27. Provided it can be done without making false progressions, passing notes, double, triple, or even quadruple, may be taken both above and beneath notes of chords (Ex. 29).

Ex. 29.

Ex. 29—*continued.*

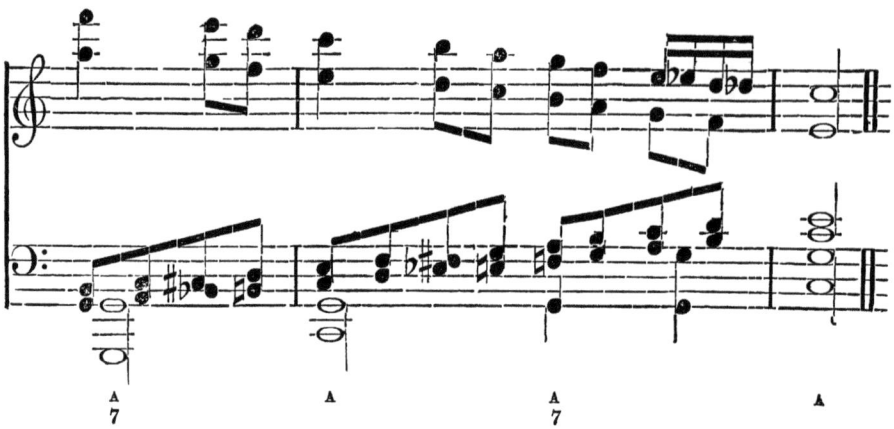

28. Although rules have been given above regulating the progression of double chromatic passing notes in similar motion, also of chromatic passing notes in contrary motion, yet both the one and the other should be used very sparingly, as, however well managed, the effect is rarely agreeable.*

Ex. 30.

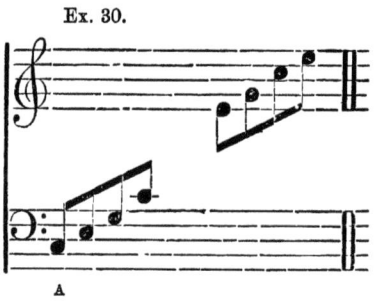

29. An arpeggio is when the notes of a chord are sounded successively, instead of simultaneously (Ex. 30).

30. Arpeggios may be divided into two kinds : I, in which the different notes form real parts, and the parts progress as though the entire chord were struck at once and not divided (Ex. 31) ;

Ex. 31.

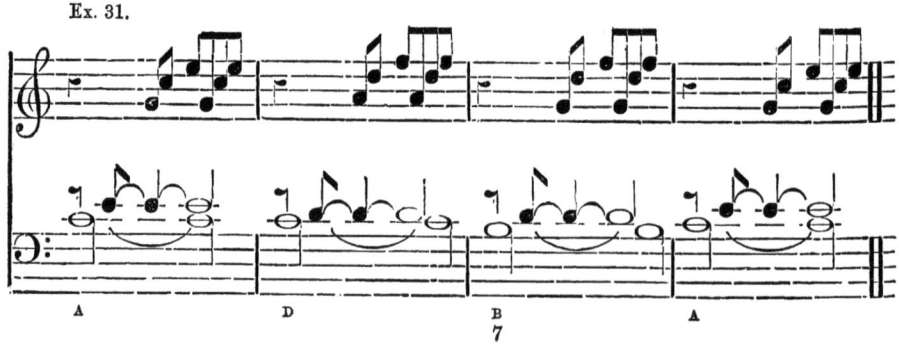

---

* Appendix FFF.

II, in which they do not form real parts (Ex. 32);

Ex. 32.

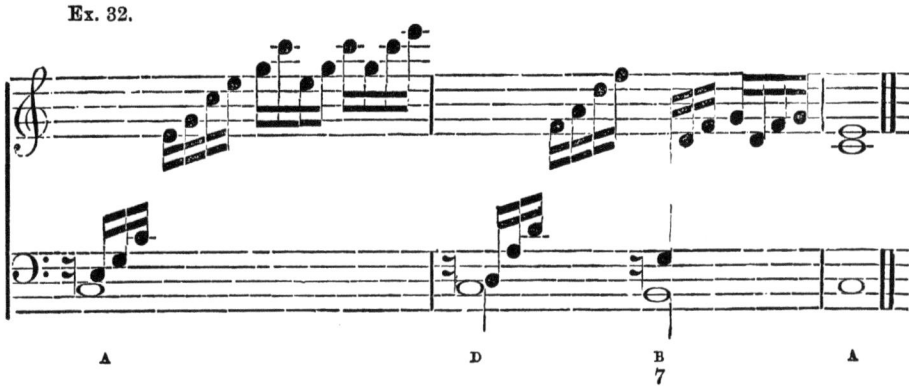

Passing notes may be taken by step or by skip between one note of an arpeggio and another (Ex. 33).

Ex. 33.

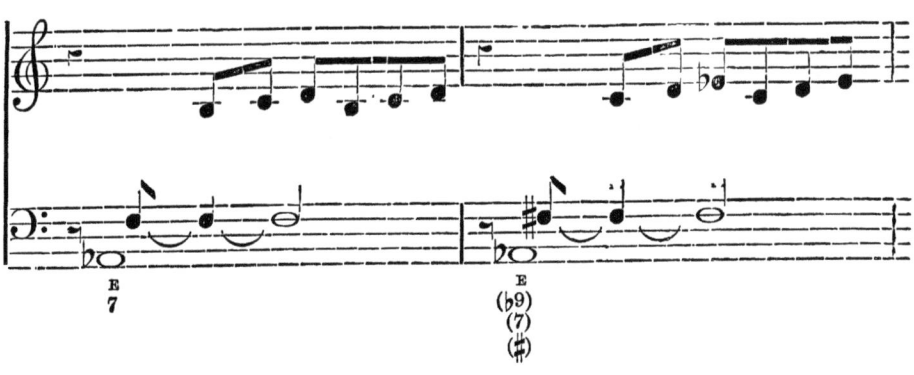

31. With regard to the second kind, in which the different notes do not form real parts, the arpeggio may commence and terminate on any note of the chord, and the lowest note of the chord, whether part of the arpeggio or not, is the actual bass (Ex. 34).

Ex. 34.

32. Any note of an arpeggio, whether it be a concord, or a suspended, essential, transitory, or fundamental discord, may be doubled (Ex. 35). It is recommended that the *interval* of the augmented sixth be never inverted, and that the major third be not taken above the major ninth.

Ex. 35.

Ex. 35—*continued.*

33. Parts in arpeggio may proceed in similar motion (Ex. 36), or in

Ex. 36.

contrary motion (Ex. 37), or while other parts sustain (Ex. 38).

Ex. 37.

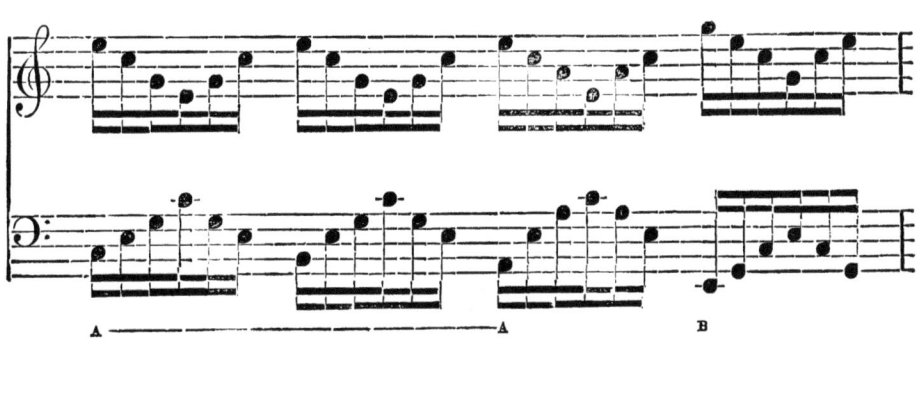

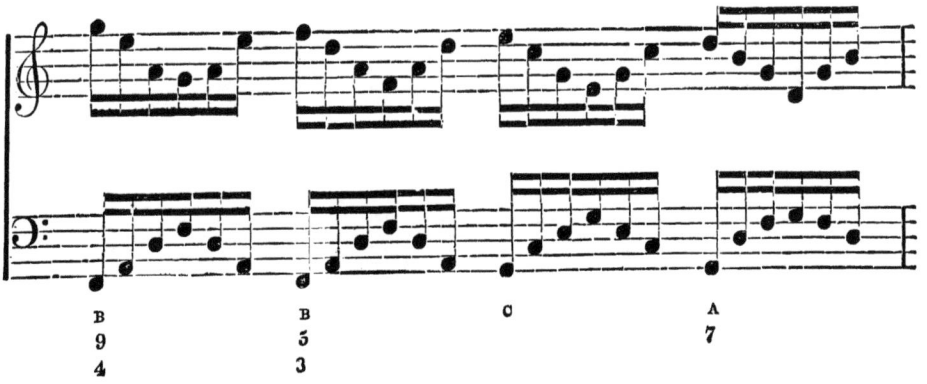

Ex. 37—*continued.*

Ex. 38.

Ex. 38—*continued.*

CHAPTER XXVI.

OF PEDALS IN THE FREE STYLE.

INTRODUCTION.

THE laws affecting pedals have hitherto been lax and ill-defined. This circumstance, joined with false notation, has left a vague idea that a pedal can be only the tonic or the dominant of the key in which any piece or distinct portion of a piece of music may be; but that on these pedals may be taken any chords whatever, whether belonging to such key or not. That this is not the case is endeavoured to be shown in this chapter; and the limits to harmonies on either tonic or dominant pedal, or both, are distinctly marked out. Probably the best way to test the harmonies on a pedal would be to write all the roots of the chords beneath the pedal.

SECTION 1. As in diatonic harmony, a pedal note is one note continued through several chords.

2. Such pedal may either be an essential portion of the harmony, or it may not.

3. When it is not an essential portion of the harmony, the part immediately above it must form a good bass in itself, that is, must be regular in its progression as a bass; but when such pedal note is an essential portion of the harmony, the part immediately above it need not form a good bass in itself, but may stand as an inner part, provided always that if the pedal note be an essential portion of one chord and not of the next, the part immediately above such pedal must be regular in its progression as a bass, from the first of such chords to the second; thus Ex. 1 is good and Ex. 2 is bad.*

Ex. 1.

---

* Appendix GGG.

Ex 2.

4. Only the key note and dominant may be taken as pedals.

5. In free compositions a double pedal, that is, both key note and dominant together, may be taken, provided the key note be the lower note

6. On the tonic pedal all the harmonies belonging to the key may be taken, with their several resolutions.

7. On the dominant all the harmonies belonging to the key may be taken. More than this, the dominant may be so far considered as a key note as to admit on it all the chromatic harmonies of the major sixth of the scale that is, the major common chord, and the chords of the seventh, ninth, and thirteenth; provided always that these chords do not resolve on the major harmony of the supertonic.†

8. All the harmonies, with their resolutions into the key, may be taken on the double pedal (Ex. 3).

Ex. 3.

† Appendix HHH.

N

Ex. 3—*continued.*

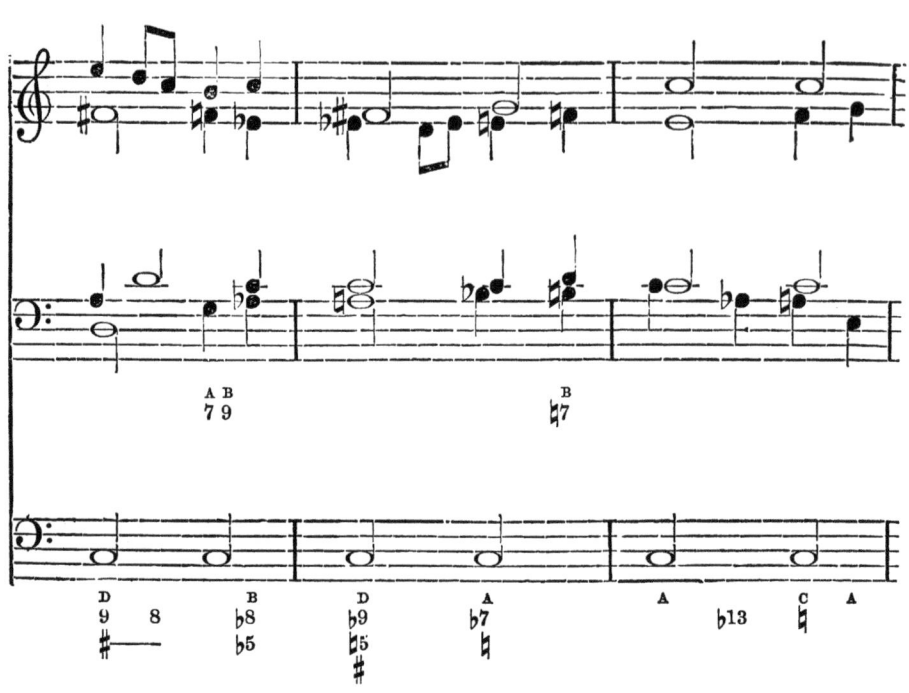

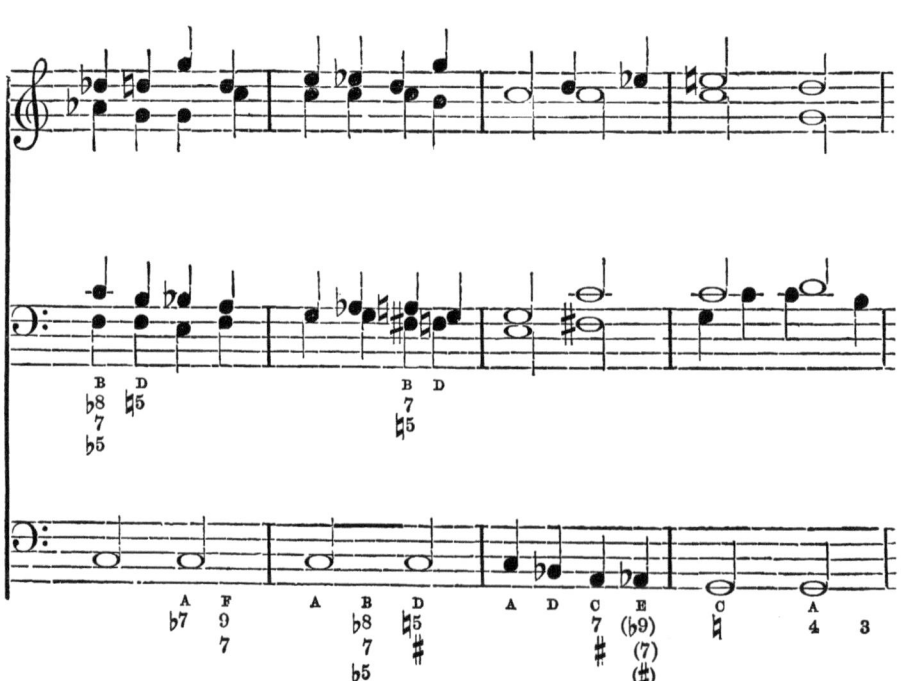

Ex. 3—*continued.*

Ex. 3—*continued.*

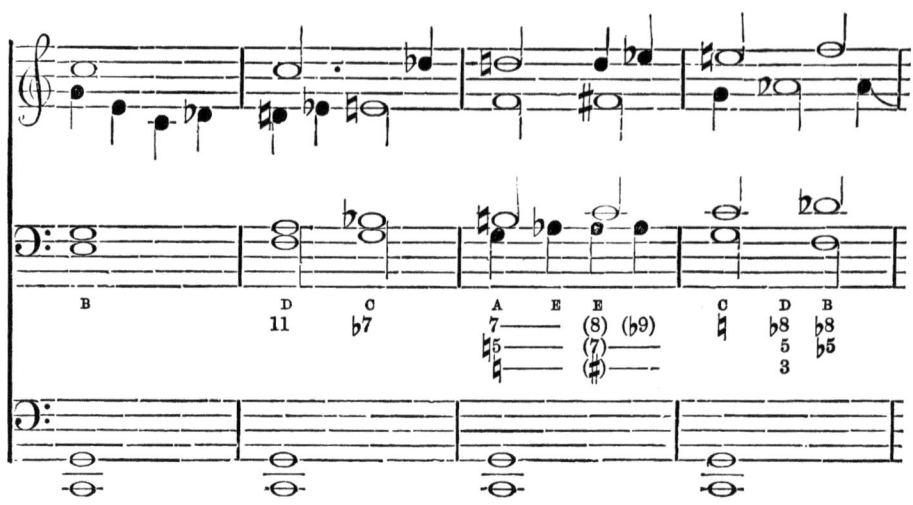

9. Pedals, whether single or double, may be taken either in the bass or in any other part (the key note being always the lower note of the two in a double pedal) ; the only restriction being that none of the other parts pass through them.*

---

* This restriction does not always apply to orchestral scores, in which the different qualities of tone in the several instruments frequently prevent any confusion of parts when notes pass through an inverted pedal.

CHAPTER XXVII.

OF MODULATION IN THE FREE STYLE.

INTRODUCTION.

THIS chapter contains all the principles by which modulation can be made. The variety to be obtained by following these principles through their application is almost boundless.

SECTION 1. Major and minor common chords, or their first inversions, may be treated as diatonic or chromatic chords in the key *to* which, instead of *from* which, the modulation is made.

2. Every major common chord or its first inversion may be a diatonic harmony in the keys of which the root of the chord is the key note, subdominant or dominant; or in the minor keys of which it is the dominant or submediant; or a chromatic chord in the major keys in which it is the supertonic, or the minor sixth, or the minor second; or in the minor keys of which it is the supertonic or the minor second (Ex. 1).

Ex. 1.

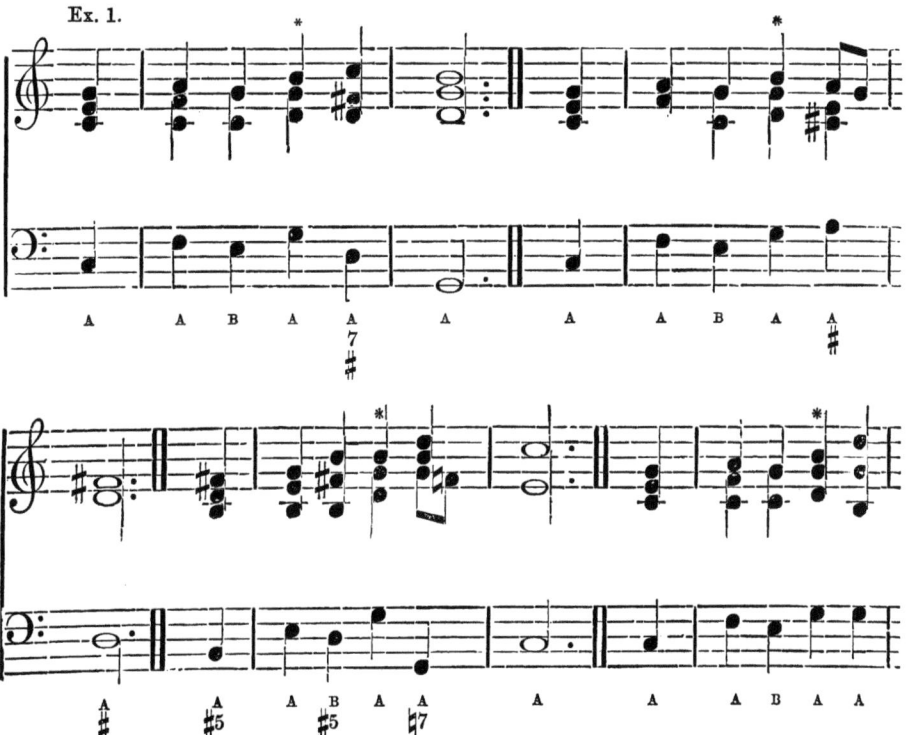

Ex. 1.—continued.

3. The fundamental seventh, minor or major ninth, eleventh, and minor or major thirteenth, may be added to each major common chord, and provided no false progressions be made, the chords may be treated in the same way, that is, as chords in the key *to* which, instead of *from* which, the modulation is made (Ex. 2).

Ex. 2.

4. Every minor common chord, or its first inversion, may be a diatonic harmony in the minor keys of which the root of the chord is either the first or fourth, or the major keys of which it is either the second or sixth† (Ex. 3).

Ex. 3.

5. Every chord of the minor ninth or its inversions may belong to the three major or three minor keys of which its root is the dominant, or super-tonic, or tonic (Ex. 4).‡

Ex. 4.

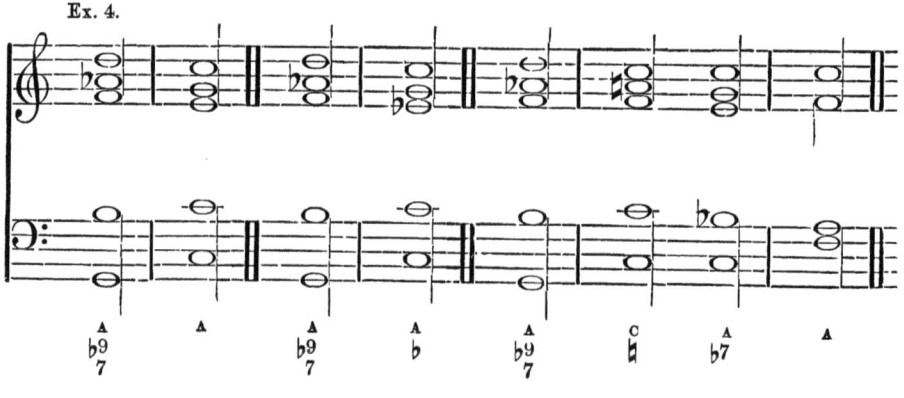

---

† Appendix III.   ‡ Appendix JJJ.

Ex. 4.—*continued.*

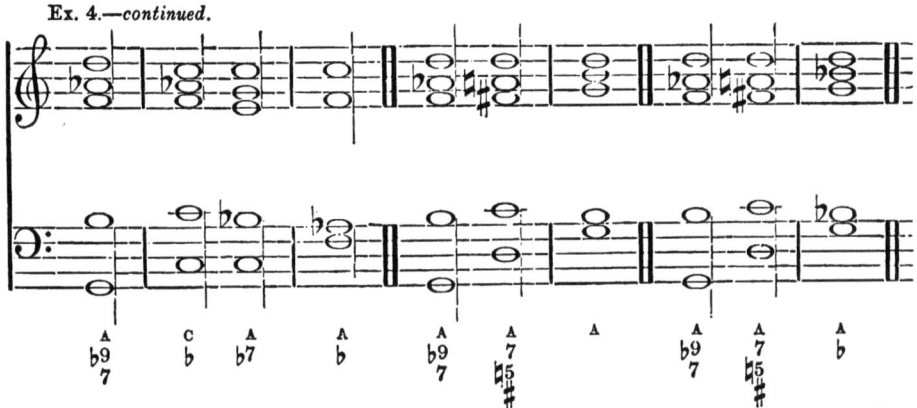

6. Enharmonic modulation is when modulation is effected by changing the name of one or more notes of a chord, and then resolving it according to the proper resolution of the chord as newly named, or else resolving the chord (without changing the names of the notes) as though they had been changed. In Ex. 5 the F in the chord of seventh of G is changed into E♯,

Ex. 5.

the chord forming then the augmented sixth of G, which is resolved on the second inversion of the major common chord of B (Ex. 5). In Ex. 6 the chord of the seventh of G resolves at once on the second inversion of the major common chord of B, the resolution being as though the F had been changed into E♯ before resolution.

Ex. 6.

7. Every chord of the minor ninth without the root may, by enharmonic change, be written in four different ways (Ex. 7), therefore every inverted chord of the minor ninth may resolve into any of the twelve major or twelve minor keys.

Ex. 7.

8. Any note of a major common chord, or of a fundamental chord of the seventh, minor or major ninth, eleventh, minor or major thirteenth, or augmented sixth, may remain to become any other interval of any other of those chords, excepting that neither minor or major ninth can ever remain as the primary root of the chord of the augmented sixth (Ex. 8).

Ex. 8.

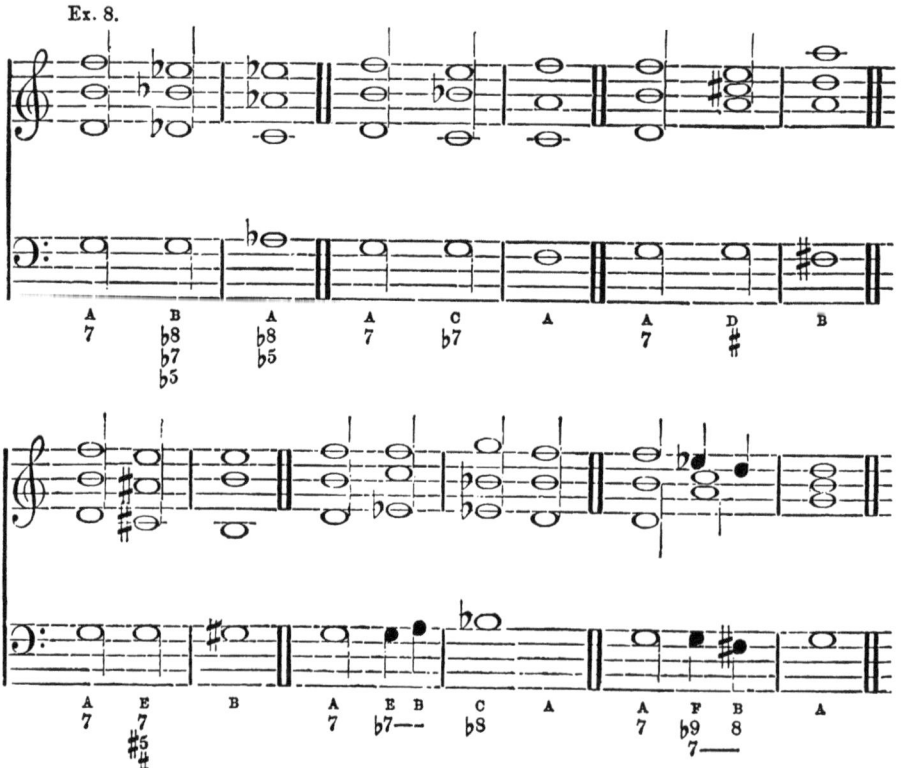

Ex. 8—*continued.*

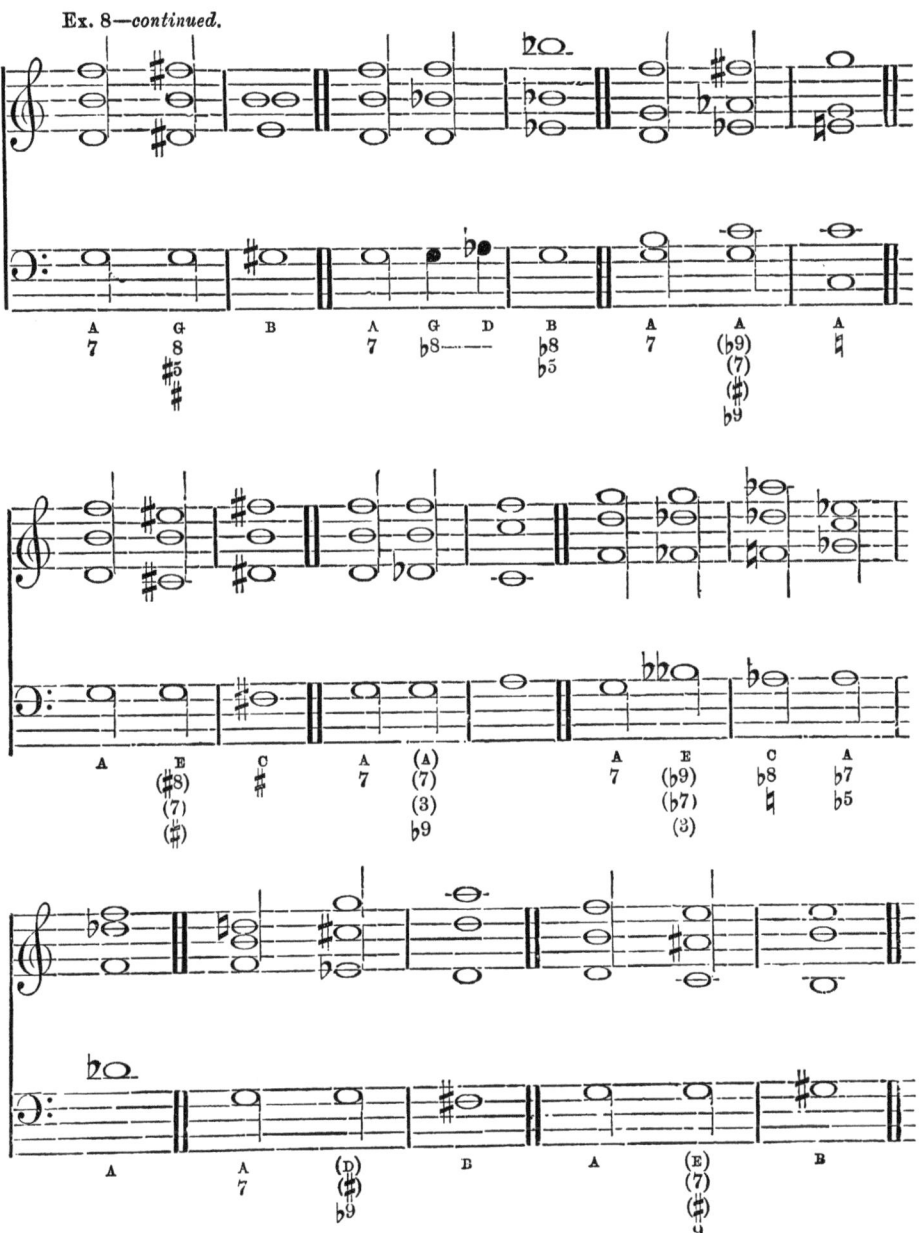

9. In Ex. 8, G, the root of the first chord in each instance remains to be successively the third, fifth, seventh, minor ninth, major ninth, eleventh, minor thirteenth, major thirteenth, each of another chord; also the primary root, primary ninth, secondary root, third (when the repeated G is in the top part, because the interval of the augmented sixth should not be inverted) seventh and ninth of the chord of augmented sixth. In the same way, with the restriction before mentioned, may any other interval of any other chord be treated.

APPENDIX.

PART I.

A.—CHAP. I., SECT. 15.

THE following table shows the relative numbers of vibrations of all the notes of the diatonic scale in the major and minor forms of a key, derived as described in the Introduction to Chapter II. In ordinary cases, the supertonic only is variable according to the harmony in which it occurs; in particular instances the mediant also varies in both major and minor keys, namely, when it bears a suspended fifth which has to be resolved upward (Chap. VII., sects. 23, 24); and when it is the apparent root of an essential discord (Chap. VIII., sects. 17, 18, 19); the mediant is then the thirteenth of the dominant, which is fully treated in the second part of this book, and therefore not regarded in the following table. The ratios in the table are all reckoned from the tonic, and the high number of 360 is assigned to this note in order to avoid the use of fractions, and not for the sake of defining the pitch. Comparison of any degree of the scale with any other shows the relative ratios of the two.

TONIC, root of major or minor chord, 3rd of Submediant minor and Submediant major, and 5th of Subdominant 360
SUPERTONIC I. ($\frac{9}{8}$) major tone of Tonic and 5th of Dominant 405
SUPERTONIC II. ($\frac{10}{9}$) minor tone of Tonic and root of minor chord 400
MEDIANT MINOR ($\frac{6}{5}$) minor 3rd of Tonic and 5th of Submediant minor 432
MEDIANT MAJOR ($\frac{5}{4}$) major 3rd of Tonic and 5th of Submediant major 450
SUBDOMINANT ($\frac{4}{3}$) perfect 4th of Tonic, root of major or minor chord, and 3rd of Supertonic II. 480
DOMINANT ($\frac{3}{2}$) 5th of Tonic and root of major chord 540
SUBMEDIANT MINOR ($\frac{8}{5}$) minor 6th of Tonic, root of major chord, and minor 3rd of Subdominant 576
SUBMEDIANT MAJOR ($\frac{5}{3}$) major 6th of Tonic, root of minor chord, major 3rd of Subdominant, and 5th of Supertonic II. 600
MINOR SEVENTH ($\frac{16}{9}$) minor 7th of Tonic,* and inverted minor 3rd of Dominant 640
LEADING NOTE ($\frac{15}{8}$) major 7th of Tonic, and major 3rd of Dominant 675

The eighth above any note has double the number of vibrations that the note has from which such eighth is reckoned, as $\frac{720}{360}$, $\frac{810}{405}$, &c. All the notes in the above table are available for any of the four species of discords in the major or minor key to which each belongs.

B.—CHAP. II., GENERAL INTRODUCTION.

Certain of all the arguments in the present and subsequent chapters that establish the harmonic propriety of the invariable minor scale, the editor still feels that the frequent use of a variable scale by the best masters necessitates its acceptance by students, and the enunciation of rules for its employment. To distinguish it from the invariable scale advocated in the text, which may

* Appendix B, I, and O.

be called the Harmonic Minor Scale, because formed of notes available in chords, and existing in the three harmonies named in the Introduction, let the variable scale be called the Arbitrary Minor Scale, because it admits of notes which may be introduced at the composer's arbitrary will. Its first five notes, from the tonic inclusive, are the same as in the Harmonic Scale; but its sixth and seventh may both be major or both be minor as shown in the sequel (Chap. II., Sect. 15).

C.—CHAP. III., SECT. 10.

Scientists are silent on the phenomena that distinguish the perfect from the imperfect intervals, among which is the bad effect of two perfect fifths in consecution. The proposal by a musician of a reason for the speciality may well stand in a part of the blank which still remains to be completely filled. That consecutive fourths (inverted fifths) between upper parts with one or more parts moving below them have good effect, though fourths between the bass and an upper part sound as bad as fifths, is as yet unexplained. It may have some bearing upon this seeming anomaly, that the discordance of the diminished fifth and of the perfect fifth of the mediant is mitigated, if not wholly dispelled, when the discordant triads are taken in their first inversions. That the fourth between the bass and an upper part is always discordant in the diatonic style, and when not discordant in the chromatic style is limited in treatment, whereas the perfect fifth of any note except the mediant is always concordant, is another instance of the qualifying power of inversion upon the effect of an interval.

D.—CHAP. III., SECT. 18.

The rule in this section is less stringent than others in the present chapter. The approach to the octave of the bass by a wide interval of melody when the bass moves often gives unpleasant prominence to the top part; but instances are when the prominence of the note is not unpleasant, and then, therefore, the approach to it by skip escapes objection, as when the eighth is the root of a chord, especially when this is tonic, dominant or subdominant. Good taste in the composer must be trusted as a guide in making exception.

E.—CHAP. III., SECT. 19.

Two notes next to each other in alphabetical order may not be followed by an unison approached by oblique motion,

except rarely, if one of the two be a passing note.

Students are warned against the frequent use of this exception.

F.—CHAP. III., SECT. 24.

This may be received as a recommendation more than as a rule, for, though the overlapping here prohibited be certainly undesirable, it cannot always be avoided, especially in writing for many parts. Sometimes, even in two-part writing, to continue a succession of imperfect concords, and to maintain melodious progression in both parts, one overlaps the other without bad effect.

G.—CHAP. III., SECT. 25.

The last part of this rule may be read as positive; the effect of a fifth after a third, when both parts step a second, in two-part writing, being always bad.

H.—CHAP. IV., SECT. 5.

The editor has learned to differ from the rule here given. He thinks that the duplication of the third is admissible in any chord, except the chord of the dominant (Chap. II., Sect. 10). The reason may be that the greater sonority of the bass overpowers the harmonic which would induce the dissonance, but which is only obvious enough to give brilliancy to the chord. The duplication of the third in the chord of the sub-mediant (this third being the tonic) much enriches the effect of the chord. The harmonic fifth of the tonic is the dominant, which dominant may be sounded with good effect as a pedal; and therefore its suggestion by the doubling of the tonic is naturally acceptable.

I.—CHAP. IV., SECT 17.

When, in the minor key, the bass descends by seconds, from the tonic to the sub-mediant, the minor seventh of the Arbitrary Scale is often taken as the bass of a first inversion, the good effect of which, even more than its frequent use, justifies the acceptance of the variable minor scale.

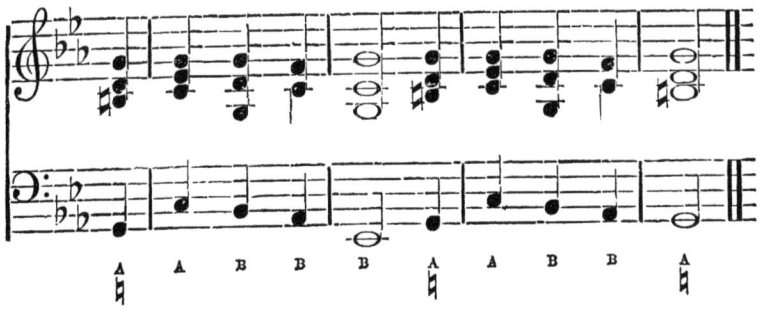

J.—Chap. IV., Sect. 21.

During the continuance of the dominant in the bass the second inversion of the common chord of the tonic may follow another chord, and must be succeeded by a further change of harmony. The whole passage may be considered as resting on a dominant pedal (Chap. XI.), and in this light it must have been regarded by the old masters in whose music it occurs.

K.—Chap. V., Sect. 1.

The word "transposition" might be substituted for "repetition" in all rules referring to sequence, with the provision that there be no change of key, and that the progression be transposed to other degrees of the same diatonic scale.

L.—Chap. VI., Sect. 7.

This rule, with the references to it in Chap. VII., Sects. 6, 10, 11, 15, and 26, must be received with great reservation. It is given rather to explain the principle than to authorise the frequent application of this principle. A dissonant note is always harshest when sounded with the note on which it is to be resolved; such harshness is, however, less when the note of resolution is in the bass than when in an upper part, and the student will do well to restrict its use in any upper part to most rare occasions, and to employ it only when some special point of melody may warrant so extreme an effect. The contraction of the interval of the ninth to that of a second (Chap. I., Sect. 5) is eminently unsatisfactory, and its occurrence in music of good writers should be regarded as a warning rather than an example; its figuring is still 9—8.*

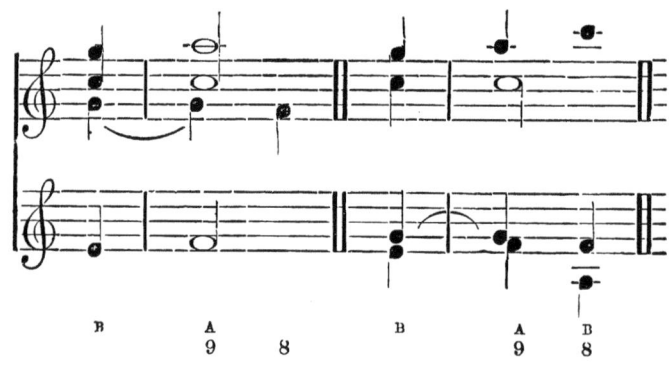

---

* Appendix E.

M.—Chap. VII., Introduction.

Whereas previous writers classed as distinct and separate suspensions those which they figured 9—8, 7—6, and $\frac{4}{2}$— or $\frac{7}{4}$— this chapter shows that

the last three are inversions of the first. In like manner $\frac{9}{6}$—8 and $\frac{5}{2}$— are shown to be inversions of 4—3. The same principle unifies the figuring of the double suspensions and their inversions. The greater clearness of regarding the several inversions as different aspects of one chord than of distinguishing each as a separate harmony must be apparent to all who perceive the relation of a common chord to its first inversion.

N.—Chap. VII., Sect. 1.

A seeming, but not real, exception from the rule that "the resolution takes place while the chord against which the discordant note forms the discord remains," is that the bass or any other parts may move to different notes of the same chord, together with the resolving of the suspended discord.

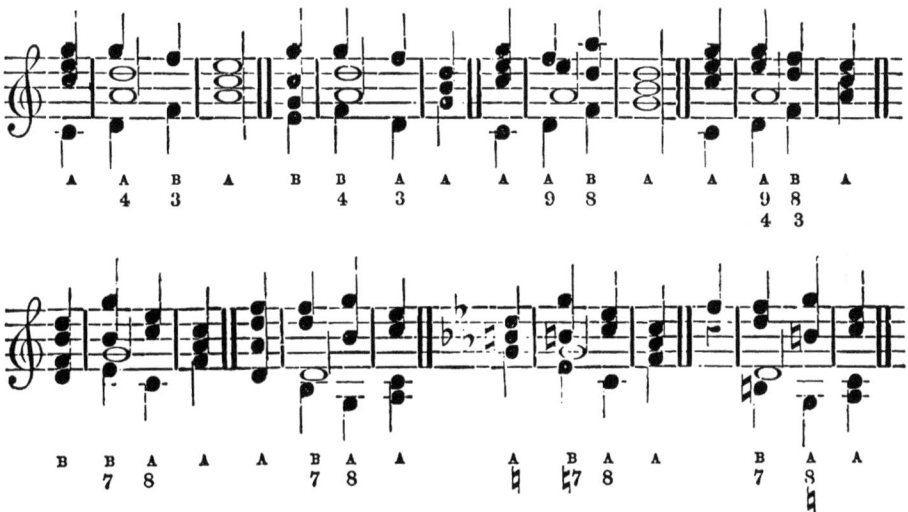

Two, and only two, exceptions from the same rule are: I. That the ninth in one chord may be resolved on the third of a chord whose root is a third below that of the suspended ninth. II. That the fourth in one chord may be resolved on the fifth of a chord whose root is a third below that of the suspended fourth; but this latter should be in the first inversion in order that the bass proceed not in similar motion to the fifth below the note that resolves the fourth.

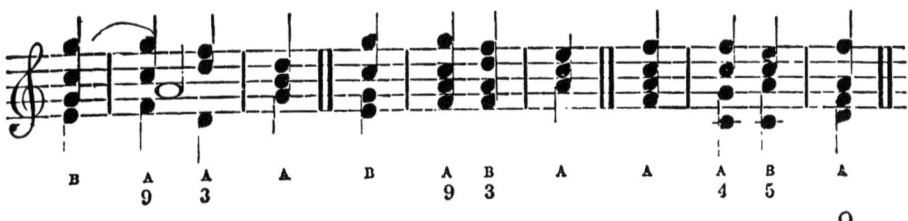

O

O.—CHAP. VIII., SECTS. 3 AND 9.

The editor differs from the author as to the third inversion of the chord of the seventh, and perceives strong distinction between this and the second inversion. In the second inversion, the fourth from the bass is the inverted root, and the bass is the fifth of the chord, both of which are concords; but they have an unsatisfactory effect because of the ambiguous character of the combination of the fourth. In the third inversion the bass is discordant and requires preparation and resolution; but not so the fourth, which is the third from the root. Nothing is ambiguous as to the consonance of the one and the dissonance of the other; and this justifies the employment of the third inversion in the diatonic style, examples of which may be found in the music of early masters. The bass being the seventh from the root is lettered D

and has the same treatment as if it were an upper part. Hence, though the chords of the seventh of the sub-dominant and the leading note are unavailable because the chords on which they should resolve are dissonant, the third inversion of those chords of the seventh can be used, because resolved on the first inversion of the subsequent chord; and the first inversion of those chords of the seventh also can be used if resolved on the third inversion of the chord of the seventh.

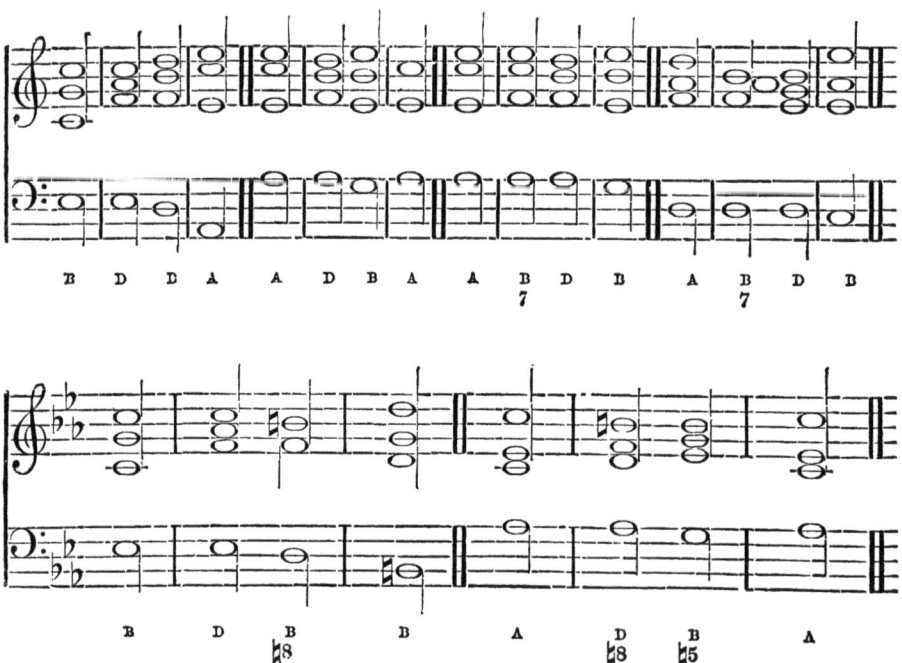

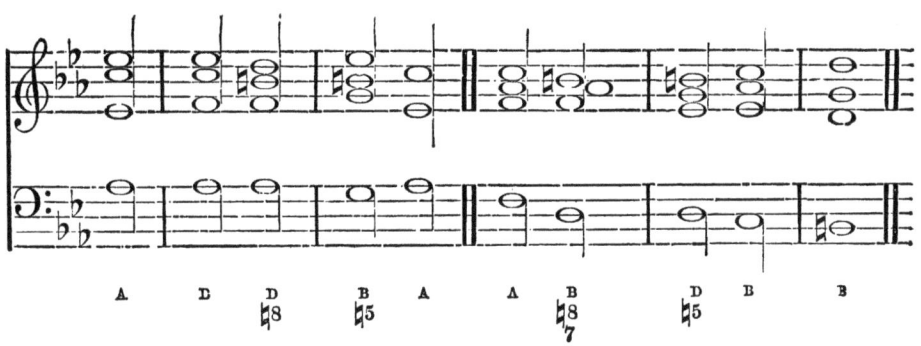

Admitting the availability of the minor seventh of a minor key (Appendix I.) as the bass of a first inversion, this note may prepare a seventh, and thus is obtained the third inversion of the chord of the seventh of the tonic.

P.—CHAP. VIII., SECT. 13.

If the last inversion of the chord of the seventh be accepted because of the discordance and the satisfactory preparation and resolution of the seventh in the bass, the third inversion of the chord of the ninth may be received on the same ground, when the context distinguishes it from a second inversion of the chord of the seventh, which consists of the same notes.

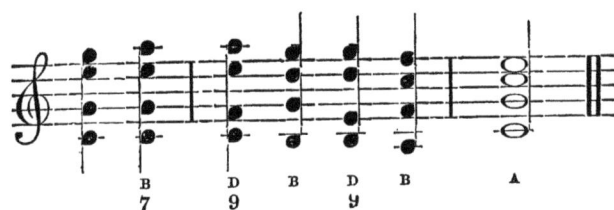

The fourth inversion of a chord of the ninth is wholly unavailable, because its resolution would be on an unallowable inversion of a chord.

Q.—CHAP. VIII., SECT. 19.

The rules for the use of the third inversion of chords of the seventh and of chords of the ninth and seventh, with consonant fifth or dissonant fifth, have been anticipated in O and P. The editor feels these inverted discords to be wholly accordant with the principles of the strict diatonic style, and their employment appropriate to compositions framed on these principles.

APPENDIX.

PART II.

R.—GENERAL INTRODUCTION.

THE term "fundamental chords" here signifies chords that consist of notes of the harmonic column naturally generated by a chosen root or fundamental note. The editor believes it to have been first used in this sense in the present work; but Rameau and Logier had earlier employed the word " fundamental" with a different meaning (Chap. XIII., sect. 4). The phrase "prepared by nature," in the last preceding sentence of the text, has given rise to objection on the ground that preparation means previously sounding. Let the word "generated" be substituted for "prepared," the fact will be beyond dispute, and the objection will fall.

S.—GENERAL INTRODUCTION.

With all regard for the author's reticence respecting the harmonic relationship to the key-note of every note available in fundamental chords, the editor offers the following table, which is an amplification of that in Appendix A, for the use of readers who may desire to verify the derivation of these chords, and of every note which each chord comprises. Every note, save one, of the chromatic scale is slightly variable: and when each is truthfully tuned the beauty of the chord to which it pertains with such intonation is greatly enhanced, and the effect of its minute ascent or descent to its resolution in the ensuing chord is a further beauty. Truthful and various intonation is obviously impracticable upon keyed instruments, and the chromatic scale of equal temperament has universal acceptance as a compromise; but the smallest gradations of pitch are possible, and are commonly practised, with voices and on bowed instruments. The notes in the table are all named, for convenience, as belonging to the key of C; but the numbers of the ratios are chosen for the sake of agreement with those in Appendix A, and refer only to the relative, not the positive, pitch of the several sounds.

C I. root of C, 5th of F, minor 3rd of A, and major 3rd of A♭	360
C II. 7th of D I.	356½
C III. 11th of G.	371¼
D♭ I. root of D♭	384
D♭ II. minor 9th of C	382½
D I. root of D major, 5th of G, and major 9th of C	405
D II. root of D minor	400
E♭ I. minor 3rd of C, and 5th of A♭	432
E♭ II. minor 9th of D, and minor 13th of G	430,$\frac{5}{16}$
E I. major 3rd of C, and 5th of A	450
E II. major 13th of G	438¾
E III. major 9th of D	455⅝
F I. root of F, major 3rd of D♭, and minor 3rd of D II.	480
F II. 7th of G	472½

F III. 11th of C	495
F♯, major 3rd of D	$506\frac{1}{4}$
G I. root of G, and 5th of C	540
G II. 11th of D.	$556\frac{7}{8}$
A♭ I. root of A♭, minor 3rd of F and 5th of D♭	576
A♭ II. minor 9th of G, and minor 13th of C	$573\frac{3}{4}$
A I. major 3rd of F, root of A minor, and 5th of D minor	600
A II. major 13th of C	585
A III.* 5th of D I., and 9th of G	$607\frac{1}{2}$
B♭ I. minor 3rd of G	648
B♭ II. minor 13th of D I.	$645\frac{15}{32}$
B♭ III. 7th of C	630
B I. major 3rd of G	675
B II. major 13th of D	$658\frac{1}{8}$

T.—General Introduction.

This sentence has by some been interpreted as denying the existence of the eleventh of the supertonic and that of the tonic; and thence has been argued the unavailability of the major and minor thirteenths of the same roots. The argument might be confuted were its basis valid; but the eleventh certainly exists in every harmonic column, though opportunities for its employment in harmonies generated by the two-named roots, occur, if ever, so rarely as to render rules for its treatment unnecessary. To prove the existence of the two elevenths in question, and to show the remote possibility of their occasional use, the editor appends to Chapter XX. some experimental progressions.

U.—Chap. XIII., Introduction.

In the first edition a paragraph follows in which all the diatonic and chromatic chords are shown to be formed of notes generated by the dominant, and the dominant itself to be generated by the tonic. According to equal temperament every note may be thus deduced; but the table in Appendix S defines the true pitch of every note and the varieties of each note, and states the several roots from which all varieties arise; and as this table supersedes the original view, the ensuing paragraph in the first edition is here omitted.

V.—Chap. XIII., Sect. 5.

The table in Appendix S shows the harmonic seventh to be less than minor, the harmonic eleventh to be more than perfect, and other intervals to be more minutely graduated than is represented by the conventional terms—perfect, major, minor, augmented, and diminished. Perplexity would arise from the employment of terms that would precisely define all the qualities of intervals, so the accepted terms are retained, which must be understood in a general, not positive, signification.

* Exceptionally (Part II., Chap. XIV., sect. 7) this note may be taken as the root or fundamental note of a harmonic column, when its major 3rd is in the ration of $\frac{5}{4}$, and its perfect 5th in that of $\frac{3}{2}$ being identical with the major 9th of D I.

W.—Chap. XIV., Sect. 4.

Similar motion by descending leap to the eighth of the bass when the bass moves a second is also allowable when such eighth is the fifth of a chord.

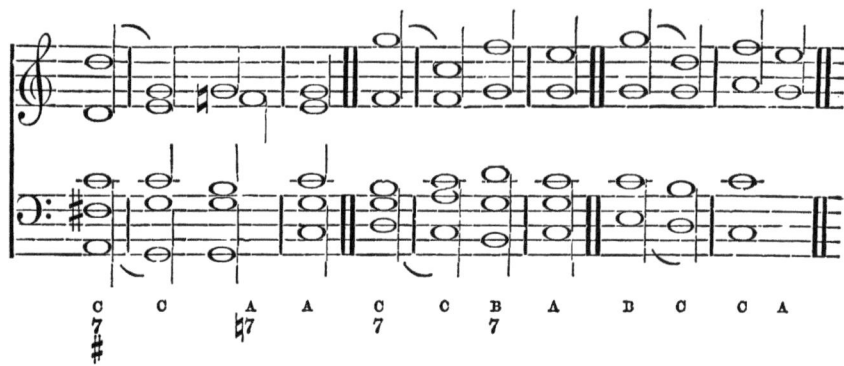

Best composers sometimes, though rarely, approach the eighth of the bass by upward leap in the top part when the bass rises to the dominant as a root, from the first inversion of any chromatic supertonic discord, bringing thus a phrase to a half-close; the precedent should scarcely be regarded as an example.

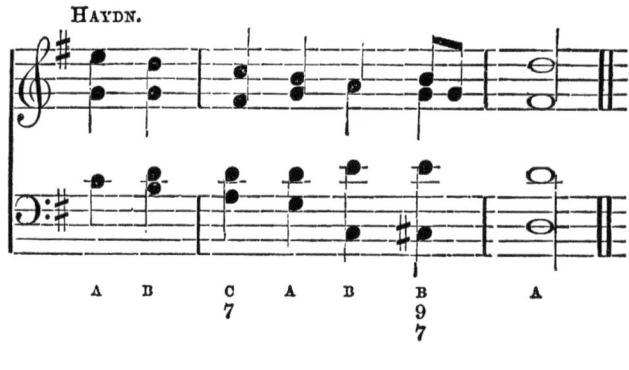

X.—Chap. XIV., Sect. 7.

Further exceptions from the rule against proceeding to an eighth by oblique motion from two notes next each other in alphabetical order are: when a fundamental minor or major ninth is resolved on the root of the same chord;

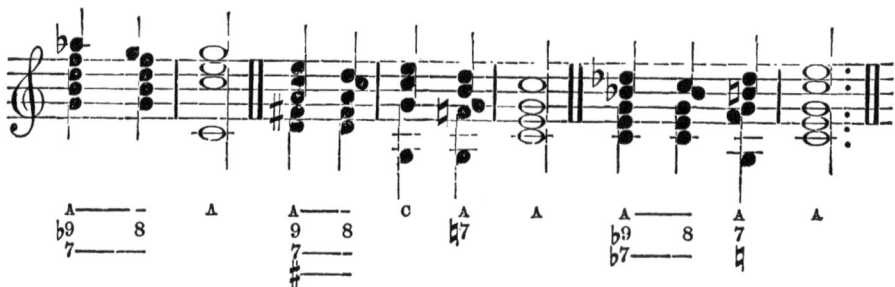

and also when a thirteenth in the bass remains to be the third in the ensuing chord, and the fifth or seventh, or both, of the former chord proceed to the doubled third of the latter chord.

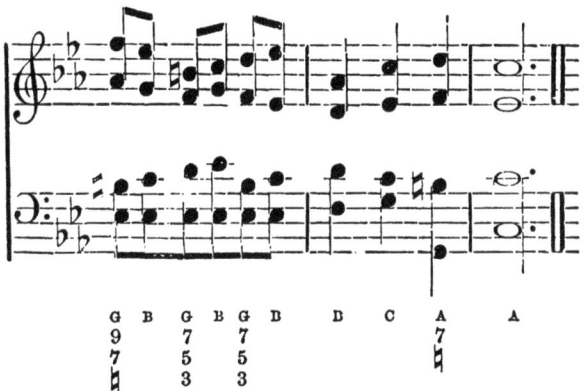

G B G B G B   D   C   A   A
9   7   7   7
7   5   5
♮   3   3

The same exceptions with regard to suspension (Chap. VII.), and passing notes (Chap. IX.), avail in the free style as in the strict.

Y.—CHAP. XIV., SECTS. 9 AND 12.

The reasoning against consecutive fifths in Chap. III., sect. 10, is confirmed by the series of rules here given for the exceptional use of the hitherto forbidden progression. The table in Appendix S shows the fifth of the subdominant in relation to that of the tonic to be perfect, as also that of the tonic in relation to that of the dominant, and likewise that of the dominant in relation to that of the chromatic chords of the supertonic. These three pairs of fifths are each thus proved to be comprised in one key, and hence the alleged passage from any key to another is not implied in their consecution. The same argument justifies the consecution of the fifths of the minor second of the key and the tonic, and also the fifths of the minor sixth of the key and the dominant; but while the allowability of these is indisputable, students are earnestly enjoined to employ them, if ever, most sparingly.

Z.—CHAP. XIV., SECT. 13.

Fourths with the bass are allowable likewise when the second fourth is an accented passing note.

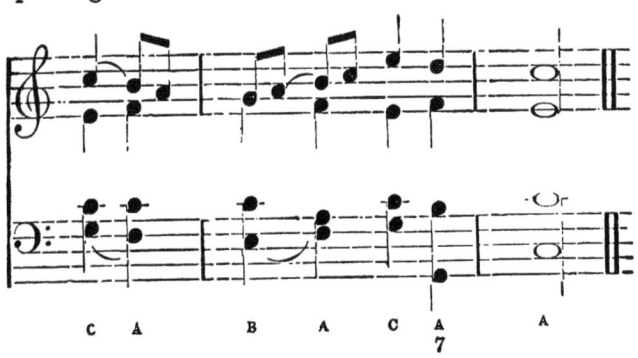

C   A   B   A   C   A   A
                                 7

AA.—Chap. XIV., Sect. 19.

An eighth may not descend to a seventh or second when one part moves a third and the other a second;

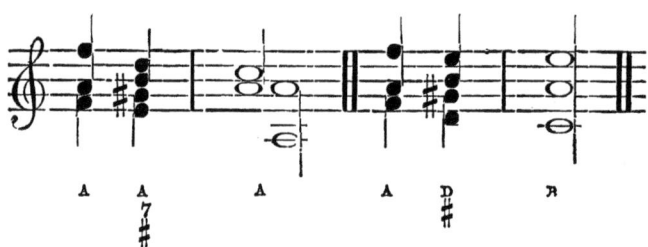

but an eighth may ascend to a seventh or second, when one part moves a second and the other a third.

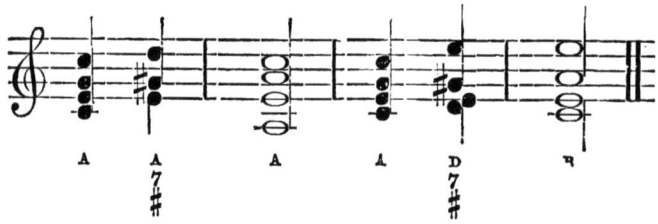

It is not allowable for the bass to descend by leap to a discordant note,

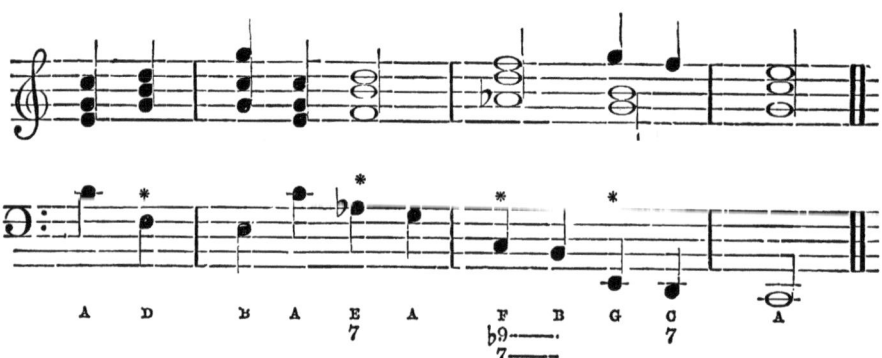

but it may descend by second or by chromatic semitone, or may ascend by leap to a discordant note.

BB.—Chap. XV., Sect. 1.

In the free style it is not false relation when two notes of different quality are sounded together, if one be a harmony-note and the other a passing note treated according to the rules in Chap. XXV.

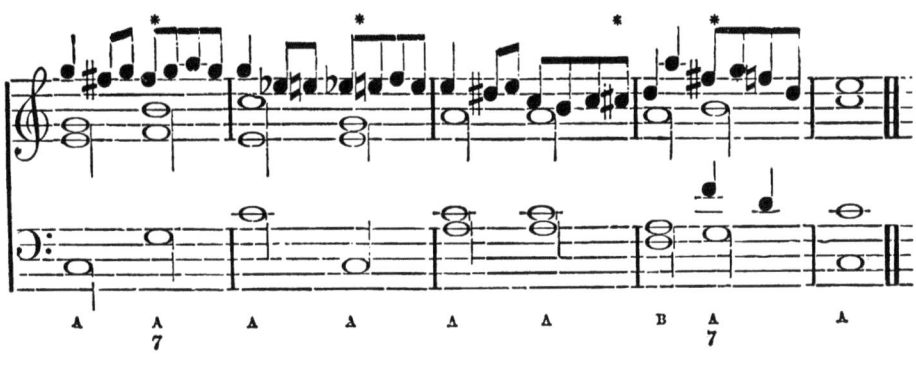

CC.—CHAP. XVI., SECT. 2.

The availability of the major chord of the tonic in a minor key is shown in Chap. IV., sect. 8. The minor chord of the tonic is allowable in a major key, provided that in one part its third proceed from the major third of the same root.

DD.—CHAP. XVI., SECT. 3.

Composers of the first half of the eighteenth century employed a major chord of the subdominant in a minor key when the melody of any part proceeded by seconds from the dominant to the leading note. However presumptuous to oppose a precept to the example of the greatest of those musicians, the undesirability must be urged of such progressions as the following :—

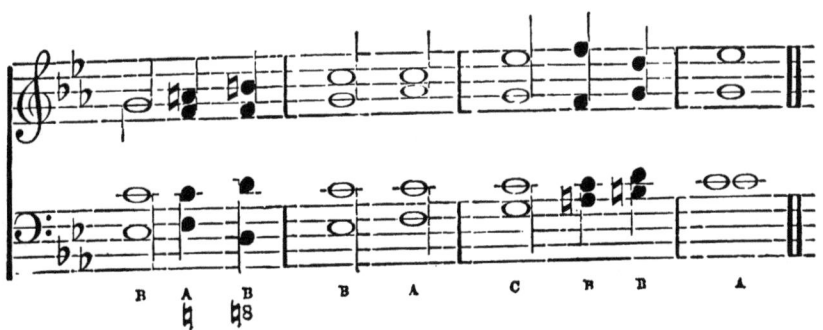

EE.—Chap. XVI., Sect. 8.

The first inversion of a diminished triad, with the subdominant for bass, ranks among the diatonic concords in a minor key. It may be taken as a chromatic concord in a major key.

Its derivation is explained in Chap. XIX., sect. 27.

FF.—Chap. XVII., Sect. 2.

In the second inversions of the chords of the tonic, subdominant, and dominant, the suspended fourth or ninth from the root may be taken. These must be prepared, suspended, and resolved according to the rules in Chap. VII.

GG.—Chap. XVII., Sect. 4.

The first instance in Ex. 1 and that in Ex. 2 show an exception from the rule that the chord of the tonic cannot follow that of the supertonic (Chap. IV., sect. 15.) When the chord of the tonic is in the second inversion it may be preceded by the chord of the supertonic, which may be direct as in the two examples, or may be in its first inversion.

HH.—Chap. XVII., Sect. 4.

It is also allowable to leap to the bass of a second inversion from the third inversion of a chord of the fundamental ninth, as explained in App. NN, PP, QQ, and Chap. XXI., sect. 24.

II.—Chap. XVII., Sect. 7.

If a chord in the second inversion be preceded by another chord on the same bass, that in the second inversion need not be on the strong accent.

JJ.—Chap. XVII., Sect. 10.

The editor ventures to differ from the author as to the disallowance of the second inversions of the concords of the minor second and the minor sixth of the key. Helmholtz assumes the chord of the minor sixth to be the source of the minor common chord of the tonic, the fifth in which latter is a secondary harmonic of the minor sixth, and this bears upon Day's original theory of the derivation of the chords of the augmented sixth (Chap. XXII.). By the same reasoning, the minor second is the source of the minor chord of the subdominant, and the minor sixth is generated by the minor second. Admitting, as the author does, the inclusion of the concords of the minor second and the minor sixth and the first inversion of each, among the available harmonies of a key, and tracing other harmonies to them, as above, there seems to be no reason against the acceptance of their second inversions. Handel and Mozart have employed the second inversion of the concord of the minor second with beautiful effect, and its use may be found, though rarely, in the writings of other musicians; it is not more their example, however, than the theoretical principle that appears to justify the admission of the chord, and the same principle applies to the second inversion of the chord of the minor sixth.

KK.—CHAP. XVIII., SECT. 5.

Fundamental chords of the seventh differ from the chords of the prepared seventh in the diatonic style, insomuch as their second inversion is available. This is because, in the modern style, the consonance of the inverted fifth is fully recognised, and its unlikeness in character and treatment to the suspended fourth, to the last inversion of the suspended ninth, and to the third inversion of chords of the prepared seventh and of the prepared ninth is established. When, in the second inversion of a fundamental chord of the seventh, the root is omitted, the incomplete chord is no longer a dissonance, because it comprises no two notes next each other in alphabetical order, and no diminished or augmented interval from the bass. In the strict style this chord is described as the first inversion of the diminished triad of the leading note (Chap. IV., sect. 17)—a fictitious assumption of course, because the diminished triad ranks not among concords; but the assumption is justifiable because the combination is treated in every respect as a first inversion. In the free style, when the root is omitted from the combination, the chord is exempt from the treatment due to a discord, and is only restricted as to the non-duplication and as to the progression of its third. Until the middle of the eighteenth century, although composers used freely the fundamental chord of the dominant seventh, used frequently that of the supertonic seventh, and used rarely that of the tonic seventh, as also the first and third inversions of all these three chords, a complete chord of the fundamental seventh in the second inversion occurs so very seldom in the music before that period as to compel the supposition that its employment was accidental rather than designed; the reason of the seemingly careful avoidance of the root by those composers may have been that the bugbear of the dissonant fourth was not yet exorcised, and that having no precept for its employment as a consonant interval they wrote no examples. The insertion of the fourth from the bass (the inverted root) in these chords, which establishes their dissonance and compels their resolution, may be regarded as marking a new epoch in musical history, and the omission of the said fourth is desiderated in music that may now be written in emulation of the earlier style.

LL.—CHAP. XVIII., SECT. 15.

This progression of the third is exceptional. When employed, the progression of the fifth (in the chord of the seventh) to that note in the chord of resolution to which the third would usually have proceeded is most desirable.

MM.—CHAP. XVIII., SECT. 16.

This progression includes the resolution of the seventh on a minor or major thirteenth from the same root, which latter discord is then resolved as though no seventh had preceded it.

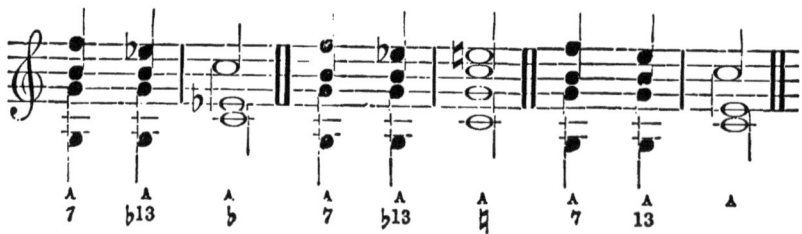

NN.—Chap. XVIII., Sect. 18.

This progression of the seventh is a parallel to that of the third described in Sect. 15, and like that is exceptional. When employed, the progression of the fifth (in the chord of the seventh) to that note in the chord of resolution to which the seventh would usually have proceeded is most desirable.

When the seventh is a note in the chord of resolution, if the fifth in the chord of the seventh leap to that note in the ensuing chord which was the seventh in the former, the progression of the seventh is free, provided it proceed not in similar motion to the eighth of the note to which the root of the chord proceeds.

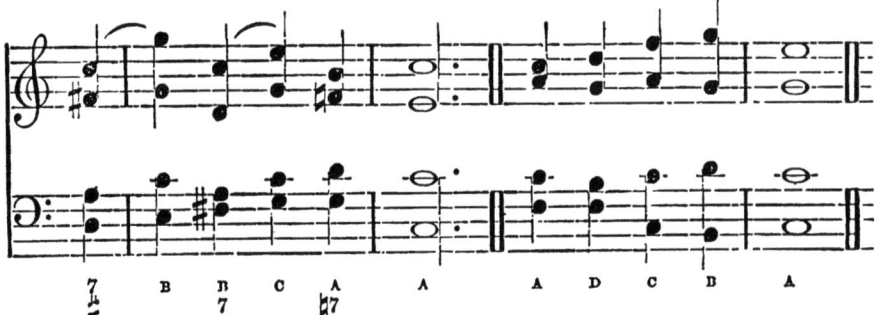

The last instance in the above example shows an exception from the rule against leaping to the bass of a chord in the second inversion from the inversion of another chord (Chap. XVII., sect. 4, App. HH and PP).

OO.—Chap. XIX., Sect. 23.

The minor ninth of any of the three available roots may resolve on the major ninth of the same; and this major ninth has then the same treatment that it would have had if the minor ninth had not preceded it:

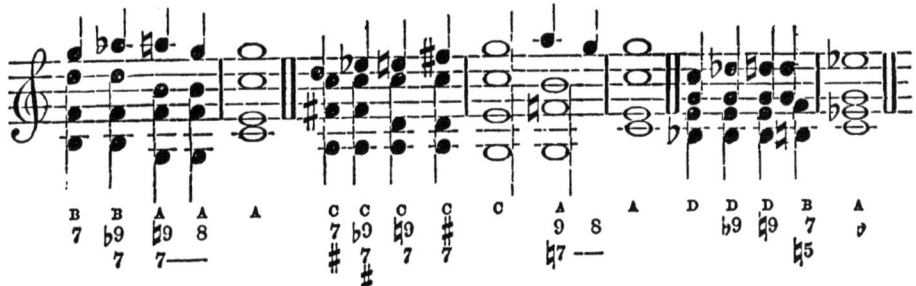

The major ninth may resolve on the minor ninth, and this minor ninth has then the same treatment that it would have had if the major ninth had not preceded it:

PP.—Chap. XIX., Sect. 27.

In the third inversion the bass may skip a fourth downwards to the root of the tonic chord, when the fifth of the dominant must rise to the third of the tonic:

or the bass may skip a fourth downwards to the fifth of the subdominant, when the fifth of the dominant must rise to the root of the subdominant:

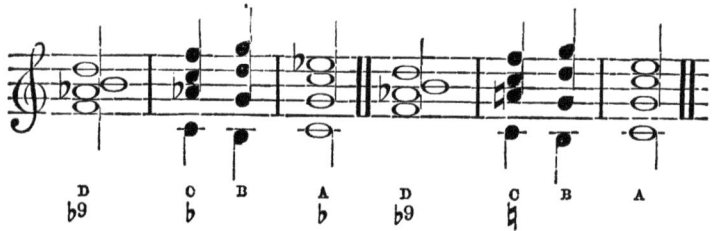

this being an exception (App. HH.) from the rule against skipping from an inverted chord to the bass of a second inversion.

QQ.—Chap. XIX., Sect. 31.

The rule in App. PP applies also to the chord of the supertonic minor ninth.

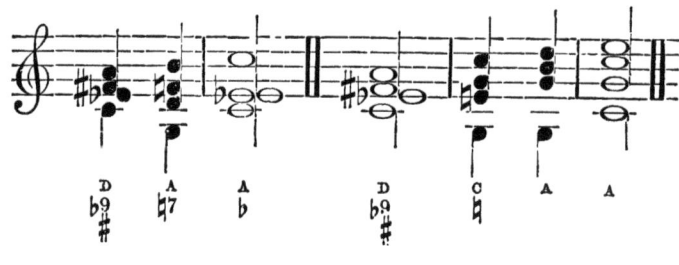

RR.—Chap. XX. Sects. 19 and 33.

Imperception of the radical derivation of the chord and of the resolution here given, has led eminent composers to a treatment of the harmony which breaks established rules, and seems to the editor unsatisfactory:

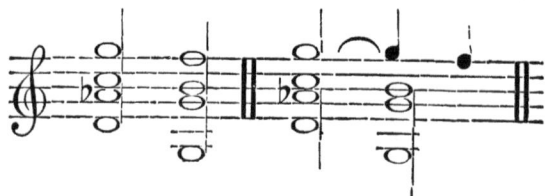

The assumption that G is the suspended fourth of D is untenable, because, as such, it must resolve on the third of D, and not on the seventh of G, and its remaining to be the root of G equally disproves it to be a suspension over D. The assumption that C is the direct seventh of D compels its normal resolution on the third of G, and this precludes the progression of A to B, because the leading-note may not be doubled. The A, if natural, may not proceed to D in perfect fifths with the bass, and, if flat, will produce an effect little less bad in progressing to this note; the consequence is either that A G proceed in sevenths below G F, or else that A is resolved on G, while G remains, both of which are forbidden by rules that are beyond dispute. The view that the inverted eleventh may rise to the fifth when the major or minor ninth is resolved on the third, and when the root proceeds to the seventh seems clearly to account for the combination and its progression, and a fully satisfactory, nay, beautiful effect is the result:

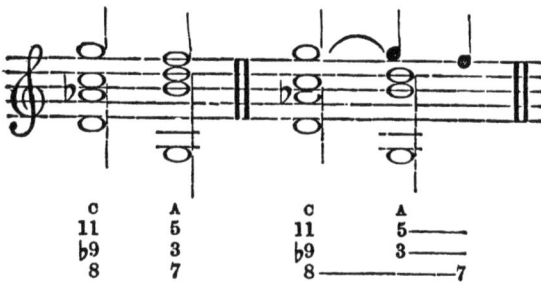

In each of these examples A may be flat or natural.

SS.—Chap. XX., Sect. 34.

The following examples, which are the result of experience subsequent to the author's death, are offered to prove that the use of the eleventh of the supertonic and of the eleventh of the tonic is possible, as being compatible with the key, but not to show the desirability of such use. Like the first instance in the example, every other is equally available in minor as in major keys.

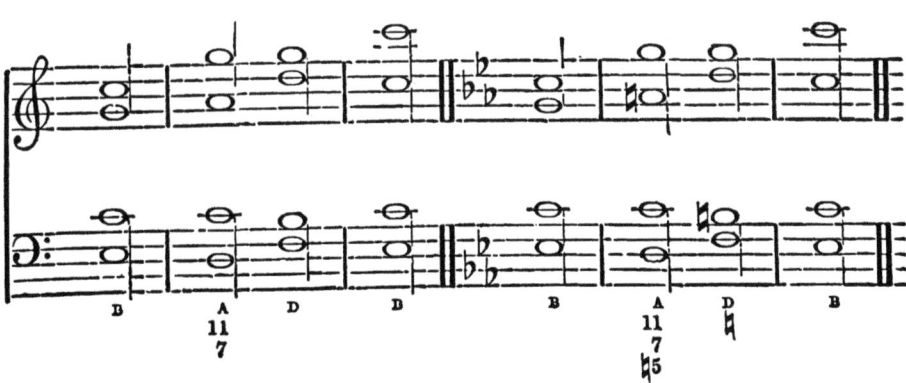

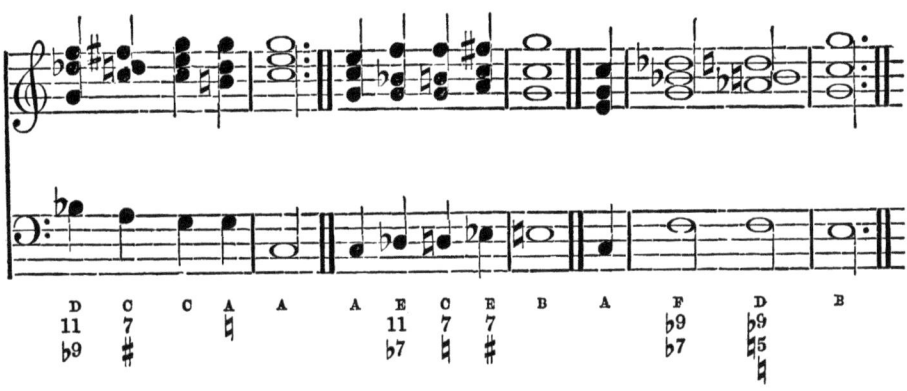

TT.—CHAP. XXI., SECT. 1 AND SECT. 29.

When a minor thirteenth is accompanied with a seventh it is desirable that the thirteenth be assigned to a higher part than the seventh, unless some peculiar effect be intended, or unless some special vocal or instrumental distribution give extraordinary prominence to the under part which bears the thirteenth. This injunction applies equally to a major thirteenth with a seventh.

UU.—CHAP. XXI., SECT. 3.

Prolonged experience convinces the editor that the minor thirteenth of the supertonic is not insusceptible of resolution on a chord derived from the same root. It may proceed to the fifth, or the seventh, or the major thirteenth.

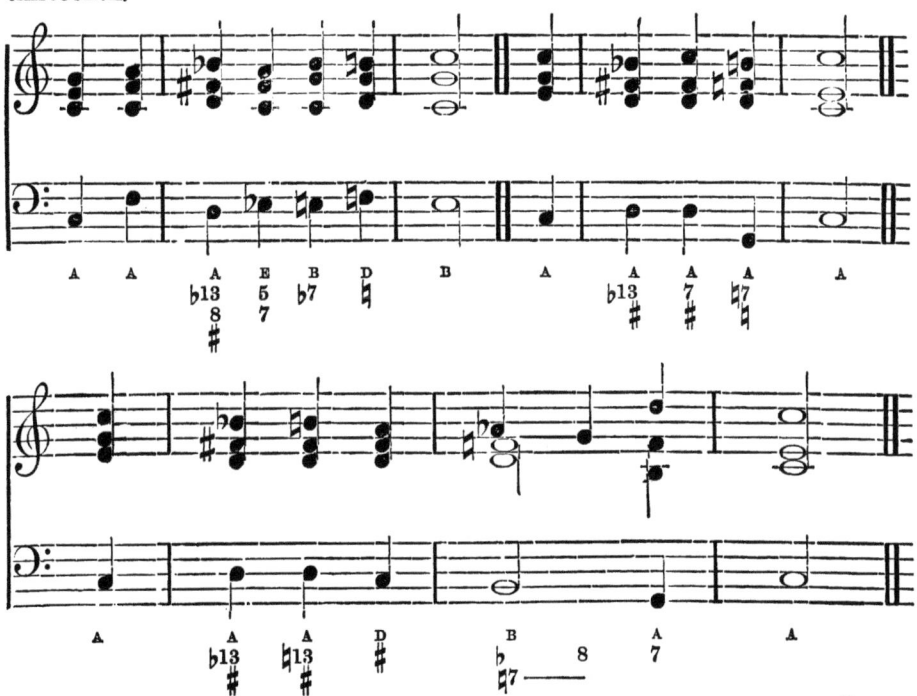

P

VV.—Chap. XXI., Sect. 3.

It may be accompanied with the root and third only; but then, when the thirteenth is resolved upon the fifth, some other note of the chord must proceed to the seventh.

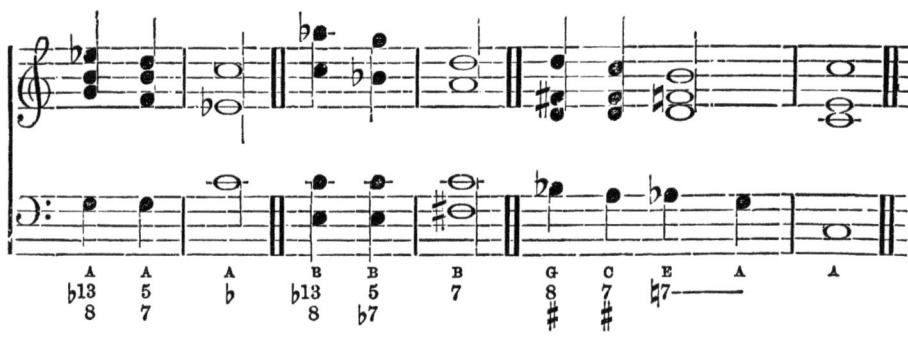

WW.—Foot-note to Chap. XXI., Sect. 16.

The minor thirteenth of the dominant, in the key of C, when written as an augmented fifth, and accompanied with the third, resembles in appearance, and to some extent in treatment, the diatonic discord of the augmented fifth of the mediant in the key of E minor (Chap. VIII., sects. 17, 18, 19). It differs from this chord in the restricted treatment of its third, and in the non-preparation of its apparent fifth, as is shown in the next two examples.

The minor thirteenth further differs from the augmented fifth, in that the latter may be accompanied with the major seventh and the former with the minor seventh.

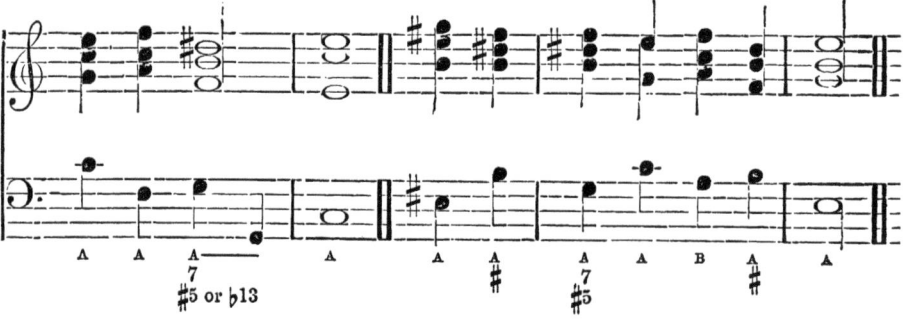

Again it differs from it, in that, if the latter be accompanied with the ninth, such ninth must be major; but the ninth with the former may be minor or major.

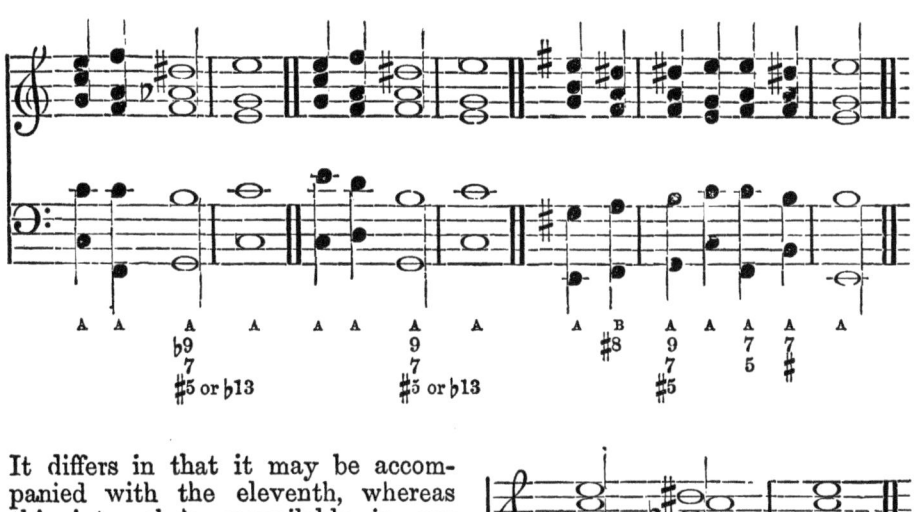

It differs in that it may be accompanied with the eleventh, whereas this interval is unavailable in any chord peculiar to the diatonic or strict style; and, again, it differs as to the passing-note that may be taken below it, which must be a tone from the augmented fifth, but a semitone from the minor thirteenth.

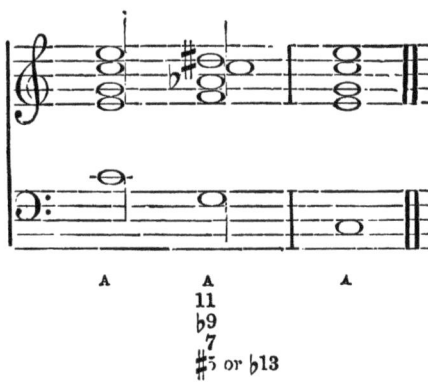

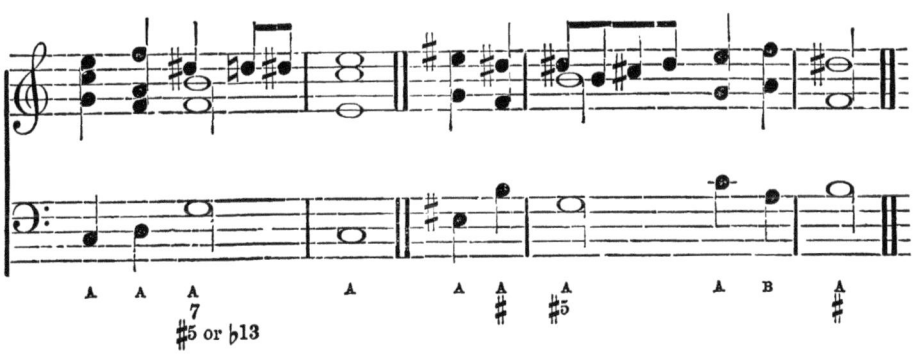

The above examples might be largely multiplied, but they should be sufficient to convince unprejudiced readers of the difference between the two chords, and the impropriety of disguising the minor thirteenth in the notation of an augmented fifth, although sometimes, in the less complete forms of its accompaniments, so to misname it may be expedient. That the two chords are in different keys, accounts for their different notation and effect.

XX.—Chap. XXI., Sect. 28.

With the third in the bass any major thirteenth, if accompanied with only the doubled root, is a discord to be resolved on the fifth while the root proceeds to the seventh. The intervals from the bass are the same as in the second inversion of a concord, but the second inversion is unavailable in any of the three instances: the first inversion of a major thirteenth is distinguished from any second inversion by its needing resolution, which the second inversion of a concord does not.

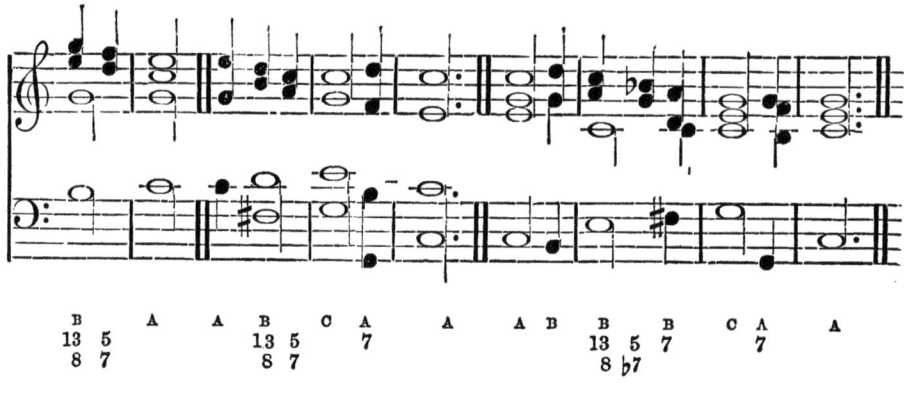

YY.—Chap. XXI., Sect. 61.

An exception must be made from the rule in Sect. 25, that "the major thirteenth of dominant and supertonic belong exclusively to the major key," and the statement of this exception has been reserved till the end of the chapter in order that it may have any clearness that may result from the reader's knowledge of other forms of resolving the major thirteenth. The major thirteenth of both dominant and tonic, accompanied with the third, fifth, and minor ninth, is available in a minor key if it descend a chromatic semitone to a note of the ensuing chord, which note may be the minor thirteenth of the same root or the minor ninth of the fifth above its root, or the minor third of the fourth above its root, the last being the least rare resolution. The chord may be employed in any of its inversions, but it is here exemplified in the sixth inversion as the one in which it is heard with best effect.

The freedom of the fifth in each of these chords of the thirteenth (D when G is the root, and G when C is the root) proves that, though it be a seventh from the bass, it is a concord in the harmony.

ZZ.—Chap. XXII., Introduction.

The derivation here given of the interval of the augmented sixth, and of its variable accompaniment, the editor believes to have been an entirely original conception of the author, which was made public in the first edition of the present work. While, for the sake of convenience, upholding the author's terminology of primary and secondary roots and primary and secondary harmonics, the editor suggests that each augmented sixth is wholly generated by its primary root, of which the primary ninth is the seventeenth harmonic, and the secondary third is the fifteenth harmonic, whose octave (the thirtieth harmonic) is the augmented sixth above the seventh harmonic. Thus regarded, the dominant and the tonic respectively are the roots of the chords of the augmented sixth of the minor sixth and the minor second of the key. These two chords comprise the only instances of the interval of the augmented sixth that appear in the chromatic scale of any key.

AAA.—Chap. XXII., Sect. 5.

The excessive harshness of the combination of the diminished third may be assigned as a practical, if not a scientific, reason for its most rare employment. The author's words "should not," applied to the use of the inversion of the interval of the augmented sixth, must be received as recommendatory rather than imperative, since instances by Weldon, Bach, and Mendelssohn prove that in extreme cases, to embody a quite extraordinary expression, the chord (so to speak) of the diminished third can be used with beautiful effect—beautiful, perhaps, because of its appropriate discordance, and because of its very seldom occurrence.

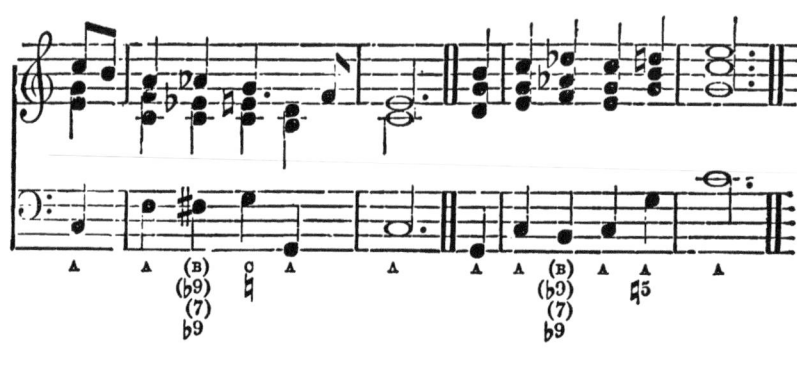

BBB.—Chap. XXII., Sect. 16.

The primary root of a chord of the augmented sixth has been used as a bass, and theory here justifies example, but the author's qualifying "should not," in Sect. 5, may emphatically be applied to the frequent employment of this form of the chord.

CCC.—Chap. XXIII., Sect. 1.

The suspension of any fundamental chord over the root or third of the ensuing chord has this important difference from diatonic suspensions: that any dissonant note may be prepared in one part and suspended in another, instead of being held or repeated in the part which prepares it.

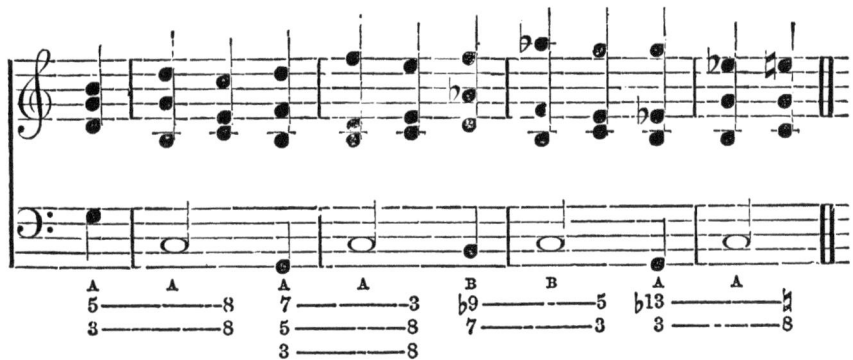

An extension of this rule is stated in Chap. XXIII., sect. 4, which shows that notes peculiar to the preparatory chord may be inserted in the suspension, though they be not included in the preparation. The word "suspension" thus applied is literally a misnomer, but the treatment of notes to which it refers is so analogous to that of diatonic suspensions that its present use may be accepted to avoid the multiplication of terms, and to direct attention to the likeness and the unlikeness of a fundamental chord over a foreign bass note, to the diatonic suspension of a complete chord.

DDD.—Chap. XXV., Sect. 3.

The author omitted to state, though his examples abundantly show, that free passing notes differ from strict as they may be either chromatic or diatonic. It is necessary for completeness further to state that a passing note to be resolved upward on the root or fifth of a chord, whether approached by leap or descent of a second, should be at a semitone from its resolution, whereas if resolved upward on the third it may be at a tone or a semitone from its resolution, and the tone below the third of a chord is often preferable; the passing note to be resolved on a fundamental seventh is better at a semitone than a tone below its resolution. The whole of this rule applies to free passages formed upon Chap, IX., sect. 6.

Comparison of the foregoing with the ensuing example shows the urgency of the rule.

A seeming exception from the above is that the note to be resolved on the fifth of a fundamental discord may be at a tone below it; but this is not truly an exception, because the said note, being the eleventh from the root, is essential in the harmony, and so not a passing note.

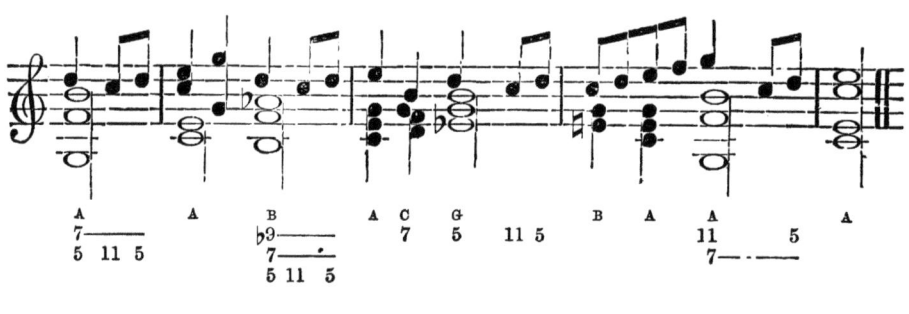

EEE.—CHAP. XXV., SECT. 18.

If two or more parts proceed simultaneously in passing notes they may not induce harmonies that are inadmissible in the prevailing key. Hence none of the combinations marked + in Ex. 1 may be used, nor might they be

Ex. 1.

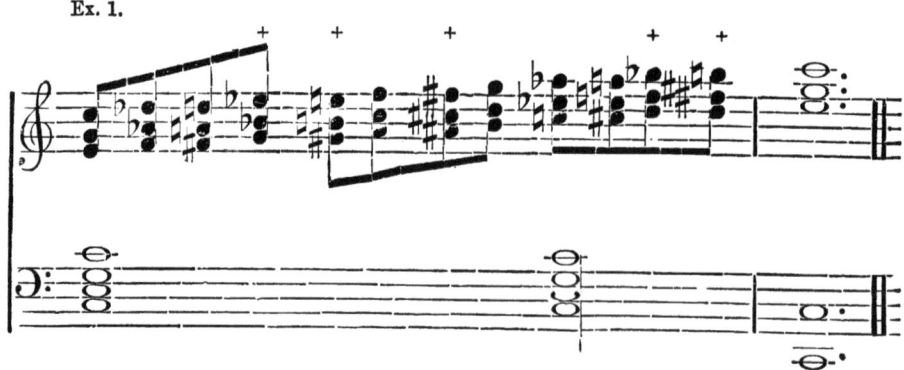

used if noted according to the chromatic scale of the key; whereas all those in Ex. 2 are available.

Ex. 2.

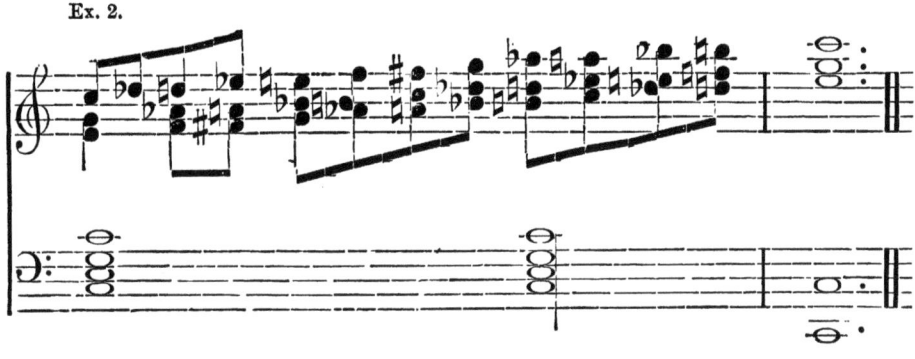

FFF.—Chap. XXV., Sect. 28.

As tending to the completion of rules for passing notes in the free style the reader is referred to "Counterpoint: a Course of Practical Study," Sects. 352 and 353, by the editor.

GGG.—Chap. XXVI., Sect. 3.

A pedal may only be quitted when it is an essential note of the harmony As an essential note of the harmony it may be consonant or dissonant, and in either case it must be treated as the note would be were it not previously sounded as a pedal. Hence it may be quitted when it is a root or any other note of a chord.

HHH.—Chap. XXVI., Sect. 7.

Examples by Mozart and Beethoven prove that the availability of the submediant as a root of fundamental discords is extensible not only to a dominant pedal but even to a tonic pedal, with as much the necessity in the one instance as in the other of its being succeeded by a harmony that comprises the subdominant and not the augmented fourth of the key. The affinity between the minor key of the supertonic and the major key of the tonic is so strong as to give that key a far better right to be styled the "relative minor" of the major key at a tone below it than has the minor key of the submediant, which has little but its ambiguous identity of signature to connect it with the major key at the sixth below it. The close intimacy of the first-named keys is indicated in the first of the following examples; is declared in the second, where the dominant pedal seems to enchain them; and is established in the third, where the tonic pedal shows that there is no departure from the primary key. Note well that no effect of false relation is in the third example. It may not be too much to assume that the seeming chord of D in each of the three examples is truly the chord of the major ninth, seventh, and fifth of G, which ninth may be resolved upon the third, or root, or minor ninth of the dominant, or may remain to be the fifth in a chromatic chord of the supertonic. The use of fundamental chords derived from the submediant is limited to major keys. The natural transformation of these examples from C to C minor and its surroundings will substitute the chords of A♭ and D♭ (which are both comprehended in the key of C minor) for those of A major and D minor.

III.—Chap. XXVII., Sect. 4.

Every fundamental chord of the seventh, or its inversions, may belong to the three major or minor keys of which its root is the dominant, supertonic, or tonic.

Every incomplete second inversion of a fundamental chord of the seventh which has been described as the first inversion of a diminished triad (Chap XVIII., sect. 5), may be interchanged with the incomplete third inversion of the fundamental minor ninth, which also has been described as the first inversion of a diminished triad (Chap. XIX., sect. 27), whose root is at a minor third below the root of the chord of the seventh.

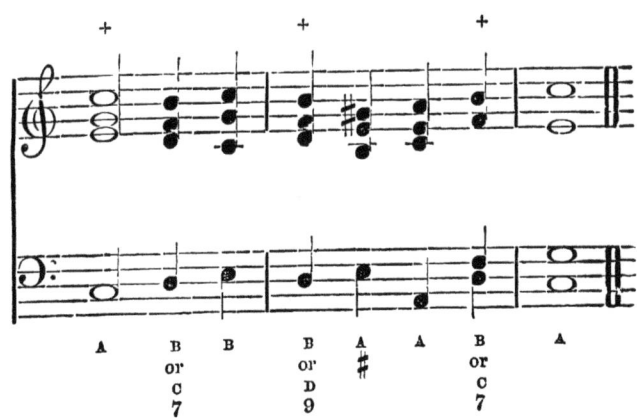

JJJ.—Chap. XXVII., Sect. 5.

Every chord of the major ninth, or its inversions, may belong to the three major keys of which its root is the dominant, supertonic or tonic, or to the minor key of which its root is the tonic.

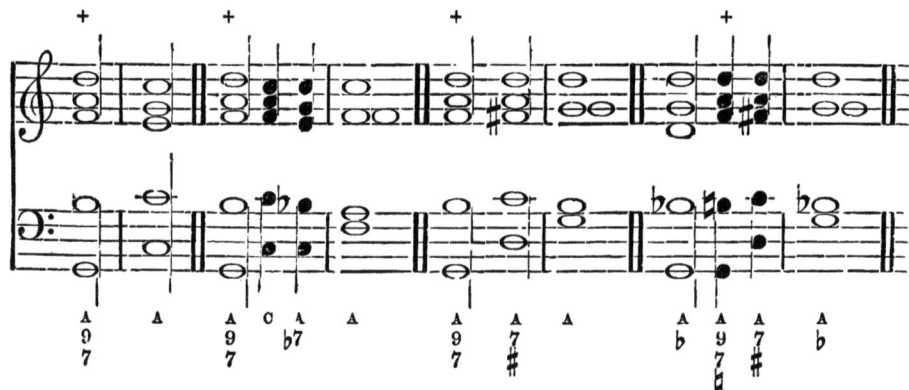

Every inversion of any chord of the major ninth may be interchanged with an inversion of the chord of the eleventh with major ninth whose root is at a minor third below that of the chord of the major ninth, provided the roots of both chords be omitted.

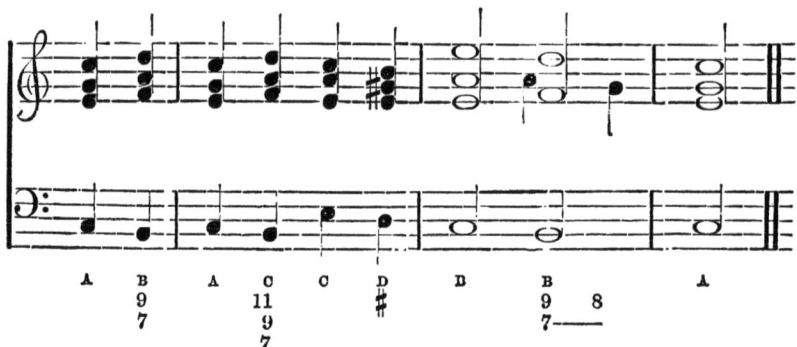

Every chord of the minor thirteenth may belong to the three major or three minor keys of which its root is the dominant, supertonic or tonic.

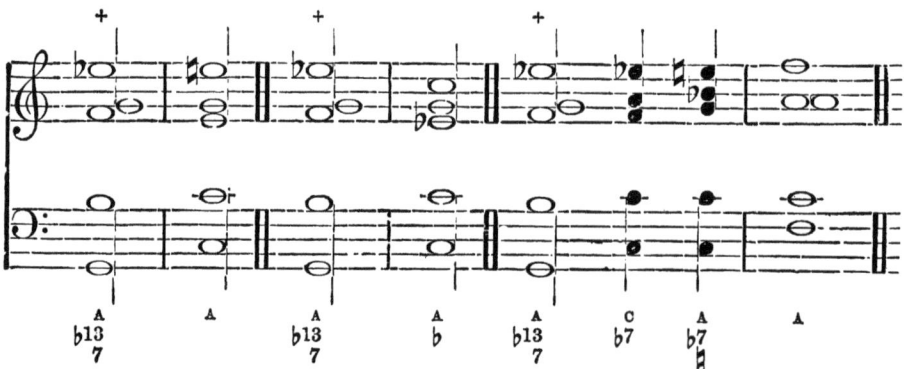

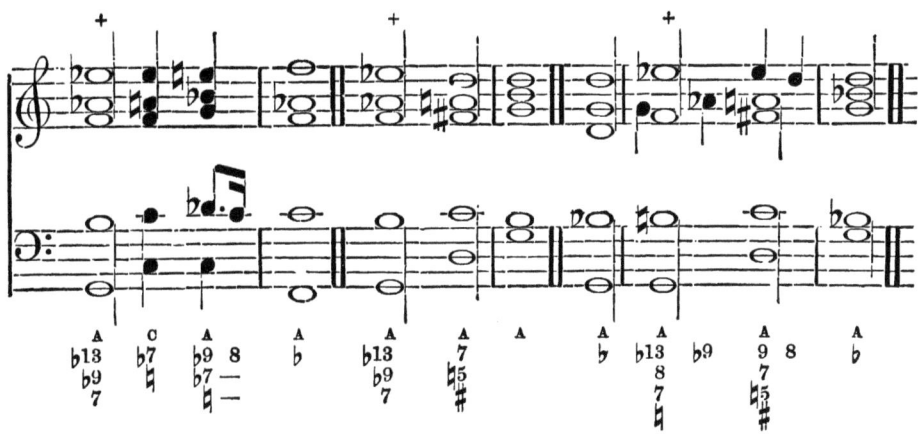

Every chord of the minor thirteenth with only the third and root may, by enharmonic change, be written in three different ways, therefore every chord of the minor thirteenth and third may resolve into nine major and nine minor keys.

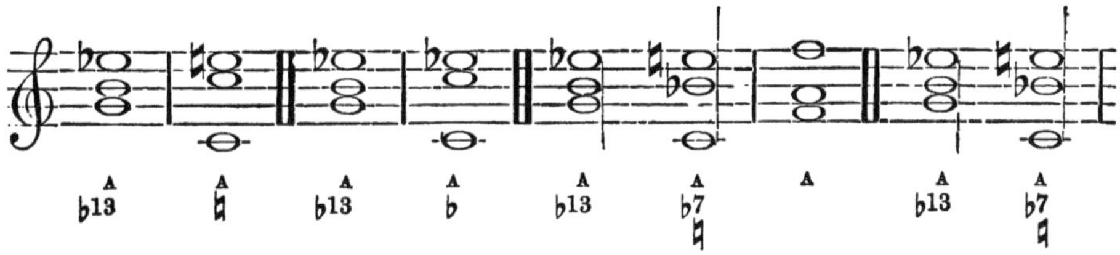

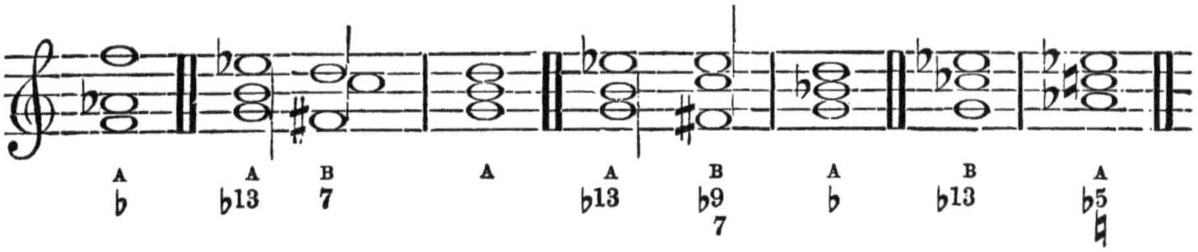

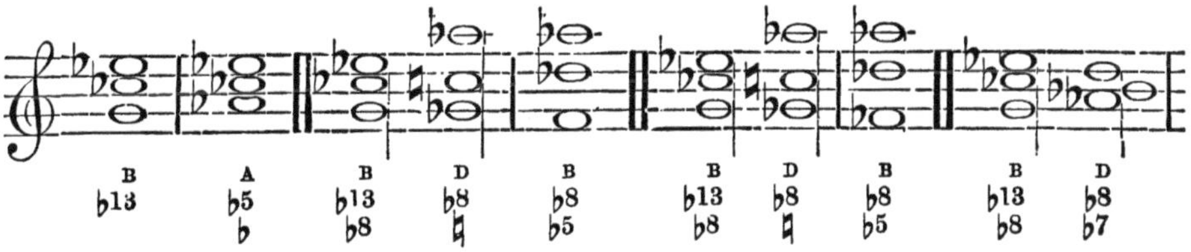

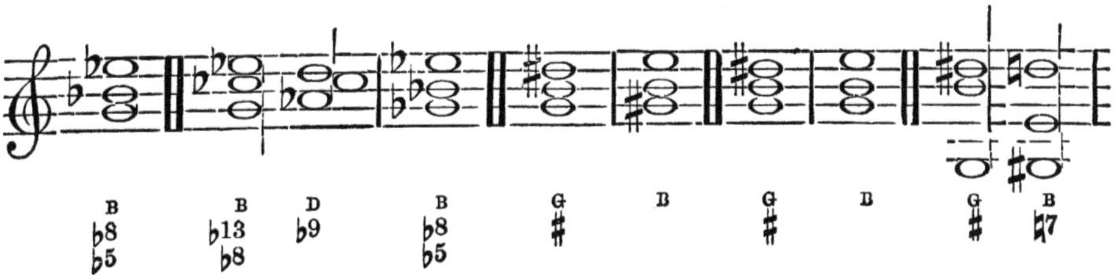

Every chord of the major thirteenth may belong to the three major keys of which the root is the dominant, supertonic, or tonic, or the minor key of which the root is the supertonic.

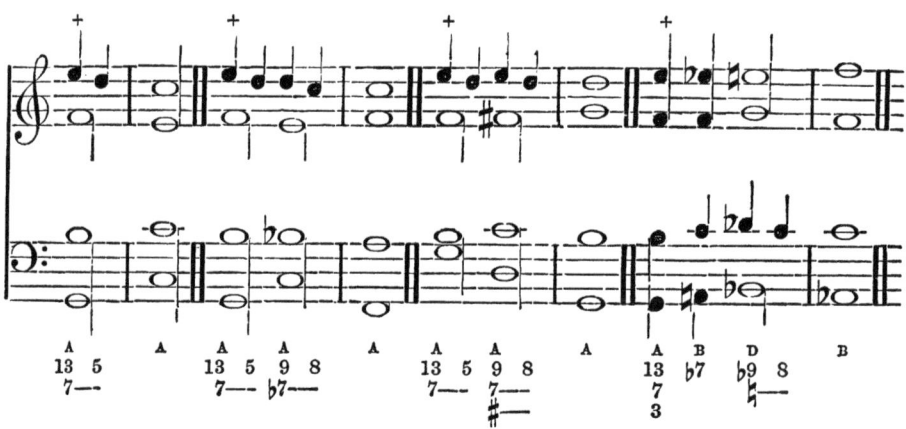

Every chord of the augmented sixth, however accompanied, may belong to the major or minor key of which its primary root is either the dominant or the tonic.

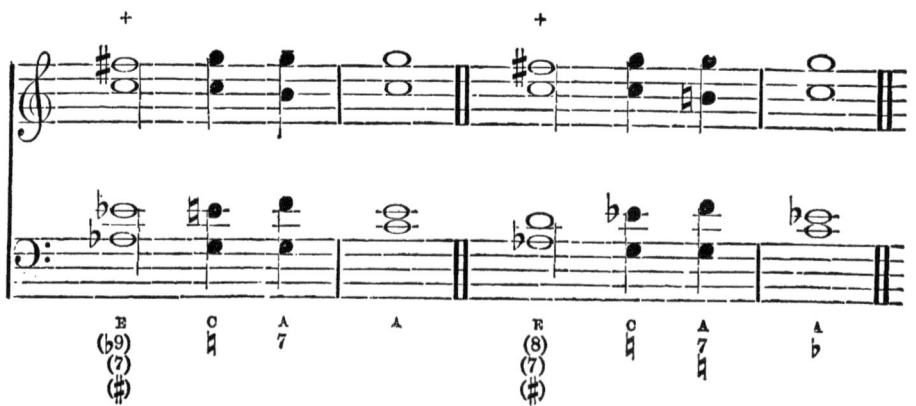

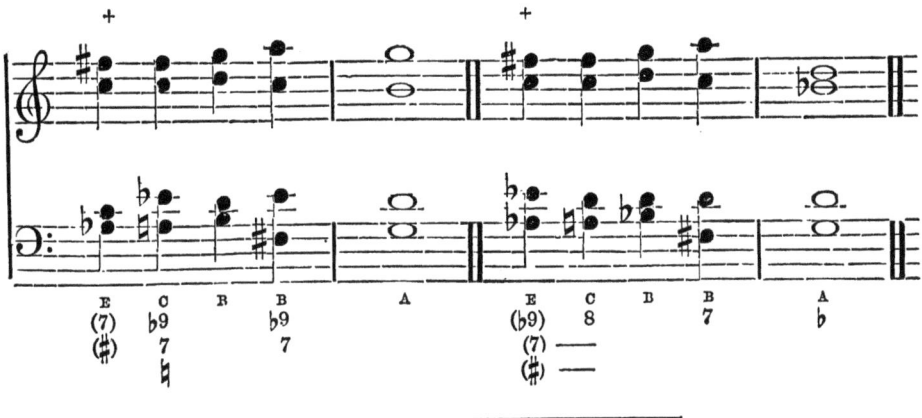

POSTSCRIPT.

Further additions are desirable to Chapters XVI. and XXIV., which are here made together because bearing on each other.

Analogous to the use of the major third of the subdominant in the minor key (Chap. XVI., sect. 3) is the permissible use of the major third of the tonic in a minor key, under the same conditions as the other, viz., that it be approached and quitted by descending semitone.

Besides the suspension of the ninth over the root of the minor second of the key (Chap. XXIV., sects. 2 and 4), the diatonic ninth may be suspended over the major chord of the subdominant or that of the tonic, and resolved on the root when the major third proceeds to the minor third.

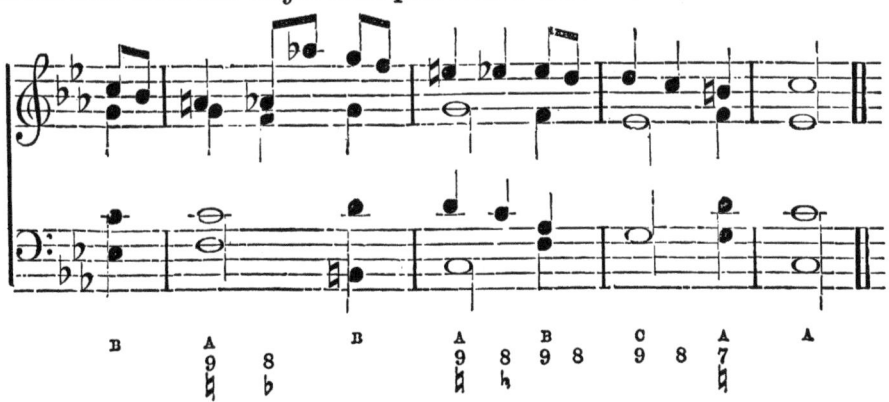

Further than this, and exceptionally from the generally necessary resolution of a suspension on a note of the chord against which it is dissonant, the suspended ninth of the subdominant may proceed to the seventh of the dominant, provided the major third of the subdominant proceed to the minor ninth of the dominant (Ex. 1), or remain to be the major ninth of the dominant (Ex. 2), or else provided that the minor third of the subdominant remain to be the minor ninth of the dominant (Ex. 3). The suspended ninth of the tonic may proceed to the seventh of the supertonic, under the same conditions as the suspended ninth of the subdominant proceeding to a dominant discord (Exs. 1, 2, and 3).

London : Harrison & Sons, Printers in Ordinary to Her Majesty, St. Martin's Lane.

For EU product safety concerns, contact us at Calle de José Abascal, 56–1°,
28003 Madrid, Spain or eugpsr@cambridge.org.

www.ingramcontent.com/pod-product-compliance
Ingram Content Group UK Ltd.
Pitfield, Milton Keynes, MK11 3LW, UK
UKHW051009240426
470322UK00018B/573